THE POLITICS OF RACE AND ETHNICITY

Series Editors Rodney E. Hero, University of Notre Dame
Katherine Tate, University of California, Irvine

Politics of Race and Ethnicity is premised on the view that understanding race and ethnicity is integral to a fuller, more complete understanding of the American political system. The goal is to provide the scholarly community at all levels with accessible texts that will introduce them to, and stimulate their thinking on, fundamental questions in this field. We are interested in books that creatively examine the meaning of American democracy for racial and ethnic groups and, conversely, what racial and ethnic groups mean and have meant for American democracy.

The Urban Voter: Group Conflict and Mayoral Voting Behavior in American Cities
Karen M. Kaufmann

Democracy's Promise: Immigrants and American Civil Institutions
Janelle S. Wong

Mark One or More: Civil Rights in Multiracial America
Kim M. Williams

MARK ONE OR MORE ✓

Civil Rights in Multiracial America

Kim M. Williams

THE UNIVERSITY OF MICHIGAN PRESS   Ann Arbor

Copyright © by the University of Michigan 2006
All rights reserved
Published in the United States of America by
The University of Michigan Press
Manufactured in the United States of America
⊗ Printed on acid-free paper

2009   2008   2007   2006   4   3   2   1

A CIP catalog record for this book is available from the British Library.

Library of Congress Cataloging-in-Publication Data

Williams, Kim M., 1968–
    Mark one or more : civil rights in multiracial America / Kim M.
Williams.
        p. cm. — (The politics of race and ethnicity)
    Includes bibliographical references and index.
    ISBN-13: 978-0-472-11442-9 (cloth : alk. paper)
    ISBN-10: 0-472-11442-5 (cloth : alk. paper)
    1. United States—Race relations.   2. Racially mixed people—
Civil rights—United States.   3. Racially mixed people—Race
identity—United States.   4. Racially mixed people—Politics and
government—United States.   5. Race awareness—United States.
6. Racism—United States.   7. Ethnicity—United States.
I. Title.   II. Series.
E184.A1W456   2006
305.8'05073—dc22   2006003033

Contents

List of Tables and Figures

Preface

The multiracial movement drew me in for reasons outside personal experience, as the term is typically used. Yet personal experience pulled me toward it nonetheless. My grandfather was born just twenty-one years after the Supreme Court's infamous ruling in *Plessy v. Ferguson* (1896), which sanctioned preexisting Jim Crow laws in his home state and paved the way for new ones beyond it. That was one connection. There was no ambiguity about where Alfornia Lewis fit into the law's black-and-white categories. Yet here was a group of people claiming the right to change their racial identities over time, the right to claim more than one race, and perhaps the right to escape from racial minority status altogether. That struck another chord. The struggles of earlier generations for first-class citizenship and equal rights bequeathed to mine powerful messages such as "I AM Somebody" and "black and proud—say it loud." They handed down the most precious of gifts: the demise of formal Jim Crow and a sense of dignity in carving the space to define oneself. I was born in Oakland, in the late 1960s, an environment that generated abundant proof that black was beautiful, powerful, and eclectic. All the while, through my parents and their idiosyncratic circle of friends and acquaintances in my increasingly international hometown, I learned from childhood to move between many worlds.

The Oakland Adult Day School where my mother, Dorothy Edwards, taught English as a second language until I was twelve brought to life the otherwise abstract notion of demographic change. In the wake of the Vietnam War, a trickle of affluent, French-speaking Vietnamese appeared in her classes, eventually followed by scores of refugees from across Southeast Asia. Iranian students enrolled after the fall of the Shah. Political upheaval in Guatemala and El Salvador brought students from these countries into her classroom and our lives. New arrivals, joining the more stable flow of Mexicans, sometimes made for overnight changes in the student body. The students and their stories spurred my interest in politics and further expanded my worldview.

My upbringing was such that I could later appreciate how people might find that monoracial categories did not fit their multiracial reality. Multiracial advocates' desire for latitude in self-identification was, on one hand, unobjectionable and even familiar. Freedom of expression and of association were inextricable from the kind of black pride that I had grown up with from childhood. On the other hand, using civil rights victories and symbolism, multiracial activists seemed to seek a flexibility that eludes most blacks. And the very notion of "multiracial recognition" had the potential to undermine federal civil rights enforcement efforts, already under considerable attack from other corners. Thus, I began a long conversation with multiracial activists, who claimed that their recognition could lessen racial polarization by enabling Americans to think differently, and more humanely, across racial boundaries.

This book explains how a social movement with powerful opponents, little money, and few active supporters could spark a series of unprecedented changes in the way Americans measure race. The new message from the government—reaching far and wide, through the promulgation of census data—is that race can be multiple and flexible; it need not be singular or rigid. If this drives a wedge into the larger debate about the changing meaning of race and the measure of progress, as argued in the book, then, contrary to conventional wisdom, the implications for civil rights thought and action are significant. Now that it has been institutionalized in the federal statistical system and in a number of states, the old but newly vindicated notion of racial mixture is not likely to go away. It further complicates matters that there is something in the multiracial idea that most of us want to hear. The window that this issue opens onto the civil rights past, present, and future is the subject of this book.

I witnessed many of the events described here firsthand, and I cannot thank the activists enough. I pursued these people for years and—a wonder to me still—they preserved a sense of humor about it. I could not have written this book without them. During the height of movement activity and beyond, I followed them to their conferences, trailed them at their solidarity marches, visited their homes, and feasted at their countless cookouts. I have had some of the most memorable race conversations of my life with multiracial activists. I am especially grateful to Nancy Brown, Charles Byrd, Reg Daniel, Edwin Darden, Ramona Douglass, Levonne Gaddy, Harold Gates, Susan Graham, Matt Kelley, Sarah Ross, and Ruth White.

Benedict Anderson, Davydd Greenwood, Theodore Lowi, and Sidney Tarrow each gave me something different; combined, I could not have wished for more in a dissertation committee. Sid's contributions are beyond enumeration; thus, I simply thank him for everything. I learned a lot in the "Invisible College of Contentious Politics," the brainchild of Ron Aminzade, Jack Goldstone, Doug McAdam, Elizabeth Perry, William Sewell, Sidney Tarrow, and Charles Tilly. My contentious junior colleagues also shared a wealth of knowledge: Lissa Bell, Pam Burke, Jorge Cadena-Roa, David Cunningham, Manali Desai, Robyn Eckhardt, John Glenn, Debbie Gould, Hyojoung Kim, Joseph Luders, Heidi Swarts, Nella Van Dyke, and Heather Williams. Thanks to Mary Katzenstein. At Harvard, Alan Altshuler, Christopher Edley Jr., Lani Guinier, Jennifer Hochschild, Al Kauffman, Jane Mansbridge, Katherine Newman, Robert Putnam, and William Julius Wilson have greatly influenced my thinking and have shown much appreciated interest in my academic growth. Special thanks to Jennifer, whose incisive questions made me look for better answers. Thanks also for her thoughtfulness and excellent advice. And I owe a great deal to the other members of the Race and Ethnic Measurement in Federal Statistics working group: Reynolds Farley, Ian Haney López, Victoria Hattam, David Hollinger, Melissa Nobles, Matthew Snipp, and Kenneth Prewitt, who, luckily for me, brought us all together.

Judy Byfield, Kim DaCosta, Terri Givens, David Harris, Regine Jackson, Deborah King, Karyn Lacy, Taeku Lee, Ann Morning, Valeria Sinclair-Chapman, John Skrentny, Guy Stuart, and Sonya Tafoya offered precious feedback. My editor, Jim Reische, was enthusiastic about the project from the start and wise in his guidance throughout. I thank him for these valuable contributions. Thanks also to my series editors, Rodney Hero and Katherine Tate, along with two anonymous reviewers, whose advice I have tried to take to heart since their counsel was so apt. Tissa Hami, Brian Min, Adamma Obele, Nnenna Ofobike, Mara Cecilia-Ostfeld, and Megan Sampson supplied invaluable administrative support. Thanks to Anders Hopperstead. The Ford Foundation provided funding at two critical junctures and gave me much more by concurrently inducting me into an extraordinary community of young scholars across the country. Additional support came from the Horowitz Foundation; Mathematica Policy Research, Inc.; Dartmouth College; and the Civil Rights Project and the Taubman Center for State and Local Government at the John F. Kennedy School of Government, both at Harvard University.

My family has been an ongoing source of solace and wisdom. My husband, Mingus Mapps, put up with years of census minutiae that surely would have brought an average man to the brink. He often helped me think through ideas, he always encouraged me to tell it like it is, and he has done so much more. My brother, Daniel Williams, offered refreshing perspectives and comic relief by way of thoughtful phone calls. Thanks to my aunts and uncles for all that they have taught me: Brad and Kaye Collins, Dean Collins, Ray Collins, Tori Collins, Jean and Emmett Richardson, Ethel and Jerry Williams, Norris Williams, Elizabeth (Cookie) Williams, and Glenn Williams. Thanks to Jack Williams. Thanks to Kenny Williams. My grandparents—Geraldine Collins, Juanita and Alfornia Lewis, and E. C. Williams—related spectacularly sad stories, screamingly funny accounts, and sundry incidents all the more remarkable because they regarded them as mundane. Everybody had an opinion. My life and my work have grown richer as a result. Most of all, I thank my parents, Dorothy and Terry Edwards, who taught me by example how to move between many worlds.

Introduction

Testifying before the U.S. House of Representatives in June 1993, a group of "multiracial movement" activists declared that race is socially constructed. The activists later described the hearings as the culmination of "years of effort . . . to gain public recognition of the multiracial/ethnic community and the injustice of denying its particular identity on official forms."[1]

In February 1994, at a high school assembly in Wedowee, Alabama, the principal told students that the school prom would be canceled if interracial couples attended. When questioned by student ReVonda Bowens about how this would apply to her, since her father was white and her mother was black, principal Hulond Humphries replied: "That's exactly my point. . . . the rule . . . is aimed at preventing mistakes like you."[2] Bowens sued. The Association of MultiEthnic Americans (AMEA), established in 1988, hoped to use the incident as a precedent to identify and legally eliminate discrimination against multiracial individuals and families. Bowens, however, eventually chose to settle out of court.

In July 1996, the first ever "multiracial solidarity march" was held on the National Mall in Washington, DC. To rally the troops, Charles Byrd, the main organizer of the event and editor of the then popular *Interracial Voice* Web site, claimed that

> The group most able to help this society bridge the gap between the race obsessed present and an ideal future of racelessness is the mixed-race contingent. There has never been an

attempt to bring together large numbers of mixed-race individuals to petition the government for anything—in this case, a multiracial census category that would allow millions of Americans to, for the first time, legally self-identify.[3]

In November 1996, the president of the National Association for the Advancement of Colored People (NAACP), Kweisi Mfume, devoted much of his weekly radio address to the issue of multiracialism. "With some figures showing 70% of African Americans fitting into a multiracial category," he said, "will we be able to identify black voters in terms of fair representation? No one should be forced to choose or reject any aspect of their heritage, but no category should be allowed to weaken others."[4]

In July 1997, Newt Gingrich, then Speaker of the House, endorsed "adding a multiracial category to census and other government forms to begin phasing out the outdated, divisive and rigid classification of Americans."[5]

In January 2001, after stepping down from his post as the head of the Census Bureau, Kenneth Prewitt said, "Census 2000 will go down in history as the event that began to redefine race in American society."[6]

This book tells the story of how a small group of activists spurred the recent restructuring of the American racial classification system. The multiracial movement is best known for its advocates' efforts to add a multiracial category to the 2000 census. This aspiration brought with it a series of unprecedented debates about race and, ultimately, unanticipated outcomes in the way race is recorded in this country. By the end of the 1990s, the federal government, along with a number of state governments, had not only devoted substantial resources to investigating the issue; eventually it agreed to document race in a new way. Although a multiracial category was not added to the 2000 census, the government made an official move away from a binary race approach and toward a multiracial one.[7] For the first time ever, a "mark one or more" (MOOM) option—allowing Americans to identify officially with as many racial groups as they saw fit—became the law of the land. Eventually, MOOM—separately and in tandem with coexisting trends—is likely to reach deep into the nation's civil rights agenda. Yet, for a variety of reasons, it was sold as a reform whose effects would scarcely be noticed.

The episodes recounted at the beginning of this chapter reflect the recurring themes of this work: the changing scope of ethnoracial identity and affiliation, the political stakes attached to those identifications, and the state's involvement in what Paul Starr aptly describes as the "political reduction of social complexity."[8] Racial classifications have been used to sustain a range of exploitative arrangements throughout most of American history. In the 1960s, however, these same classifications became useful, finally, for the laudable purpose of enforcing and monitoring civil rights laws. That is, the recent chapters of this long story spotlight the transformative use of statistics as promoted by the civil rights movement. A few decades later, the idea that there was nothing inevitable or preordained about most categories, including racial ones, began to pick up steam. As things stand now, the stakes involved in American ethnoracial categorization are considerable, yet the grounds for identifying and delimiting racial groups are increasingly suspect.

Fundamental to the civil rights movement was the idea that racism was not just a matter of personal or individual behavior but an affliction manifesting itself in systemic ways. To demonstrate the prevalence and perniciousness of institutionalized racism, civil rights advocates marshaled statistics on residential segregation, unequal educational opportunities, infant mortality and life expectancy, black and white income differentials, disparities in office holding, and so on. Not only did civil rights activists use statistics as the raw materials for demonstrating the scope of institutional discrimination, but they also used the data to generate political support for new laws and policies meant to address these documented problems.[9] The civil rights movement turned the previously oppressive function of racial data on its head.

At this level, the census is far more than an official ledger. Activists use it to highlight and correct political imbalances; black activism of the 1960s and beyond represents a prime example of this reverse dynamic at work. The outcomes of the civil rights movement meant that, for the first time, minorities—through the political leadership of civil rights organizations and a growing cadre of minority elected officials—were able to use racial counts to

before civil rights → data had oppressive function

expose, and to some extent redress, long-standing disparities. From a public policy standpoint, one sees evidence of this shift in the Civil Rights Act of 1964, the Voting Rights Act of 1965, and in the array of antipoverty programs associated with Lyndon B. Johnson's Great Society. Discussed in chapter 2, these acts and programs spurred the reallocation of millions of dollars and, to some extent, political power. In the process, racial data took on new importance, although the definition of race remained implicit in practice and vague in the law. The civil rights successes created long overdue opportunities, yet this new fusion of statistics and politics would usher in a new set of challenges.

The Actors

Four main parties dominated the debate over the inclusion of a multiracial category on the 2000 census. First there were the activists: the multiracial movement started with a handful of adult-based (that is, nonstudent) groups that formed on the West Coast in the late 1970s and early 1980s. In the mid-1990s, during the height of movement activity, I determined that there were thirty active adult-based multiracial organizations across the United States and approximately the same number of student organizations on college campuses. This book looks only at adult-based groups. In 1988, a number of these local organizations joined forces to create the AMEA, whose political objective was to push the Census Bureau to add a multiracial category on government forms. Soon after the establishment of the AMEA, two other organizations claiming national memberships and networks also came to the fore: Project RACE (Reclassify All Children Equally) and A Place For Us (APFU). The three groups' orientations and goals were divergent from the beginning. However, they shared the conviction that it was inaccurate and unacceptable to force multiracial Americans into monoracial categories. On this basis, the groups often worked together during the 1990s.

Second were the civil rights groups who, over the course of that decade, increasingly came to perceive the multiracial movement as a threat. The link between numbers and power was the driving impetus behind this concern. The civil rights community feared that a multiracial category would dilute the count of minority populations, and—although in actuality this prospect triggered different concerns for different civil rights organizations—their shared position was that a multiracial identifier would undercut existing civil rights safeguards.

Third was the Office of Management and Budget (OMB), responsible for coordinating the activities of all federal statistical agencies, including the Census Bureau. The OMB was keen to avoid the difficulty and controversy of prior censuses. Responding to ongoing criticism of the census and to rapid change in the racial and ethnic makeup of the country, the OMB launched an extensive review of the racial categorization system in 1993. Ultimately, via the MOOM decision of 1997, the OMB tried to steer a middle course on multiracial recognition. Officials in the Clinton administration's OMB and Census Bureau seemed to see this as a symbolic gesture that would not adversely affect civil rights enforcement efforts.

Elected officials in both federal and state government constitute the final set of actors. From 1992 to 1998, six states passed legislation to add a multiracial category on state forms; five other states introduced similar legislation during this period. In the states, Democrats primarily initiated multiracial category legislation. In Congress, however, it was mostly Republicans—many of whom, I argue, viewed the multiracial issue as an opportunity to undermine civil rights gains—who supported the federal-level multiracial category proposal. I explain this apparent incongruity in later chapters; for now, the important thing to keep in mind is that the multiracial idea held some appeal, albeit for different reasons, across the ideological spectrum in the 1990s.

A flurry of recent books and articles delve deeply into multiracial identity issues; the view of the multiracial experience that we get from most authors is intimate and personal.[11] *Mark One or More*, in contrast, speaks to the political effects of multiracial advocacy in relation to civil rights priorities and strategies. The few related analytical studies leave these questions wide open. Melissa Nobles's *Shades of Citizenship* hedges on the point: are we to believe that the multiracialists have demonstrated long-standing dedication to the civil rights struggle or not?[12] *The New Race Question*, the most comprehensive volume on American multiracial politics to date, leaves such questions "to others."[13]

Mark One or More focuses on these questions and advances a solution to the underlying puzzle of political commitments left unexplored by other authors. On one hand, multiracial category proponents tried to position themselves to the left of "traditional" civil rights groups. On the other hand, those same civil rights groups, along with a range of supporting minority institutions, treated the multiracial initiative as a right-wing conspiracy. Contrary to conventional wisdom, my contention is that the multiracial category effort was *not* a right-wing conspiracy; instead, powerful people with right-wing agendas appropriated it. This distinction is important. My account leaves open the otherwise foreclosed possibility of the left's productive engagement with multiracial issues. Multiracial politics need not and should not connect so tenuously to the larger civil rights project.

Undoing the Working Definition of Race

1
2 ✔
3
4
5
6

The debate over the multiracial category issue opened arguably the most probing examination of race in this country since the 1960s. Yet multiracial activists of the 1980s and 1990s did not reinvent the wheel of protest; instead, they creatively adapted and reinterpreted the tactics, ideologies, and legal outcomes available to them. The civil rights struggles of the 1950s and 1960s helped to remove fundamental barriers and produced the legal and political space for multiracial activism to take root and thrive. With this latitude, and on behalf of a generation "literally born from the successes of the civil rights movement,"[1] multiracial activists drew shrewdly on civil rights symbolism yet cast themselves as more progressive than the so-called progressives.

What Makes It a Social Movement?

Figure 1, compiled from my leadership survey data, is a map of multiracial organizations assembled from primary documents and other original sources (see appendixes A and C for details). I believe this depicts the universe of adult-based groups at the height of movement activity. These groups began and remain primarily as support networks; however—and we know this is conspicuously rare in the United States—they also serve as local entities encouraging cross-racial friendship and dialogue.

In my preliminary research, I found that the AMEA, Project

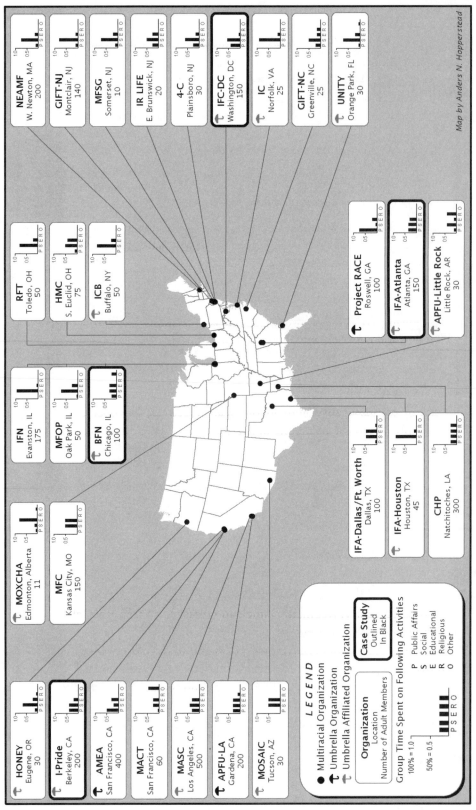

FIGURE 1. Multiracial Organizations, 1997–98

Map by Anders N. Hopperstead

NEAMF
W. Newton, MA
200

GIFT-NJ
Montclair, NJ
140

MFSG
Somerset, NJ
10

IR LIFE
E. Brunswick, NJ
20

4-C
Plainsboro, NJ
30

IFC-DC
Washington, DC
150

IC
Norfolk, VA
25

GIFT-NC
Greenville, NC
25

UNITY
Orange Park, FL
30

RFT
Toledo, OH
50

HMC
S. Euclid, OH
75

ICB
Buffalo, NY
50

Project RACE
Roswell, GA
100

IFA-Atlanta
Atlanta, GA
150

APFU-Little Rock
Little Rock, AR
30

IFN
Evanston, IL
175

MFOP
Oak Park, IL
50

BFN
Chicago, IL
100

IFA-Dallas/Ft. Worth
Dallas, TX
100

IFA-Houston
Houston, TX
45

CHP
Natchitoches, LA
300

MOXCHA
Edmonton, Alberta
11

MFC
Kansas City, MO
150

HONEY
Eugene, OR
30

I-Pride
Berkeley, CA
200

AMEA
San Francisco, CA
400

MACT
San Francisco, CA
60

MASC
Los Angeles, CA
500

APFU-LA
Gardena, CA
200

MOSAIC
Tucson, AZ
30

P S E R O

LEGEND

Organization
Location
Number of Adult Members

Case Study
Outlined In Black

● Multiracial Organization
♇ Umbrella Organization
♇ Umbrella Affiliated Organization

Group Time Spent on Following Activities

P Public Affairs
S Social
E Educational
R Religious
O Other

100% = 1.0
50% = 0.5

P S E R O

RACE, APFU, and their respective affiliates were the locus of political action.

1. AMEA took the position that multiracial people should have the right to claim their entire heritage and embrace their total identity. Its mission statement declared that the group's primary goal was education: to "promote a positive awareness of interracial and multiethnic identity, for ourselves and for society as a whole."[2] One means to that end, AMEA maintained, was multiracial recognition on the census.

2. For Project RACE, the main objective was to get a "multiracial classification on all school, employment, state, federal, local, census and medical forms requiring racial data,"[3] so that multiracial children would not have to suffer the adverse consequences of being regarded as "Other." → NO "OTHer" = goal

3. Finally, APFU viewed the "support and encouragement of interaction between anyone involved with interracial relationships" as their purpose and a "color-blind society" as their goal.[4] → color blind society = goal

Although pursuing divergent ideological objectives, together the three represented the backbone of the multiracial category effort in the 1990s.

The AMEA began in 1988 as an experiment full of hope, excitement, and talent. Its leaders sought to galvanize preexisting local grassroots groups around a common multiracial agenda. They wanted many things—respect, recognition, an end to racism, and a multiracial designator on the U.S. census. At the founding meeting, held in Berkeley, California, representatives from the fourteen charter member organizations (see table 1) elected AMEA's first president, Carlos Alejandro Fernández; vice president, Ramona Douglass; secretary, Reginald Daniel; and treasurer, Sarah Ross, all of whom also held leadership positions in their respective local groups. AMEA's leaders moved with dispatch to develop two-year and five-year plans. Within five years, advocates expected to establish "an educational and/or legal defense fund; create a multicultural resource center or institute; staff a political action committee to lobby for changing official forms; and establish an AMEA hotline/switchboard to disseminate information and provide solutions to interracial/multiracial problems that arise across the nation."[5]

Many of these ideas did not make it past the drawing board. Still, within six years, AMEA had testified before Congress, incorporated with 501(c) (3) nonprofit status, and assembled an erudite advisory board packed with accomplished professionals whose opinions were increasingly sought by the media. The board of directors was and is liberal and secular; many of the organization's founders held advanced degrees. In his debut "Message from the President," written for AMEA's first newsletter, *Mélange*, Carlos Fernández invited readers to approach multiracialism as a collective vision of progress to be shared by all principled Americans. Confronting the "poisonous" ideology of racism, he wrote, was a matter of vital national interest, for it "infects every ethnic community in this country, even those who are its traditional victims."[6] The charge was that minorities could be racists, too, and that multiracial families could serve as a positive, progressive example for us all.

This was a far cry from the message of an earlier generation of scientists and academics, whose studies of racial mixture feverishly sought to prove that mulattos, quadroons, and octoroons were physically and mentally inferior to whites and doomed to extinction. AMEA's founders made no explicit reference to this past. Instead, very much in the language of their day, they spoke of rights and recognition. To secure both, the activists reasoned, they needed lobbyists in Washington. Indeed, by the time its founders launched AMEA in 1988, the changing mix of strategies used by most American rights groups had tilted decidedly in the direction of professional advocacy and markedly away from mass protest.[7] AMEA's political development is very much part of this broader wave of late twentieth-century advocacy. However, many American advocacy groups had long since abandoned the kind of nationwide, chapter-based network envisioned by AMEA in 1988.

In its first year of existence, AMEA pressed the federal government to add a new category "principally for individuals of mixed race backgrounds and those who want the option of specifically stating a unique identification," according to Sally Katzen, administrator in the OMB's Office of Information and Regulatory Affairs. The AMEA proposal—which would have required an

"Other" category and classification by self-identification—was, according to Katzen, supported by "many multi-racial and multi-ethnic groups and some educational institutions"[8] but was met with a blaze of opposition from civil rights forces inside and outside of government. Falling back on the need for more testing, the OMB ultimately dropped the issue. AMEA, however, did not, and early in 1989 Fernández, a lawyer, opened discussions with the American Civil Liberties Union (ACLU) to explore the possibility of obtaining a federal court order to make the change.[9] Fernández also began to look aggressively for court cases around the country that might provide a precedent, but no such case materialized.[10]

APFU, a Christian-focused group, had an altogether different focus and constituency. Ruth and Steve White started APFU in 1986 after their minister would not marry them: he is white and she is black. Eventually, they became ministers themselves and began to provide counseling services, to perform marriages, to organize workshops, and to coordinate Bible studies for interracial Christian couples in Southern California. A few years later, when AMEA established its base of operation in Northern California, APFU extended a guarded welcome. "Although interracial organizations share a common interest, there could be the potential [for] separation,"[11] warned the *Peacemaker*, APFU's intermittently published newsletter.

In spite of this lukewarm reception, which quietly tried to limit AMEA's relative status, APFU actually became one of AMEA's affiliate groups before declaring itself a national organization in its own right (table 1). The two fledgling entities collaborated on a number of minor initiatives that never got off the ground, including the 1989 Douglass-White Proposal, a vaguely defined call to eliminate the "one-drop rule" as sanctioned by the government. The one-drop rule holds that anyone who is known to have a black ancestor is black. Operating in different eras as a means of controlling and augmenting the slave population, as legal diktat, and as social definition, the one-drop rule has long been the American answer to the ambiguity of intermediate racial identity. For blacks, that is. "Not only does the one-drop rule apply to no other group than American blacks, but apparently the rule is unique in that it is found only in the United States and not in any other nation in the world,"[12] wrote F. James Davis in 1991. Multiracial advocates opposed government policies based on a binary understanding of race and acknowledging nothing in between.

On its own, APFU also attempted to stage a sunrise event on January 1, 1990, called the "Love Chain." "Each participant will pledge not to judge others by the color of their skin, but by the content of their character." APFU dedicated the Love Chain to Barbara Bush, who "publicly stated that she would like to see a color-blind society."[13] Plans for the event were abandoned after Ruth and Steve White realized that sunrise on New Year's Day was not the most opportune moment to stage a demonstration.

Eight months into that year, a group of white youth attacked a multiracial teenager in Southern California. As reported in the *Orange County Register*, Amber Jefferson was "bashed in the knees with a baseball bat [and] suffered a severe gash from her hairline to her chin when she was hit with a large piece of glass."[14] Declaring this a hate crime, APFU issued its first press release, which served as both a response and warning to interracial families: "to [those of you] who haven't yet experienced the sting of racism, and who think there's no need to get involved in this kind of movement: don't wait! There may well be a future time when you will need this kind of aid, and what goes around comes around."[15] At this point, APFU also revised its mission statement to include a new goal— "to work with other multiracial groups to establish a multiracial category"—with a qualifier:("*until all racial categories are eliminated.*"[16]) Ruth and Steve White began to appear on television and radio shows discussing the Jefferson case and a variety of other issues that they deemed relevant to interracial family life.

That same year, finding no suitable category for her son on the 1990 census form, Susan Graham of Marietta, Georgia, called the Census Bureau for instruction. "They kept putting me on hold, then coming back. Finally [the bureau representative] tells me 'I got with the supervisor,' and his voice became very hushed. 'Your children would take the race of the mother,' he said. When I asked why, he said, 'Because in cases like these, we always know who the mother is and not the father.'"[17] Graham, a white woman in her mid-forties, founded Project RACE in 1991 with the intent of getting a multiracial category added to all government forms calling for racial identification. Her husband, Gordon Graham, helped to publicize the effort (he was a CNN anchor at the time). Project RACE and AMEA soon settled into a productive division of labor: Project RACE focused on lobbying state legislatures, while AMEA concentrated on the federal government. APFU, meanwhile, made a number of dramatic entrances and exits from the scene.

RACE → lobbying state legislatures APFU →
AMEA → federal government inconsistent

The Local Groups

Beyond conducting a survey of all group leaders across the country (fig. 1), I planned to select a few of the affiliates of each umbrella organization for case study analysis, since these groups were the driving force behind the political articulation of multiracial claims. However, exhaustive research determined that Project RACE and APFU did not *have* affiliates. Although both groups listed affiliate organizations on their stationery and referred to "their members" in various conversations, further investigation showed that these "affiliates" either were unreachable (disconnected phone numbers, invalid addresses, etc.) or comprised only one or two people in each location. This meant that AMEA was the only organization with an active network of affiliates at the time of my research. Accordingly, my case studies of local organizations were all AMEA affiliates. Table 1 shows the fourteen organizations with which AMEA started in 1988. I selected the Interracial Family Circle, or IFC (Washington, DC); Interracial/Intercultural-Pride, or I-Pride (San Francisco/Berkeley); the Biracial Family Network, or BFN (Chicago); and the Interracial Family Alliance, or IFA (Atlanta), for case study, based on several criteria.[18]

What makes this a social movement? Multiracial politics has flowered in unexpected places in recent years, yet it is a social movement not because the multiracial idea is becoming culturally accepted or ubiquitous but rather because the push for multiracial recognition has involved a series of interactions between the state and challenging groups. Political effort on the part of the latter— with some response from the former—can be traced back to at least 1979. AMEA's affiliates joined forces in the late 1980s with many goals: among them was altering public policy. They targeted progressive local school boards in Northern California and later set their sights on the Census Bureau and the OMB. Years of institu-

social movement

tion building, letter writing, demonstrations, lobbying, groups and Web sites launched and folded, ambitious plans devised and dropped, and encounters with state and federal officials make it a social movement.

In most circumstances, and by most calculations, the odds are against social movements bringing about change at any level of government. Yet sometimes they do. How do we explain this? The "resource mobilization" approach suggests that social movements with a preponderance of resources (money, large memberships, and relatively high levels of internal professionalization) enjoy the

TABLE 1.   AMEA's Charter Organizations

West	Midwest	South	East
A Place For Us Ministry (Gardena, CA)[b] est. 1984	Biracial Family Network (Chicago, IL) est. 1980	Interracial Connection (Norfolk, VA) est. 1982	Interracial Club of Buffalo (NY) est. 1983
Honor Our Ethnic Youth, or HONEY (Eugene, OR) est. 1983	Parents of Interracial Children (Omaha, NE)[a]	Interracial Family Alliance (Atlanta, GA) est. 1983	Interracial Family Circle (Washington, DC) est. 1984
IMAGE (San Diego, CA)[a]		Interracial Family Alliance (Houston, TX) est. 1982	Interracial Families, Inc. (Pittsburgh, PA)[a]
Interracial Network[a] (Seattle, WA)			
Interracial/Intercultural-Pride or I-Pride (San Francisco/ Berkeley, CA) est. 1979			
Multiracial Americans of Southern California, or MASC (Los Angeles, CA) est. 1987			

Note: Shaded cells indicate case studies. See appendix A for details.
[a]Defunct as of 1997.
[b]Eventually, Ruth and Steve White declared A Place For Us a national organization, but it became so in name only.

most success.[19] Think of resources as actual or potential. *Actual* resources include assets like money in the bank, paid staff to keep things on track, or a readily mobilized constituency. *Potential* resources include less concrete advantages such as popular sympathy or elite support, which, if they can be marshaled, may further the cause.

The number of people to whom a multiracial movement would most plausibly appeal has increased as interracial dating and marriage have become more common. Even closer to the matter at hand, the increase in the number of multiracial organizations over the past twenty years would seem to support a resource mobilization line of reasoning. In 1979, there was one active adult-based multiracial organization: I-Pride, in Berkeley, California. By 1984, twelve multiracial groups existed across the country; by 1994, there were twenty, and soon after, forty.[20] Although some of these groups later disbanded, the number of multiracial organizations has continued to grow. The biggest increase occurred when the federal government and many states began to take the multiracial category idea seriously—that is, after 1993. The capacities of most multiracial organizations have also grown (albeit modestly) over the past two decades, if measured by membership rates, professionalization, and financial reserves.

Yet I found little bearing between the actual resources of multiracial organizations and any of the policy outcomes, as discussed in coming chapters. All three of the "umbrella" organizations—again, AMEA was the only operation with a real network of affiliates—maneuvered on shoestring budgets. If gauged by its overall membership base, the multiracial movement involved only about 3,500 adult members spread across the country at the height of activity.[21] Joined loosely together through the infrastructure depicted in figure 1, participants were generally more interested in gaining social support than in changing the census. Only a handful of multiracial movement leaders—*about twenty people*—pushed the multiracial category effort forward in the 1990s. Unsurprisingly, organizational capacity was in short supply. Two years after AMEA's first testimony before Congress, Ramona Douglass, the organization's new president, wrote to her predecessor, "our mailbox pick-up has been less than reliable lately, and we cannot afford to have a response from Bill Clinton go unanswered due to lack of consistent pick-up or delivery of our mail."[22] Clearly, the multiracial movement did not muscle its way to victory.

The "resource mobilization" idea had toppled classical theories of social movements, supplanting them with the notion that movement behavior was as rational as other forms of social action. This was a serious blow to the pluralist implication that sane political action was necessarily institutionalized political action. Instead, resource mobilization positioned social movements as a political phenomenon. Yet, if social movement participants were so rational, then why did they participate at all? Why didn't they free ride on the efforts of others? By the late 1970s, the cost-benefit calculus in social movement studies was shifting toward an expanded view of "rationality" and toward a more nuanced depiction of resources.

Political Opportunities

Here the resources of most consequence are those upon which movements capitalize but by no means control. Again, challengers face enormous odds under ordinary circumstances, but weakness is not the same thing as powerlessness. Sometimes the powerful are vulnerable to attack. In this way, writes Doug McAdam in *Political Process and the Development of Black Insurgency, 1930–1970*, movements are products of opportunities afforded to insurgents and their ability to exploit them.[23] Both of these come and go. To understand timing and outcomes, the "political process" model focuses on the role of the state and its rules of allocation. "Not only when reform is pending, but when institutional access opens, when alignments shift, when conflicts emerge among elites and when allies become available, will challengers find favorable opportunities,"[24] writes movement scholar Sidney Tarrow. Considered alongside more stable institutional features, such as the nature of the party system and the strength or weakness of the state, windows of political opportunity temporarily reduce power disparities and give challengers a reason for hope.

The multiracial movement, despite all its limitations, had the significant advantage of dealing with a census bureau already under considerable stress. Coping with mounting scrutiny and escalating criticism, the U.S. Census Bureau has never been in charge of its own fate. Begun in the Department of the Interior, the bureau was transferred to the Department of Commerce and Labor in 1903. When Commerce separated from Labor in 1913, the Census Bureau became a permanent part of the former. Thus, the director of the Census Bureau is a presidential appointee who reports to the secretary of commerce. The OMB, which reviews and decides upon budget requests from the bureau, exerts further control. This leaves the bureau in a difficult spot: it is the public face of the nation's statistical system, and, as such, it is the most obvious target for complaint. However, much of the public's criticism of the bureau is focused on decisions over which the bureau has marginal influence.

This point comes to life in the ferocious and chronic debate about whether to adjust the results of the decennial census to compensate for the undercount of minorities. Experts concur that a systematic undercount of minorities exists; the dispute revolves around what to do about it. Through postenumeration surveys and other techniques, the Census Bureau estimates how many people it missed in the official enumeration. Missed persons are considered to be "undercounted"; the undercount usually represents between 1 and 3 percent of the population. Race enters the picture because the bureau consistently misses a disproportionately large fraction of poor, urban, and minority populations. Thus, complain urban mayors, leaders of minority organizations, and members of Congress representing these constituencies, the undercount has its biggest impact upon large cities, resulting in a steady loss of state and federal dollars and political representation. The undercount debate and its controversial remedy, sampling, amount to an ongoing problem for the bureau and its parent agency.

In one way or another, the bureau's biggest problems in the current era revolve around race. But as Peter Skerry points out, there is a "pervasive tendency at the Census Bureau and at the Office of Management and Budget to downplay racial matters and even to deny their importance."[25] How can both statements be true? The answer lies in the distance between a "bookish" bureau of statisticians, demographers, and other highly trained professionals striving to cultivate an apolitical image, on one hand, and advocacy groups, city governments, and state politicians clamoring for rectification of the bureau's (self-measured) flaws, on the other. To put this in perspective, briefly consider the major controversies of contemporary American census taking.

major controversies of census taking *(handwritten)*

1970

"When the 1970 census was taken, the bureau was deluged by complaints,"[26] writes Harvey Choldin. Much of the criticism had to do with the fact that the 1970 census was the first to be administered by mail. In previous censuses, enumerators went door to door to conduct an interview at every household. Although the new system helped to solve some problems (for instance, it allowed for racial self-identification; before 1970, the enumerator determined the race of the respondent through "observer identification"), it led to other difficulties. Critics of the new system believed that the mailing lists were incomplete and that Americans were unlikely to fill in and mail back questionnaires. Questions and lawsuits arose about how people speaking and writing in languages other than English would deal with the forms.[27] When the bureau released the undercount figures for 1970, it estimated that it had missed 5.3 million people, or about 2.5 percent of the total population. Breaking that figure down by race, however, over four times as many blacks (7.7 percent) as whites (1.9 percent) were missed in 1970.[28] Mayors from big cities with large black populations complained about the undercount, as did other minority spokespersons. Researchers began to take interest in the undercount phenomenon and its political implications for the "Fact-finder of the Nation."

(handwritten margin note: undercount 7.7% blacks)

1980

Things got worse in 1980. The Census Bureau stepped up efforts to reach hard-to-count populations, but, ultimately, "fifty-four municipalities or other entities brought suit against the bureau, generating more litigation than any prior United States census."[29] The difference in net undercount between blacks and whites was about 5 percent in 1980.[30] The plaintiffs demanded adjustment and insisted that their cities were suffering due to the census count. Although the bureau lost none of these cases, it cannot be said to

(handwritten note: bureau lost none of 54 cases → didn't really win them either.)

have won them either. As Margo Anderson and Stephen Feinberg explain, "going into the census in the beginning of 1980 [census officials] had faced disgruntled state and local officials and some scholars who wanted them to adjust for the differential undercount. Despite having prevailed in court, five years later they faced the same dissatisfied state and local officials and an increasingly expert group of survey statisticians who pressured for adjustment of the undercount."[31]

1990

These now familiar problems resurfaced again in 1990. In that year, the bureau reported a nationwide undercount of 2.1 percent, but the figures for blacks (4.8 percent), Hispanics (5.2 percent), and American Indians (5 percent) were over twice the national average. The bureau also reported an undercount above the national average in 1990 for Asians (3.1 percent). The census director, Barbara Bryant, recommended adjustment to the secretary of commerce, Robert Mosbacher, but Mosbacher, breaking a tradition of deferral to the census director on technical issues, declined. In March 1996, the Supreme Court handed down a decision in favor of Mosbacher's position. The litigation relating to the undercount and sampling in the 1990 census (twenty-one suits in total) went on for eight years, almost up to the point at which the 2000 census was conducted.[32]

Clearly, the Census Bureau's difficulties existed well before the multiracial movement began pressing its concerns. These troubles trace back to the institutional placement of the bureau within the federal bureaucracy and to the culture of the bureau itself. The lack of autonomy, epitomized by the 1990 fiasco, adds to these problems and is a central reason for the high turnover of Census Bureau directors. The position has remained unoccupied for long stretches of time. Peter Skerry notes that during Janet Norwood's uninterrupted twelve-year tenure as commissioner of the Bureau of Labor Statistics, the Census Bureau went through seven leadership changes (four directors plus three interim acting directors).[33] And there was no census director for nearly the first two years of the Clinton presidency, notes Barbara Bryant, who held the position

high turnover rate of Census Bureau Directors

during the first Bush administration.[34] (The post had been vacant for eleven months before she took the helm.) Along with William Dunn, Bryant describes the deteriorating situation in *Moving Power and Money: The Politics of Census Taking*. Tracing the "takeover"[35] of the Census Bureau by the Commerce Department to the Reagan years, Bryant complains that lawsuits "moved adjustment decisions away from the purely statistical arena."[36]

In 1980, the decision to adjust the results of the census to correct for the known undercount was left up to the Census Bureau director, but by 1987 the situation had changed. The year 1987 was a turning point beyond even the divisive adjustment issue. Harvey Choldin reports how in that same year, on the grounds of protecting privacy and striving toward smaller government, President Reagan's OMB attempted to delete questions and "truncate the sample size for long-form questionnaires,"[37] protests from within the Census Bureau notwithstanding. Eventually, the statistical agencies prevailed against this intrusion, but OMB did succeed in pressing the bureau to alter the design of the sample, forcing the deletion of three housing questions.[38] The Census Bureau, rather than emanating an air of objectivity, brings to mind politics and lawsuits.

Memorably, Peter Skerry describes the bureau as resembling "a graduate school as much as a government agency."[39] In other words, the bureau has shown a dearth of political savvy (which, I would add, says little for graduate school). Skerry reports that the bureau's professional statisticians and demographers, in their struggle to maintain an image of dispassionate impartiality, tend to be averse to politics (even in the midst of political chaos) and race (although the chaos is inextricable from racial considerations). Martha Riche, Clinton's first Census Bureau director, seems to fit this mold. As she explained to me, "there is a space between demographic change and politics, and our highest priority is to protect it."[40] Yet it also seems plausible that the bureau's avoidance of political relationships makes a bad situation worse.

Another complication appeared on the horizon in the early 1990s. "Growing racial and ethnic diversity of the American population [and] changing attitudes about race and ethnicity,"[41] the OMB admitted, did not square well with the existing framework (discussed later) for delineating the population by race. In part as an effort to avoid the conflicts and lawsuits like those that arose in the wake of the prior three censuses, the OMB requested that Congress hold hearings on the standards for racial and ethnic classification to be used in 2000. Angling for an invitation to testify in these hearings, AMEA staged its first major event in June 1992: a commemoration of the twenty-fifth anniversary of the Supreme Court's *Loving v. Virginia* decision, which overturned the sixteen remaining antimiscegenation laws in the United States. While in Washington for this event, AMEA leaders managed to schedule a meeting with Congressman Thomas Sawyer (D-OH), chair of the Subcommittee on Census, Statistics, and Postal Personnel of the House Committee on Post Office and Civil Service, and Nampeo McKinney, then assistant division chief of special populations for the Census Bureau. As Congressman Sawyer was responsible for organizing the hearings requested by the OMB and slated for the coming year, AMEA leaders pressed further and arranged a subsequent meeting a few days later with his staff director, TerriAnn Lowenthal, who informed AMEA representatives that she herself had a biracial daughter and was sympathetic to the group's position.[42] Within a month of the Washington meetings, AMEA received an invitation to participate in congressional hearings to be held the following year. AMEA (and the other multiracial organizations that would soon join in) now found itself in an auspicious position. The OMB was openly acknowledging the need for a reassessment of the status quo, and AMEA was part of the process. As former AMEA secretary and IMAGE founder (table 1) Jan Carpenter Tucker said in a personal interview, "we were all so excited . . . we felt we were making history."[43]

Unstable electoral alliances further served to amplify the call for a multiracial category on the census. The 104th Congress was the first in forty years in which the Republican Party controlled the House of Representatives and the first Republican Congress in forty-six years to face a Democratic president. Representative Newt Gingrich and other conservatives supported the addition of a multiracial category; however, recognition ultimately came from the Clinton administration. Think of it this way: Democrats wanted multiracial recognition *without* adverse civil rights consequences; Republicans wanted multiracial recognition *with* adverse civil rights consequences. I elaborate and substantiate this claim in *[handwritten margin notes: white-black = white / black-white = black { 1990 census }]*

the coming chapters; for now, I simply point out that, under divided government, multiracial advocates found allies across the ideological spectrum.

Meanwhile, growing racial complexity had already cast the bureau in an embarrassing light.

> For the 1990 census, people who wrote that they were "multiracial" or "bi-racial" were left in the "Other" race classification. Respondents who wrote "black-white" were counted as blacks; those who wrote "white-black" were counted as whites. Finally, imputation processes . . . are used to assign a standard race to more complicated cases. This usually involves checking the racial responses of other people in the same household or similar households in the neighborhood.[44]

Arguably just as bad, in cases where individuals disregarded the instructions altogether in 1990 and marked more than one box, former census director Kenneth Prewitt is reported to have heard that "the darker mark got it."[45] Vulnerable policies, unstable political alignments, elites divided on census policy and eventually on multiracial recognition itself: the political opportunities for multiracial activists in the 1990s were abundant.

[handwritten margin note: political ops for mult activ]

Racial Statistics and Minority Empowerment

Throughout American history, the U.S. government has used racial designations as a tool of dominance, serving to separate and penalize those not defined as white. To "ground the authority of the state in the sovereignty of the people,"[46] the framers of the Constitution used population counts to determine state representation in Congress. This made it necessary to clarify whether slaves were equivalent to free persons, and the framers concluded that they were not. Slaves—both property and people—were "discounted to 60 percent of the free"[47] for the allocation of seats among the states in the House of Representatives and for tax assessment purposes. The Three-Fifths Compromise, in this way, temporarily settled one of the most pressing administrative and political hurdles of early American nation building.

By 1820, this bargain was at a breaking point. The changing demographics of slavery and the entry of new states to the union threatened to cost the original thirteen colonies their majority of seats. Federalists tried unsuccessfully to change the ratio. The Missouri Compromise, another makeshift arrangement, closed two years of debate about the ratio, the future of slavery in the West, and other inflammatory topics. This compromise brought Maine and Missouri into the union—one free, one slave—in a move that escalated the conflict that ultimately led to the Civil War. The demography of slavery and freedom, continually in flux due to westward expansion, hastened the collapse of compromise.

After the war, the principle emerged from Reconstruction that governments must treat all persons equally. Key statutory and constitutional acts backed this ideal—the Civil Rights Acts of 1866, 1870, 1871, and 1875, along with the bedrock Thirteenth, Fourteenth, and Fifteenth Amendments—but another compromise brought this momentum to a halt. The deadlocked presidential election of 1876 was resolved in favor of Republican Rutherford B. Hayes, whom Southerners supported on the condition that he relax Reconstruction efforts. True to his word, the troops were pulled out—at a steep cost to blacks, barely a decade removed from slavery. Census data fueled antebellum racial attitudes, later facilitated the hasty retreat from racial equality, and even served to legitimate this shift. Consider the circumstances of the introduction of the mulatto category in 1850. Added initially as a means by which to test Josiah C. Nott's theory that blacks and whites were separate species, he believed the progeny of interracial unions to be frailer and, thus, to live shorter lives. They will "follow the fate of the Indians," he prophesied.[48] "Mulatto" appeared on all subsequent censuses through 1890—at which point "Quadroon" and "Octoroon" made one-time appearances—after which it was dropped in 1900 and reappeared in 1910. After a final census appearance in 1920, the decades-long search for evidence that mulattos were susceptible to early death was finally abandoned.

The fact that white men contributed considerably to the abundance of mulattos in the first place did not deter white supremacists from exploiting fears of interracial sex via the inveterate trope of white women's virtue, on one hand, and black men's bestiality, on the other. The power of this myth is often underestimated. Accord-

↑ power of myth is often underestimated.

ing to Gunnar Myrdal, Randall Kennedy, and Rachel Moran, for instance, much of the arc of American race relations can be traced back to this. "Maryland enacted the first antimiscegenation statute in 1661 and Virginia followed suit one year later," Moran reports.[49] The anxieties of white men regarding interracial sex amounted to "perhaps *the* major justification for subverting the civil and political rights that had been granted to blacks" [after the First Reconstruction] and "*the* major reason for confining blacks to their degraded 'place' at the bottom of the social hierarchy" during Jim Crow, writes Kennedy.[50] Indeed, as Moran's important book *Interracial Intimacy: The Regulation of Race and Romance* points out, fourteen years before notoriously upholding the legality of segregation in *Plessy v. Ferguson* (1896), the U.S. Supreme Court employed comparable logic in *Pace v. Alabama* (1882). In *Pace*, the Court gave credence to a "separate but equal" principle in sexual and marital regulation. The justices concurred unanimously: "[interracial adultery or fornication] cannot be committed without involving the persons of both races in the same punishment. . . . the punishment of each offending person, whether white or black, is the same."[51] This desperately thin interpretation of Fourteenth Amendment equality left to the states the right to regulate sex and marriage. Antimiscegenation laws proliferated anew, and governments soon extended the segregation principle to railroads, libraries, parks, schools, and most other areas of American public life.

The *Plessy* decision, having sanctioned segregation on railroads, also drew a solid, if arbitrary, line between black and white. Homer Plessy, light-skinned enough to remain undetected, sat in a car for whites and informed the conductor: "I have to tell you that, according to Louisiana law, I am a colored man."[52] This did two things at once: it affirmed the right of colored people to equal facilities, and it mocked the imposition of assigned racial designations. In 1896—just six years after "Quadroon" and "Octoroon" appeared in the census—the Court rejected the nuance: Homer Plessy was colored and had no say in the matter. Further, the Court determined that racially segregated facilities did not violate the principle of equal protection under law. In his famous dissent, Justice Harlan said the law was intended "not so much to exclude white persons from railroad cars occupied by blacks, as to exclude colored people from coaches occupied by . . . white persons."[53] In other words, the *Plessy* ruling sought to preserve the "virtue" of white women—by putatively keeping them away from black men of all hues—as it codified the one-drop rule. Jim Crow segregation would remain fundamentally intact for over fifty years.

Famously, *Plessy* was finally overturned in 1954 (*Brown v. Board of Education*), but the Supreme Court did not decriminalize interracial marriage (*Loving v. Virginia*) until thirteen years later, in 1967. In between, the Civil Rights Act of 1964 and the Voting Rights Act of 1965 stand as towering achievements; together, they dismantled the structure of black disenfranchisement in the South and various types of public and private discrimination throughout the United States. In the process, racial statistics became valuable to American minority groups in new ways. In implementing and regulating the Civil Rights Act, for instance, racial statistics became important in order to identify the number of minorities employed in firms and the racial composition of schools. Section 2 of the Voting Rights Act mandated that racial minorities have an equal opportunity to elect representatives of their choice; enforcement of the act required population tabulations by race to the level of the city block.

Likewise, many of the social welfare programs of the era, in their efforts to improve living conditions in cities and to address the problems faced by disadvantaged groups, distributed funds by means of statistically driven grant-in-aid formulas. According to Harvey Choldin, more than one hundred such programs were under way by 1978, using some measure of population to allocate funds for programs from preschool education to urban mass transportation.[54] With redistricting and new funding driven by federal census counts, "across the country communities and minorities began to examine closely their population numbers. Each one had the same goal: to maximize its own numbers."[55] Hence, the fierce battles surrounding the undercount.

By the 1990s, the fundamental civil rights concern about a multiracial census option was its potential to obscure the documentation of persistent patterns of inequality and discrimination. In employment cases, for instance, statistics usually enter the picture as a means to compare the racial composition of a firm versus that of proximate labor markets. Although this represents only one piece of evidence toward establishing a pattern or practice of discrimination in civil rights employment law, when statistics *are* used, only gross statistical disparities constitute prima facie proof. Such statistical disparities are measured in standard deviations, for example, *Hazlewood School District v. United States* (1977); in tests of significance, for example, *Albemarle Paper Co. v. Moody* (1975); and in other big-picture calculations such as the 80% + 1 rule, for example, *Guinyard et al. v. City of New York et al.* (1992).[56] In this light, some have argued that the multiple-race option ultimately settled upon by the OMB is immaterial to antidiscrimination efforts, due to the size and status (not a protected class) of this population. On the other hand, as Hilary Shelton of the NAACP has pointed out, the new policy could introduce fresh disputes over the definition of the racial composition of, say, a firm or a labor pool.[57]

Enforcement of the Voting Rights Act is more directly reliant upon census data than other areas of civil rights law. The issue raised by a multiracial census in a voting rights context is dilution. The Supreme Court's 1986 *Thornburg v. Gingles* decision established three preconditions that plaintiffs asserting a vote dilution claim under Section 2 must prove. The minority group must be sufficiently large and geographically compact; it must exhibit political cohesion (that is, its members must vote in a similar fashion); and the white electorate must vote in a bloc, enabling whites usually to defeat the preferred candidate of minority groups. *Johnson v. De Grandy* (1994) established these as necessary but not sufficient circumstances, and subsequent cases added more conditions. Nevertheless, *Gingles* remains a controlling precedent for litigation involving Section 2, and statistical evidence in Section 2 litigation turns on patterns broadly thought to be unaffected by the multiple race option, again because the ranks of self-identified multiracial Americans are small as currently measured.[58] Even were the numbers significantly larger[59] there is no evidence presently available to suggest that multiracial voters would vote differently enough from monoracial minorities to trigger apprehension about the political cohesion of minority communities in voting districts. In this context, interestingly, the third *Gingles* condition seems to mirror the second. For now, it is implausible that the multiracial option might obscure otherwise appreciable (to the point of polarized) patterns of white bloc voting.

geographically compact?

It is also worth noting that the Supreme Court has not provided "definitive guidance to courts grappling with population-base issues in redistricting cases," according to Bruce Clark and Timothy Reagan, who point out that *Gingles* does not define with precision what constitutes a majority or what kind of majority in a single-member district the minority group must constitute.[60] Rapid growth in the nonwhite, noncitizen population adds weight and relevance to both issues. The disparities between total resident, citizen, and registered voter populations broken down by race and ethnicity are stunning and troubling in a growing number of districts. In districts in which no one group can meet the majority requirement independently, the issue has come up as to whether different minority populations can be combined to meet the precondition, for instance, in *Sanchez v. Colorado* (1996).

The thread running through all of this is that the old, familiar, and binary view of race is showing considerable signs of strain, as are some assumptions about the relative strength of race as a predictor of preferences or behavior.[61] Growing racial diversity poses tremendous questions for contemporary civil rights thought and action. One key issue involves the fact that civil rights enforcement requires clear-cut racial categories. The Equal Employment Opportunity Commission (EEOC), created by the Civil Rights Act of 1964, sought to develop quantitative indicators of the extent to which blacks were subject to discrimination. Underfunded, understaffed, and initially denied cease-and-desist authority, the early EEOC had few resources and prudently chose to focus government attention on the most flagrant discriminators.[62] To this end, the EEOC developed the EEO-1 form, which solicited information from employers about the racial, ethnic, and gender breakdown of their workforces. Later, with this form as a guide, the OMB standardized ethnic and racial data collection across government agencies in 1977. Statistical Directive No. 15 stipulated the protocol. "OMB 15," as it came to be known, mandated the use of four standard racial categories:

1. *American Indian or Alaskan Native:* A person having origins in any of the original peoples of North America and who maintains cultural identification through tribal affiliations or community recognition.

2. *Asian or Pacific Islander:* A person having origins in any of the original peoples of the Far East, Southeast Asia, the Indian sub-continent, or the Pacific Islands. This area includes, for example, China, India, Japan, Korea, the Philippine Islands, and Samoa.

3. *Black:* A person having origins in any of the black racial groups of Africa.

4. *White:* A person having origins in any of the original peoples of Europe, North Africa, or the Middle East.

And it included one ethnic category inclusive of all races:

5. *Hispanic:* A person of Mexican, Puerto Rican, Cuban, Central or South American, or other Spanish culture or origin, regardless of race.[63]

This would serve as the final word on the administrative collection and reporting of American racial data for the next twenty years.

Before its adoption, agencies often used different nomenclature or different categories altogether. A uniform set of classifications was badly needed. OMB 15 filled this role, and, as such, it facilitated civil rights enforcement efforts on a national scale. The directive moved away from race as biological—the mandated categories should not be "interpreted as . . . scientific or anthropological in nature"[64]—but not so far as to suggest that Americans could be of more than one race. The implication was that these categories, developed to meet expressed congressional and executive needs, were intended as political instruments. Indeed, by formally articulating the official racial categories in this way, the OMB gave lobbying groups an identifiable target through which to pressure the federal government to consider categorical modifications.

Along these lines, a few improbable precedents might have seemed encouraging to multiracial activists by the late 1980s. As part of a budding effort to woo Hispanics to the Republican Party, for instance, the Nixon administration literally stopped the presses to add an untested question on Hispanic origins to the 1970 census. This came close on the heels of the recently inaugurated "Hispanic

Heritage Week." Peter Skerry describes former bureau official Conrad Taeuber's shock at the last-minute edict: "the order came down that we were to ask a direct question, have the people identify themselves as Hispanics. . . . [T]he 5-percent schedule had barely started at the printers when we pulled it back and threw in the question which hadn't been tested in the field—under orders."[65]

In another example, Reynolds Farley reports the tremendous and practically single-handed influence of one member of Congress, Representative Robert Matsui of California, to ensure that a "substantial list of Asian and Pacific Islander origins is presented to the American public on the census schedule."[66] Indeed, the census form separates Asian race categories by national origin but then lumps them together when the bureau presents its race figures. Some categorical aspirants, in a countervailing trend, have wanted out. Before the 2001 terrorist attacks, the Arab American Institute had been trying for some time to convince the government to reassign persons of Middle Eastern origin from "White" to a new "Middle Eastern" category. Understandably, Helen Samhan, executive director of the Arab American Institute, said in 2002, "this is not the time to have any segregated category. I don't know when the time will be."[67] The Celtic Coalition and the Society for German American Studies pressed the bureau to disaggregate the white category in 1990 and again in 2000, to no avail.[68] Facing political activism and fearing lawsuits and other difficulties, the OMB began a comprehensive review of its 1977 race directive in 1993. By the 1990s, terms used in the 1977 directive—such as "majority race" and "principal minority race" to refer to whites and blacks respectively—were a world away from contemporary realities.

Race-as-Construct: Then and Now

Reasonable people can and do disagree about what multiracial politics means and how it will matter. In the search for clarity, it is helpful to think about what it is that the multiracial movement exemplifies. I consider it an example of mobilization around the idea of race-as-construct. Placed in this context, it is not the only such contemporary case. Panethnicity, after all, is similar in that its key descriptive involves a shift in the scale of identification from a smaller group boundary to a larger one. What makes Chinese or Puerto Ricans, respectively, Asians or Latinos? Panethnicity focuses attention on the ways in which previously diverse or unrelated groups identify common interests and assume a shared identity. While one manifestation of this (multiracialism) appears to be on the rise, the other prominent example of it (panethnicity) currently shows considerable signs of strain. Together, the emergence of multiracialism and the decline of panethnicity offer important clues about the future of the color line.

The transformation of Slavs, Greeks, Italians, Irish, and so on, into "whites" stands as a classic American example of the broader principle that racial boundaries are historically contingent. The political arrangements of the early twentieth century—through racial origins quotas and the endorsement of scientists and other elites—positioned southern and eastern Europeans as an inferior form of white. However, by the latter half of the century, things had changed: groups that hovered earlier on the margins of whiteness were brought into the fold. That is, abutting Polish and Greek enclaves became "white" neighborhoods; white ethnic differentials along occupational and educational lines faded considerably; and the English-Italian marriage became more common and eventually ceased to be referred to as "mixed." Americans have defined racial membership in different ways over time; in this sense, race-as-construct is not new.

Arguably, however, the civil rights movement set in motion a series of new American relationships to it. That contemporary panethnicity refers primarily to the consolidation of America's racial minority groups is one indication of this. Asian and Latino advocates of panethnicity in the 1970s and 1980s, ideologically aligned with third world struggle and solidarity among "people of color," fostered cultural ties and related them to political and economic circumstance. Proponents understood panethnic identity as an appeal to a core, shared reality of economic disadvantage and to a common experience of exclusion from political institutions. At the same time, antidiscrimination legislation, affirmative action, and related government policies adopted in the wake of the civil rights revolution opened political opportunities for these groups—as groups.[69] By the early 1970s, as white ethnic markers ebbed, Latino and Asian panethnicity grew.

In the decades since, Latino and Asian panethnicity has become a recognized feature of American racial and ethnic politics (its early promoters had hoped it would), and current-day panethnic lobbies, alongside other established groups—often with crosscutting incentives—have successfully pushed to maintain liberal immigration policies. This convergence of interests has brought in many newcomers who tend to share neither material nor legal statuses in common nor perhaps much enthusiasm for panethnic affiliation. The strongest panethnic proponents, who tend to be native born, middle class, and well educated, will likely see the concept stretched thinner.[70]

There are signs beyond immigration trends that suggest Latino and Asian panethnicity could be fraying. Interracial marriages in the United States grew from about 150,000 in 1960 to almost 1.5 million in 2000.[71] Viewed from one perspective, such marriages are still rare. Considered from a different angle, it nonetheless defies common thinking about race in this country to hear that, according to demographer Joshua Goldstein, about one in seven whites, one in three blacks, four in five Asians, and more than nineteen in twenty American Indians are closely related to someone of a different racial group.[72] Those related by blood or marriage do not inevitably form close emotional bonds; still, interracial kin relations make it more likely that warm attachments will develop among individuals who might otherwise have little to do with one another. In this way, interracial marriage patterns could signal encouraging social change. That is, to the extent that it undercuts social distance and enables individuals to think differently, and more humanely, about racial boundaries, intermarriage is a positive development.

Given that individuals grouped into racial and ethnic categories do not intermarry at comparable rates, however, a less optimistic reading is also plausible. Table 2, compiled by Frank Bean and Gillian Stevens from the Current Population Survey (1995–2001), shows that whites are least likely to marry blacks and most likely to marry Latinos, with Asians falling in between.

Thinking about it the other way around, *almost 30 percent of Asians (27.2 percent) and Latinos (28.4 percent) are intermarried overall, with 86.8 and 90 percent of these intermarriages, respectively, being to a white person.* Note also that Asians and Latinos, although geographically concentrated in many of the same states and cities, are not marrying each other. Nor are they marrying blacks. The prevailing trend is toward white/nonwhite marriage, as opposed to increasing unions across racial and ethnic minority groups. Blacks are the outlier in table 2. Only 10.2 percent of blacks, overall, are intermarried, and of these people, only 69.1 percent are married to whites, significantly less than the comparable figures for Asians and Latinos. At this rate, per Bean and Stevens, the intermarriage patterns of Asians and Latinos "will parallel those of European immigrants and their descendants over the course of the twentieth century."[73]

Black isolation stands out conspicuously amid countervailing trends. What is more, Bean and Stevens partly attribute what little black-white intermarriage there is to "higher levels of acceptance of foreign-born than native-born blacks by native-born whites."[74] Like European ethnics before them, contemporary Asians and Latinos could be moving to the white side of the color line. If so, the boundaries of whiteness will expand yet again. The less-discussed corollary is that the ranks of Asians and Latinos, as we currently conceive of them, will gradually diminish in this scenario. We tend to think that current levels of immigration from Latin America and Asia will inexorably make for more Latinos and Asians. It seems straightforward. Yet the reverse could be true for reasons just discussed. The panethnic shift from a smaller to a larger collective—say, from "Mexican" to "Latino"—might not stop there. The next stage, presumably most readily available to the native born, could be whiteness. At the same time, the "new" Asians and Latinos who, through immigration, would ostensibly replenish the ranks, do not seem particularly eager to embrace American ethnoracial labels. If increasing numbers of native *and* foreign-born Latinos and Asians opt out of these designations, then, contrary to conventional wisdom, their ranks will in meaningful ways contract.[75]

Is it easy? that easy!

TABLE 2. Rates of Exogamy among Marriages Containing at Least One Member of the Racial or Ethnic Group

	White		Black		Asian		Latino		Other	
	Rate (%)	N	Rate (%)	N	Rate (%)	N	Rate (%)	N	Rate (%)	N
Total marriages	100.0	155,534	100.0	11,593	100.0	7,313	100.0	28,993	100.0	2,342
Same race	94.2	143,596	89.8	10,190	72.8	5,152	71.6	20,180	25.8	761
Intermarried	5.8	11,938	10.2	1,403	27.2	2,161	28.4	8,813	74.2	1,581
Racial or ethnic group										
White	—	—	69.1	848	86.8	1,788	90.0	7,949	88.4	1,353
Black	11.0	848	—	—	4.8	85	5.3	432	3.2	38
Asian	20.7	1,788	7.2	85	—	—	3.0	265	1.3	23
Hispanic	55.2	7,949	20.7	432	7.6	265	—	—	7.2	167
Other	13.1	1,353	3.0	38	0.8	23	1.7	167	—	—

Source: Frank Bean and Gillian Stevens, *America's Newcomers and the Dynamics of Diversity* (New York: Russell Sage Foundation, 2003), 239. Adapted from the Current Population Survey (1995–2001).

MARK ONE OR MORE

A general theory as to how the race-as-construct dynamic is likely to play out in American politics would be nice, but a litany of unknowns make it unrealistic to advance one.[76] Even so, a few broad observations may guide us in this direction. First, in this emotionally charged discussion—given the statistically minor part that black-white intermarriage plays in the unfolding drama—the black-white divide seems to loom larger than life. What is more, as discussed in later chapters, most proponents of the multiracial cause in the 1990s did not view themselves as multiracial and only a few claimed to be perceived as such by outsiders. Their concept of racial fluidity began with their children. This points to one of many ironies of multiracial advocates' reasoning, inasmuch as it treats race as primarily biological. Besides, a logic that identifies a subset of unions as "interracial" implies that all other unions are between two people of the same pure race. I return to these discrepancies later; the point for now is that race-as-construct is not to be confused with "post-race."

not post-race

A second, related observation is this: perhaps black-white and Asian-white individuals, for instance, may yet coalesce around a "panmultiracial" identity, but that is not the story of this book. There is little to suggest that outsiders make the connection. The need for racial order—betrayed by the boorish "what are you?" question—implies that outsiders, instead of lumping multiracials together as such, are inclined to fumble for alternatives that are more familiar. In a seminal article, David Lopez and Yen Espiritu drive the blunt point home. Unless "subgroups 'look alike' from the perspective of the outsider,"[77] panethnic affiliations are not likely to thrive. This fundamental tenet of panethnicity—that "external" defining processes reinforce "internal" solidarity—seems increasingly uncertain for many Latinos and Asians and, surely, for multiracials. Multiracial children even within the same family often settle on different racial identities, and multiracial youth report various racial affiliations depending on context.[78] A commonality, yes, but a unifying one? To the extent that panmultiracialism—the formation of alliances and sympathies across the far-flung span of the multiracial experience—is emerging, it is happening on college campuses. This is where the next phase of the debate over meaning and action in multiracial advocacy is now unfolding. As such, the absence of systemic information about college-based groups makes for a considerable gap in the literature. Interestingly enough, panethnicity took root on many of these same college campuses in the 1970s.

According to bureau estimates, in 2001, just after the nation experienced its first multiple-race census, Latinos displaced blacks as America's new majority-minority group. Taken separately, each of these developments is of uncertain consequence. But considered together, the MOOM option adds a new layer of complexity to an already complex situation. MOOM's impact could be most far-reaching, ultimately, in the ways in which it interacts with high levels of immigration.[79] Another set of questions, therefore, involves how modern-day race-as-construct mobilization, with some semblance to the situation at the turn of the last century, is taking place against a rapidly changing demographic backdrop. The influx of immigrants to the United States between 1970 and 2000 was comparable in scope to the massive migration stream from Europe between 1880 and 1920. It has become commonplace to refer to the contemporary racial landscape of the United States as "unprecedented," however, because most of today's immigrants are not coming from Europe. By 2000, 10.4 percent of the U.S. population was foreign born and 76.5 percent of immigrants came to the United States from Latin America, the Caribbean, or Asia.[80] The result has been moderate growth in the overall U.S. population and a substantial increase in the nonwhite share thereof. Native-born black population growth, over the same period, has remained relatively flat.

Yet the civil rights movement made modern-day race-as-construct mobilization possible. The former has served as the central example for the latter in most every way. Thus do we come to the matter of linked trajectories. Any number of factors involved in the rise of a social movement and its success are obviously beyond the direct control of the activists involved. Movements can ride the wave of political opportunity, and they can benefit from broader structural circumstances, such as demographic shifts; but they cannot ordain such things. Focusing on the elements of their environment that activists do control, including ideological framing and the choice of tactics for drawing attention to their cause, the influence of the civil rights movement on multiracial activism is unmistakable. Indeed, activists sought to package the official recognition of multiracial people as the "next logical step in civil rights."[81]

The Racial Harmony Hall of Fame award and the ambitious plans attached to it serve as a case in point. Rita Frazier, chief national director of APFU, envisioned an award to honor those who have "put their lives on the line to promote racial equality and unity."[82] The first honorees, inducted in 1995, included civil rights leader Ralph David Abernathy Jr. and Richard and Mildred Loving,[83] whose 1967 Supreme Court case dismantled the remaining interracial marriage bans in the United States. *New People* and *Interrace* magazines, along with the IFA in Dallas–Forth Worth, sponsored the awards ceremony.[84] Next, setting their sights on a more lasting tribute, Ruth and Steve White, along with Frazier, began plans to establish a Racial Harmony Hall in Little Rock, Arkansas. "As the Civil Rights museum is only two hours away in Memphis, Tennessee—The Racial Harmony Hall of Fame will start you out with some positive examples of history that have been overlooked."[85]

[In order to explain the rise of multiracial activism post-*Loving*, one must look at specific ways in which the political climate became less hostile, and eventually even favorable, to a politicized concept of multiracial identity. These opportunities were opened up by civil rights outcomes. After all, until the implementation of antisegregation laws and the repeal of antimiscegenation laws, there was little opportunity for a multiracial movement to materialize and grow.[86] The American legal system, by the end of the 1960s, had evolved from an attitude of overt hostility toward interracial contact and unions to one in which such contact was at least not regarded as criminal activity.]

I conducted interviews—often multiple interviews—with every major leader of the multiracial movement. All of these spokespeople conveyed a vision of official multiracial recognition as related to, but somehow transcending, the civil rights movement. Susan Graham, president of Project RACE, informed me that "Our objective is civil rights and equality for all."[87] Ruth White said that this country should judge people by the content of the character, not the color of the skin. Ramona Douglass, AMEA's second president, recalled how she had "been a part of the civil rights movement since the early 1970s and marched in the South with the Ku Klux Klan dancing in my face."[88]

The reliance of multiracial advocates on the civil rights example is also apparent in their choice of tactics. Over the past two decades, active multiracial organizations have joined forces to stage solidarity marches; to write and deliver position papers; to organize forums; to arrange symbolic commemorations; and to plan street boycotts. Activists have relied upon a repertoire that was clearly inspired by the mid-twentieth-century struggle for civil rights. One very noticeable example was the pair of marches held by multiracial groups in Washington, DC, in 1996 and in Los Angeles in 1997. The first of the two was even named a "March on Washington," a name universally associated with civil rights efforts. Multiracial advocates boldly adopted and reframed the tactical tools and ideological arguments of the civil rights movement as they capitalized on the legal precedents established in the context of that earlier set of struggles.

It is one thing to assert that a group deserves acknowledgment. It is yet another thing to look to the state for that recognition. Even from very early on, multiracial advocates sought recognition in one form or another from the local, state, or federal government. To put this in context, we must look back to the outcomes of the civil rights movement, which facilitated the entry of not only blacks but also Latinos, Asian Americans, American Indians, women, and gays and lesbians into the political process. Their entry, in turn, revamped the dynamics of racial and sexual politics and acted as a catalyst for political transformation. Whether talking about features of the multiracial movement that were purposely cultivated by its leaders (tactics and symbols) or those that were beyond their direct control (the context set by the repeal of antimiscegenation laws), the multiracial movement has civil rights origins.

The Multiracial Census

From 1993 to 1997, the federal government conducted a comprehensive review of the racial categories to be used in the 2000 census. Although a variety of issues was considered, the review eventually focused on the multiracial category proposal. The result was that, in 1997, the official prism through which race had been viewed in this country gave way to a new system. Before then, identification with more than one race was not allowed. After 1997, the OMB gave everyone the option to identify with as many races as they wished. The resulting race data are unlike any before. Elites from both parties took up the cause, but Republicans and Democrats apparently saw different opportunities in the same trend.

The 1993 Hearings

As mentioned in chapter 2, the OMB had previously considered a multiracial option. According to Sally Katzen, an administrator in the OMB's Office of Information and Regulatory Affairs, a 1988 proposal was dropped in response to opposition from federal agencies, including the EEOC[1] and the Civil Rights Division of the Department of Justice. In 1993, Katzen explained what happened five years earlier:

> Those who opposed the change asserted that the present system provided adequate data, an issue we could discuss; that any

changes would disrupt historical continuity, a very important consideration; and that the proposed changes could be expensive and potentially divisive, again something which probably could be thought through and handled in a mature fashion.[2]

Here we see the reverse of the sampling/undercount dynamic: civil rights forces are telling us the system is workable as is, while the OMB is telling us it is not.

Representative Tom Sawyer (D-OH) encouraged Katherine Wallman, statistical policy chief of OMB's Office of Information and Regulatory Affairs, to request that Congress conduct hearings.[3] The OMB asked, and Sawyer, who was chair of the House Subcommittee on Census, Statistics, and Postal Personnel, obliged by scheduling a series of hearings on "federal measurements of race and ethnicity" in 1993.[4] Citing ongoing criticism of the census and rapid changes in the country's racial and ethnic makeup, Representative Sawyer spelled out why the hearings were needed. He also signaled that the government would "preserve the suitability of [racial and ethnic] data for . . . important [civil rights] applications." But he also said that the current categories, "in the view of many, have become misleading over time."[5] OMB administrator Katzen reinforced the latter point by explaining how she had "received pictures of children with questions. 'How shall I record this child's ethnicity?' 'How shall I record this child's race?' The kids are cute. The questions are real and very pressing." Emphasizing the "very profound and sincere human concerns that have been voiced in letters by citizens across the country," Katzen said the time had come to have a "comprehensive review of all the categories."[6] Conveying a sense of control over the process, she promised that the review would be a "fairly speedy process for something this complex"[7] and that the racial data necessary for federal government functions, including civil rights monitoring and enforcement, would still be collected. The tone was of a reasonable balance struck: the existing arrangement deserved examination, but that examination would not be allowed to fundamentally disrupt existing arrangements.

Related work in this field[8] tends to hurry past or altogether overlook an important point: both federal and state policy outcomes were basically (intended to be) symbolic. In other words, the prospect of multiracial recognition *without* adverse civil rights con-

sequences was attractive to the <u>Clinton-era</u> OMB. Like Katzen,
Sawyer set the expectation that a balance could be achieved
between ongoing racial and ethnic data needs and growing racial
diversity. I emphasize this detail: although a proposal to create a
federal multiracial category was on the table from the beginning, it
does not appear as if the OMB ever really intended to go that route.
Katzen indicated as much in 1993, when answering in the affirmative to questioning from Representative Thomas Petri (a Republican subcommittee member) as to whether a change would likely
result in a "compromise in how the figures are massaged rather
than how the public is forced to categorize."[9] This brings us back
to where we started: Democrats drove the process and ultimately
offered what they seem to have regarded as symbolic recognition.

In 1993, Harry Scarr, acting director of the Census Bureau (the
post was officially vacant), testified that growing racial diversity,
fueled by high levels of immigration, made extensive testing and
research a necessity for the 2000 count.[10] The strong consensus in
this first round of hearings was reflected in the widespread call for
"more testing." The involved civil rights forces—including the
Mexican American Legal Defense and Educational Fund
(MALDEF), the National Council of La Raza (NCLR), the
National Urban League (NUL), the National Coalition for an
Accurate Count of Asians and Pacific Islanders, and the National
Congress of American Indians (the NAACP got involved later)—
found themselves backing the "extensive testing" argument for a
variety of reasons, not least because all of them had been insisting
for years that the bureau and the OMB improve their count.

Consequently, although Billy Tidwell of the NUL worried
that a multiracial designation might "effectively [turn] the clock
back" for blacks, he also said that "significant adjustments in the
measurement of race and ethnicity may be in order."[11] Sonia Pérez,
a senior policy analyst at NCLR, stressed the need for accurate
racial and ethnic data on the Hispanic population while also
describing that population as multiracial "by nature." (She referred
the subcommittee to Census Bureau analyst Manuel de la Puente's
work, which showed that "as a whole, Hispanics view race as a continuum, not simply as white or black.")[12] Mixed messages also came
from Stephen Carbo, then staff attorney for MALDEF, who said,
"the continued collection of race and ethnicity data in the census is

fundamental . . . [and] any changes to the collection of data on race and ethnicity must be strictly scrutinized to ensure that the integrity of our civil rights laws are not compromised."[13] However, asked by Sawyer whether increasing the number of choices would help, Carbo replied, "I'm hard pressed to find a situation where understanding diversity better, understanding complexity better, is a hindrance."[14] The logic of conducting more testing to track new trends and correct known flaws was difficult to resist.

Between 1960 and 1990, the American Indian population grew by 255 percent, a rate demographically impossible without immigration, yet there had been no influx of American Indian–identified immigrants. Instead, according to demographer Jeffrey Passel, the "extraordinary growth was achieved through changing patterns of racial self-identification on the part of people with only partial or distant American Indian ancestry," along with "relatively high fertility and improving mortality."[15] But in 1993, Rachel Joseph of the National Congress of American Indians, testified that her constituents had no major objections to the quality of the 1990 census count of Indian and Alaska Native people. Joseph said that Indian tribes and organizations would be "very reluctant to change the race question without extensive testing and clear evidence that any proposed change would lead to improvements in the quality of the Indian data."[16] Except for the testing part, Joseph lost this argument.

Despite the contradictions, the civil rights community delivered a bottom-line message to Congress: a multiracial category would imperil the statistics needed to enforce civil rights laws. Testimony from civil rights forces within the government was more pointed on at least one issue. Arthur Fletcher, chairperson of the U.S. Commission on Civil Rights, said that he could "see a whole host of light-skinned black Americans running for the door the minute they have another choice."[17] Aside from the fact that it is misleading to think of multiracial identification primarily in black-white terms—a point to which I return—this is an astounding comment from Fletcher, who would seemingly prefer racial assignment divorced from consent and personal identification. However, he, too, joined the call for more testing. At this juncture, the civil rights position converged with that of the OMB, if warily: the existing arrangement may have needed examination, but ultimately it should be left unchanged.

As reported in the *AMEA Networking News*, AMEA tried to contact the NAACP, the Urban League, and MALDEF before the 1993 hearings "to advise them of our position and to seek their support." The newsletter reports that only MALDEF bothered to respond, and President Antonia Hernández "offered her personal support, although no official organizational support was forthcoming."[18] Either multiracial proponents did not perceive a civil rights dilemma or they refused to come to terms with it. "The changes we advocate . . . can be effected immediately with minimal or no adverse impact on anyone or any group and with enormous benefit to everyone,"[19] Carlos Fernández testified before the subcommittee. AMEA and Project RACE, to some extent, wanted the same protections that other minority groups enjoyed, and both maintained that these protections would come at little or no cost. The benefits, they said, were potentially far-reaching. Without government acceptance of a multiracial concept, we "enshrine racial and ethnic divisions."[20] but multi doesn't?

but they were already minorities

Multiracial proponents in fact advocated different format changes. Susan Graham of Project RACE objected to "any format that does not include the term 'multiracial,'" taking this position in light of the self-esteem of multiracial children.

> I'm not a scholar, attorney, or lawmaker. I'm just a mother, a mother who cares about children and whether I like it or not, I realize that self-esteem is directly tied to accurate racial identity. [Ironically [due to different classification schemes] my child has been [regarded as] white on the U.S. census, black at school, and multiracial at home, all at the same time.[21]

but kids aren't taking the census

Project RACE insisted on a stand-alone multiracial classification without further breakdown. AMEA, on the other hand, endorsed a multiracial category "followed by a listing of the racial and/or ethnic groups appearing on the main list."[22] AMEA would later vacillate on this question, but in 1993 the two organizations agreed that every "multiethnic/interracial" person had the "same right as any other person to assert an identity that embraces the fullness and integrity of their actual ancestry,"[23] as Carlos Fernández testified before the subcommittee. ↳ does "multi" do that?

One problem here is that a multiracial person, according to

[margin annotation: logic on bio rational]

both AMEA and Project RACE, is someone with two monoracial parents. In calling for a tally in which multiracial individuals could identify "accurately," their logic fell back on a biological rationale. One finds a similar contradiction in the multiracial claim that misdiagnoses in health applications represented a grave problem that a federal multiracial category would solve. And why, in the case of the Project RACE proposal, would it be more accurate to lump responses into a catchall multiracial category? While both groups emphasized the societal benefits of multiracial recognition—"our very identity is a challenge to this deeply ingrained prejudice of a divided world," argued Fernández[24]—their visions were abstract. Multiracial advocates agreed that a monoracial census forced unacceptable and avoidable decisions upon individuals and families. They also shared the conviction that a growing community of multiracial people and families could help to alleviate racial strife. Beyond this, their claims were diffuse and contradictory.

Members of Congress both testified and heard testimony in 1993. Those who testified were not particularly interested in debating the pros and cons of a multiracial category. Representative Sawyer opened the second session on July 29, again underscoring the necessity and value of racial data with a philosophical caveat: these "categories of convenience . . . convey an illusion of specificity that fails to capture the dynamic patterns of our population."[25] Senator Daniel Akaka (D-HI) followed with a case in point. Stating that his proposal was supported "by the entire Hawaii congressional delegation, Hawaii's Governor John Waihee, Native Hawaiian organizations, and the National Coalition for an Accurate Count of Asians and Pacific Islanders," Akaka requested a separate classification for Native Hawaiians. "We have literally fallen through the cracks," he testified, "between definition as Native Americans in many Federal laws and classification as Asian or Pacific Islanders in Federal forms."[26] Akaka won his argument: a new Native Hawaiian and Other Pacific Islander (NHOPI) category was created in 2000 (population 874,414).[27]

Representative Norman Mineta (D-CA) proposed two additional items for the agenda. First, he wanted to put a stop to the Census Bureau's plan to collapse the separate ethnic categories for Asian-Pacific Americans (this would have eliminated the check-off format that had been used previously). Second, Mineta wanted respect. "Until the bureau recognizes [us] as a constituency to be served rather than a problem to be dealt with, this estrangement will persist."[28] He succeeded in his first goal; it is less clear whether his second demand was met. Representative Barney Frank (D-MA) said he "wouldn't be here . . . if we knew exactly what percentage" of the people in New Bedford and southeastern Massachusetts were of Cape Verdean ancestry. "People have a problem out there," said Frank. "Are they African-American? Are they Black? Are they Cape Verdean?"[29] Absorbed in other issues, congressional Democrats paid little attention to the multiracial category proposal in 1993.

However, the lone Republican on the subcommittee, hailing from an overwhelmingly white district in Wisconsin, was thinking about the possibilities. On June 30, subcommittee member Thomas Petri asked the civil rights witnesses:

> [Are you] worried that if [a multiracial category was instituted] and you have to have—when you get into court, if they establish discrimination by comparing with the pool in the community and if it drops from ten percent to eight percent because there's a new multiracial category this might somehow make it harder to win a case or something?[30]

Stephen Carbo of MALDEF responded that he was "not sure" but he "[understood] the question."[31] Later, Petri opined, "when you create a new category it may complicate litigation and protection in the civil rights area."[32]

Stunningly, within a year of the 1993 hearings, Republicans gained control of the House of Representatives for the first time in forty years. As a result, House committees were reorganized, and the Committee on Government Reform and Oversight assumed the responsibilities of the Committee on Post Office and Civil Service. Representative Petri, wasting no time, introduced H.R. 3920 as an amendment to the Paperwork Reduction Act during the 104th Congress. The bill would have required that respondents have an opportunity to "specify, respectively, 'multiracial' [in the case of a list of racial classifications], or 'multiethnic' [in the case of

Rep gained control of House

a list of ethnic classifications] in the collection of information."[33] During the 105th Congress, Petri reintroduced this tabled measure as H.R. 830 (calling it the "Tiger Woods Bill").[34] Incidentally, Tiger Woods never associated with the multiracial movement, despite fervent efforts to bring him on board.

Tiger Woods Bill

The Research Agenda

The OMB delivered on its promise to thoroughly investigate the matter of racial categorization. In March 1994, it established the Interagency Committee for the Review of Racial and Ethnic Standards, the most important of the numerous committees and workshops established toward this end. The committee, made up of a group of representatives from more than thirty federal agencies, would eventually submit final recommendations to the OMB. One of its first acts was to create a Research Working Group, cochaired by the Census Bureau and the Bureau of Labor Statistics (BLS), which would outline an appropriate agenda for research and testing. The Research Working Group identified five central issues:

1. *Reporting of multiple races.* What are the possible effects of including a multiple-race response option or a multiracial category in data collections that ask individuals to identify their race and ethnicity?

2. *Combining of questions on race and Hispanic origin.* Should a combined race and Hispanic origin question be used instead of separate questions on race and Hispanic origin?

3. *Concepts of race, ethnicity, and ancestry.* Should the concepts of race, ethnicity, and ancestry be combined and include, for example, a follow-up, open-ended question with no fixed categories? How well does the public understand these three concepts?

4. *Terminology.* Should any of the current terminology for the racial and ethnic categories be replaced or modified?

5. *New classifications.* Should new racial or ethnic categories be developed for specific population groups and be added to the minimum basic set of categories?[35]

The agenda itself represented a victory for multiracial activists, as almost all of the major issues identified for exploration related directly to their concerns. Soon after, the Research Working Group announced its major plans for the continuing review, including public hearings in 1994 to solicit commentary on a number of potential changes to OMB 15, which had stipulated the standard classifications since 1977. Then, in May 1995, the BLS would sponsor the Supplement on Race and Ethnicity to the Current Population Survey (CPS). The Census Bureau would test alternative approaches to collecting data on race and Hispanic origin in the March 1996 National Content Test (NCT). (Note that the NCT was called the National Content Survey [NCS] when it was being conducted.) And, finally, in June 1996, the bureau would conduct a Race and Ethnic Targeted Test (RAETT) to assess the effects of possible changes on smaller populations.[36] All of this was good news for multiracial advocates, but by late 1993, as reported in *AMEA Networking News*, multiracial advocates would become "quite aware of the political, bureaucratic and traditional cultural forces we are up against."[37]

Civil rights groups began to take the multiracial category proposal much more seriously after the Research Working Group laid out its agenda. In response to the OMB's stated plans, a number of civil rights organizations circulated a 1994 "Coalition Statement," signed by the Lawyer's Committee for Civil Rights Under Law, the NAACP, the National Urban League, and the Joint Center for Political and Economic Studies. This coalition was

Concerned that the addition of a multiracial category may have unanticipated adverse consequences, resulting in Blacks being placed even lower in the existing American hierarchy. . . . [The multiracial initiative has] potential disorganizing and negative effects on Black Americans [and would] distort public understanding of their condition. . . . Directive 15 is appropriately viewed as part of the judicial, legislative, and administrative machinery that has been constructed over time to combat and eradicate racial discrimination. It is important to remind ourselves that this anti-discrimination capability was achieved at great cost. The sacrifices of the Civil Rights Movement . . . were not in vain. . . . We are opposed to any action by OMB which will result in the disaggregation of the current Black population.[38]

The black civil rights stance was unequivocal: the multiracial proposal was not progressive (although it might have appeared to be) and would do considerably more harm than help. AMEA and Project RACE disagreed.

> This statement is alarmist in tone, and implies that a multiracial category, in and of itself, has the "power" to upset the racial/ethnic status quo. . . . Civil rights gains sought by any minority group in the history of the United States have never been without risk, and have been well worth changes in existing policies. The multiracial community is no less discriminated against and no less deserving of its rights than any other racial or ethnic community. The interracial community sees the rigidity of these existing categories as a means of shutting out its people from receiving the same benefits, protections, and considerations under the law as the representatives of the "coalition" wish to retain. . . . [Your] stance merely perpetuates the myth that races and ethnic groups cannot mix. It encourages a continued atmosphere of antagonism, elitism, and suspicion which allowed anti-miscegenation laws to stay on record in sixteen states up until 1967. . . . Let there be no doubt, this issue is as much an economic numbers game to the groups resisting the addition of a new category as it is a discussion of lofty socio-political ideals. How are the civil rights of the interracial community being properly served if you continue to ignore these families and their offspring?[39]

In the hearings, and in virtually all other available outlets, multiracial activists persistently touted the transformative and even revolutionary possibilities of their efforts. But here that claim is muted or even absent. Instead, the AMEA and Project RACE response features the interest group aspirations of multiracial activists. The advocates wanted it both ways: they wanted a piece of the pie (as a separate ethnoracial group), even as they sought to undermine the notion of separate ethnoracial groups.

A few months later came the Wedowee, Alabama, incident described in chapter 1. The principal's ban on interracial couples at the school prom once again drew national attention to the multiracial cause. And once more, Carlos Fernández, now AMEA's outgoing president, thought he had found the perfect case. It was "specifically her multiracial status that earned [ReVonda Bowens] the abuse of principal Hulond Humphries."[40] Along with the Southern Poverty Law Center, Fernández was disappointed when Bowens settled out of court.

In August 1995, the OMB issued a *Federal Register* notice to provide an interim report on the review process. Having received oral testimony from ninety-four witnesses and the opinions of nearly eight hundred letter writers, the *Federal Register* indicated that many of these comments proposed allowing individuals who self-identified with more than one race to "check all that apply" from the list of preexisting options.[41] In response to the interim report, AMEA and Project RACE sent a joint letter to Katherine Wallman, chief of statistical policy for the OMB: "'mark all that apply' or 'check as many as applicable' would still render a multiracial person invisible, and merely serve to collapse numbers back into the five existing categories."[42] AMEA and Project RACE now stood for a multiracial category designator and nothing less. Although leading multiracial advocates viewed the "mark all that apply" suggestion as a potential setback, within a few months they found themselves incorporated into the process. In November 1995, following up on the recommendation of Ron Brown, then secretary of commerce, Martha Riche—who filled the long-vacant position of Census Bureau director in October 1994—interviewed Ramona Douglass and, based on that meeting, granted AMEA a seat on the 2000 Census Advisory Committee.

Outside experts have provided advice to the government on census planning for over 150 years. In the late 1840s, members of the American Statistical Association and the American Geographical and Statistical Society actually helped to draw up the census forms that gave us "mulatto" in 1850. Since then, the advisory role has grown less relevant, if more democratic. The 1980 census marked the first with a role for minority advisory committees. Established to advise on minority outreach and surely to reduce litigation, by 1976 committees had been created for the black, Asian and Pacific Islander, and Hispanic communities.[43] But, as discussed in chapter 2, instead of easing the pressures of litigation, the 1980 census brought about a record number of lawsuits against the bureau. In part, this is because advisory committees are just that: *advisory*.[44] By the mid-1990s, even the census director's recommendations had become publicly expendable, as shown by Secretary of Commerce Mosbacher's decision, subsequently validated by the Supreme Court, to override census director Bryant's recommendation that adjustment would improve accuracy.[45]

Not all multiracial activists agreed that movement strategy should hinge on legal maneuverings and staid meetings in Washington. Some wanted to take the issue to the streets. In that same year, 1994, Charles Michael Byrd, a limousine driver-cum-multiracial activist based in Queens, New York, launched a Web site called *Interracial Voice*. It soon became the major means for circulating information within the activist multiracial community. As the Web site—which billed itself as "The Voice of the Global Mixed-Race/Interracial Movement"—grew in popularity, Byrd felt more inclined to broadcast his own opinions. He single-handedly organized the first multiracial solidarity march, held on the Mall on July 20, 1996. Byrd did not lead or even actively participate in any of the established multiracial organizations. Using the Web site as his platform, he began planning the solidarity event against the wishes of AMEA and other involved actors.[46] While his stated objective was to petition the government for a multiracial category on the 2000 census, Byrd also had other objectives, including

> Repudiating the rising tide of separatist ideology that is engulfing the traditional civil rights organizations and their leaders

> Signaling the beginning of the end of "race" as the social construct that divides humanity

end of race

> Unmasking hypodescent . . . a.k.a. the infamous "one drop rule," for what it is: one of the most vicious aspects of American racism

> **Multiracial Solidarity!**

> **Multiracial Power!**[47]

Eventually, Byrd managed to collect seventeen, sometimes begrudging, endorsements for the march on Washington from multiracial organizations across the country and, in a Herculean effort, arranged for fourteen speakers to deliver speeches at the event. Ruth and Steve White, Susan Graham, and—particularly lacking in enthusiasm—Ramona Douglass, AMEA's new president, were in attendance. Before the march, Douglass complained, "I believe the pen is mightier than the picket line . . . my demonstration days are numbered . . . the board room is where lasting decisions can be made, not in the streets. This isn't Selma in the 'sixties."[48] At the march, many of the sentiments advanced by multiracial activists on paper seemed to materialize before my eyes. A man walked quietly around the perimeter of the small crowd, his two young children in tow, carrying a sign that read: I AM THE FATHER OF MY CHILDREN. Often, the parents of multiracial children are presumed to be unrelated to them or to each other. A young interracial couple happily informed me that they intended to hold hands all day, which they rarely felt comfortable doing. An older black woman sitting on the grass with her white husband held a placard that read: I AM NOT THE MAID.

The speakers voiced dissimilar policy preferences and articulated divergent ideological commitments, but no one seemed to notice. Instead, the small crowd seemed inspired by the poignant assertion that the multiracial community could highlight the best of American race relations. Precious few occasions in the United States draw a group like the one assembled on the Mall that day in July. This was the first multiracial event that I personally attended, and, as would be the case repeatedly over the years, I found the moment encouraging. The demonstration was also typical, however, in that it did little to clarify the movement's political commitments. Details went unspecified, and difficult questions were dodged. While the speakers maintained that multiracial families and individuals could recast racial politics toward more progressive ends, they steered clear of a much-needed discussion about potential allies in the quest to realize their hazy objectives.

Byrd wanted the event taken seriously, but with a generous estimate of approximately three hundred people in attendance, his ambition went painfully unrealized. Until this point, multiracial activists had been referring to their growing numbers, and to their millions of potential supporters, without ever having taken it upon themselves to actually call the roll. Making matters even worse, the media covered the march extensively. I counted three major networks there to cover what Clarence Page referred to in the *Chicago Tribune* as a "hundred person picnic."[49] By now, the multiracial issue was regularly making headlines in newspapers and on television programs across the country. Leading up to the 1997 hearings, the issue of racial mixture made the front page of the *New York Times*, was featured on the cover of *Time* magazine, was discussed on CNN and NPR, and was covered in the major black periodicals: *Ebony, Essence, Jet,* and *Emerge* magazines. Meanwhile, since 1992, a number of states had passed legislation to add a multiracial category on state forms, and similar legislation was pending in others (see chap. 4). The media brought the debate to the attention of a wide range of Americans, but clearly this "hundred person picnic" would need further help from somewhere.

The CPS test results—a monthly national sample survey of approximately 60,000 households—provided a first look at the potential impact of a multiracial category. Extensive media coverage was being devoted to a growing but still very small population inclined to identify as such. Given the opportunity, approximately 1.5 percent of respondents identified as multiracial in the 1995 survey.[50] In the 1996 National Content Survey (NCS), mailed out to 94,500 households, four of the thirteen panels tested for the effects of adding a multiracial or biracial category and reached a similar conclusion. About "one percent of persons reported as multiracial in the versions of the race question that included a multiracial or biracial response category"[51] in the NCS. Both tests showed that a multiracial category would impact the Asian and Native American/Alaskan Native counts more than that of blacks, but the impact of a multiracial category was not statistically significant for any minority group in either test.

The 1997 Hearings

In the fall of 1996, just after the first solidarity march, multiracial advocates learned that they would have one last opportunity to assert their views before Congress, in a second set of hearings slated for 1997. The Interagency Committee would then submit its

final recommendations to the OMB. Since the OMB would most
likely act in accordance with the committee's recommendations, multiracial advocates recognized this as a critical moment. Early in the year, however, their efforts were frustrated. In February, with the first of the three hearing dates just two months away, Ramona Douglass voiced her displeasure with what she saw as her marginalized role on the Census Advisory Committee. AMEA had been relegated to a subcommittee, the Committee on Special Populations, which met separately from the larger group. She wrote to *Interracial Voice* editor Charles Byrd for help, complaining that the "challenges posed by the Committee on Special Populations and their continuing efforts to shut out a multiracial perspective being heard by the committee or the full 2000 Census Advisory Committee [are formidable]. . . . The NAACP and the Urban League have been instrumental in this attempted shut out."[52] However, AMEA's call for a "flood of e-mail, faxes, and letters to carry us into the congressional hearings on this subject with strong community support"[53] went unheeded.

Another frustration was that, in spite of a concerted effort to get their testimony scheduled into the first round of hearings (April 23), multiracial groups were not allowed to present their statements until the second scheduled date (May 22). Fearing that the cause had been railroaded, Douglass, who describes herself as being of African, Italian, and Native American descent, expressed her disappointment in a torrent of speeches and press releases. At the University of Michigan, she complained:

> When Dr. Martin Luther King Jr. delivered his "I Have A Dream" speech, and spoke of a day when men and women would be judged "not by the color of their skins but by the content of their character," I don't believe that any part of that dream or speech mentioned the protection of government entitlements, beefing up racial "numbers," or increasing federal funding. . . . Dr. King was about the business of preserving Human Rights, be they Black, White, Brown, Red, Yellow, or somewhere in between. . . . What we in the interracial/multiethnic community are saying today is that it is no longer acceptable that political expediency or the self-serving agendas of special interest groups [thwart our efforts].[54]

Also discouraging was the fact that only a few nationally recognized groups had stepped forward to endorse any part of the multiracial platform. The Japanese American Citizens League (JACL) supported a multiple check-off scheme,[55] not a stand-alone multiracial category. The Libertarian Party, after bigger fish, sought to eliminate racial classifications from all government forms. "If millions of Americans withheld their racial data from the government," national chair Steve Dasbash wrote in July 1997, "the politicians' framework for American Apartheid would crash to the ground."[56]

Newt Gingrich and Thomas Petri

Just before the final round of hearings began, a number of conservative Republicans surfaced to boost the multiracial category effort. The most sweeping gesture came from Representative Thomas Petri, who, without consulting any of the multiracial advocates, introduced H.R. 830 in February 1997. If passed, it would have required that the OMB add a "multiracial" or "multiethnic" designation on the 2000 census, had the OMB not taken such action of its own volition. In an interview with multiracial activist Charles Byrd of *Interracial Voice*, Petri, conceding that his own constituency "happens to be one of the more homogeneous in the country,"[57] avoided explaining why he had not consulted multiracial activists about the bill. When Byrd asked him to comment on the civil rights issues at stake, Petri, whose voting record on civil rights–related legislation is poor (table 3), replied, "I understand that those organizations' [civil rights groups] goal is to deal with the problem, and the bigger the problem is, the happier they are I guess—from the point of view of having something to organize around and raise money for and protest."[58]

Susan Graham happened to live in Newt Gingrich's district and met with him two months before the hearings began. (Although the two had never been introduced, Gingrich knew of Graham's successful effort to get a multiracial category added to Georgia state forms three years prior.) Recounting her meeting with the Speaker of the House, Graham reported that she had "waited two years [for the opportunity to meet him]. I was told I had TEN MINUTES to talk with him. I quickly outlined the problem. . . . I handed Newt a bound report with the history of the movement and statistics. He quickly flipped through the report, put it aside, and said 'This is the right thing to do for the children.'"[59] After this brisk deliberation, Gingrich threw his full support behind the multiracial category initiative. In the eight-week period after his meeting with Graham and before the hearings, the Speaker issued a number of statements advocating the addition of a multiracial category to the census. "I would like to add my voice by saying that I strongly believe that including a multiracial option on federal forms and in the 2000 census would significantly help to ensure a more accurate reflection of the racial makeup of the United States," he wrote to Franklin Raines, then head of the OMB.[60] Gingrich also made time to attend the 1997 hearings in person. The Speaker said:

> We should . . . stop forcing Americans into inaccurate categories aimed at building divisive subgroups and allow them the option of selecting the category "multiracial," which I believe will be an important step toward transcending racial division and reflecting the melting pot which is America.[61] *melting pot ideal*

Gingrich went even further, announcing ten "practical steps for building a better America," among which included "adding a multiracial category to the census" and "doing away with affirmative action."[62]

Other Members of Congress on Multiracialism

The 1997 hearings differed from those held in 1993 in three notable ways. First, as mentioned earlier, Republicans had just gained control of the House of Representatives for the first time in four decades. Thus, the 1997 hearings took place under the auspices of a different committee—Government Reform—with a new chairman, Stephen Horn (R-CA). Second, the multiracial category issue had become the driving force of the comprehensive review promised and delivered by the OMB. In response, the NAACP became involved, as did a number of black legislators (none had testified in 1993). Third, if the OMB decided not to implement the category, H.R. 830 offered one last route to a multiracial designator on the 2000 census.

Representative Horn commenced the hearings, entitled "Federal Measures of Race and Ethnicity and the Implications for the 2000 Census," before the Subcommittee on Government Management, Information, and Technology on April 23, 1997. Representatives Thomas Sawyer (chair of the 1993 hearings) and Thomas Petri (ranking member on the 1993 subcommittee), both having had much occasion to ponder their views on the matter, testified on different sides of the issue. Sawyer, setting aside prior philosophical musings, did not equivocate: a multiracial category would "undermin[e] the primary purposes for which we collect the data,"[63] and the "ample opportunity for differing perceptions that a 'multi-racial' category presents [would place] the consistency of all of the data at risk."[64] Petri, apprised of the risks, contended that the exclusion of an "entire category of people on a government form such as the census [denied their] unique place in society."[65] What made multiracials a "category" or a "group" or a "community" (he referred to them as all three) Petri did not say, although, as witnesses made clear in 1993 and again in 1997, this is an important and unsettled question. Given his voting record, it is difficult to avoid the conclusion that Petri, along with his conservative Republican colleagues, had ulterior motives.

Because H.R. 830 never came to a vote, there is no comprehensive record of legislative preference on the matter. However, almost all of the congressional Democrats who expressed their views on the issue were opposed to a multiracial category on the census; all of the Republicans who did so were in favor. The cleavage along partisan lines is striking, as is the sole exception.

Table 3 reflects Leadership Conference on Civil Rights (LCCR) report card ratings for the members of Congress who testified in the hearings or, to my knowledge, otherwise expressed their views of the multiracial category proposal publicly while it was under consideration. Many legislators testifying in the hearings did not comment on the multiracial category issue. As far as I can tell, *not one Republican in support of the multiracial category addition said one thing* as to how it might be implemented without jeopardizing the enforcement of civil rights. Carrie Meek (D-FL) reminded the committee of the importance of this work.

I understand how Tiger Woods and the rest of them feel, but no matter how they feel from a personal standpoint, we're thinking about the census and reporting accuracy, so that government and other agencies can make accurate decisions. . . . The multiracial category will just make it more difficult to identify where discrimination has taken place and where it has not taken place, because it will cloud census counts of discrete minorities who have been restricted to certain neighborhoods and, as a consequence, to certain schools. . . . It will cloud the census count of discrete minorities kept out of certain occupations or whose progress toward seniority or promotion has been skewered. The list goes on and on, Mr. Chairman. . . . Last . . . multiracial categories will reduce the level of political representation for minorities.[66]

The big surprise here is John Conyers, the ranking Democrat on the Judiciary Committee and a founder of the Congressional Black Caucus. Recognizing that his "solution to this problem [would not] be welcomed by all of my Congressional Black Caucus colleagues," Conyers "[felt] very strongly that people of mixed ancestry must have a way to identify themselves on the census if they desire to do so" and that we "undermine these rights for which

TABLE 3. Partisan Patterns of Congressional Support

In Support of a Multiracial Category			Opposed to a Multiracial Category		
Legislator	Party	Voting in Favor of Civil Rights	Legislator	Party	Voting in Favor of Civil Rights
Conyers (MI)[a]	D	100% of the time	Davis (IL)	D	90% of the time
Gingrich (GA)	R	0%	Maloney (NY)	D	95%
			Meek (FL)[b]	D	72%
			Sawyer (OH)[a]	D	100%
Petri (WI)	R	15%			
Sessions (TX)	R	8%	Waters (CA)[a]	D	100%
Sununu (NH)	R	12%			
Average rating		27%			93%
Median rating		12%			98%

Note: Legislators are identified as pro or con based on congressional testimonies (where applicable) and their comments on the multiracial issue as reported in the media. Unless otherwise noted, voting scores are from the Leadership Conference on Civil Rights (LCCR) Voting Scorecards for the 104th and 105th Congresses.

[a]LCCR Voting Scorecard, 107th Congress.
[b]NAACP Legislative Report Card, 107th Congress.

so many battles have been fought" if we allow people to pick only one racial category. Conyers proposed a multiracial category with subidentifiers. He would "include a multiracial category on the next census AND within the same question allow people to check all of the racial categories with which they identify."[67] This was essentially the format first endorsed by AMEA in 1993. As discussed in later chapters, Senator Carol Moseley-Braun was also sympathetic to the multiracial cause, as was Ralph Abernathy III, son of the famous civil rights leader.

Tabulation

The NAACP did not testify in the 1993 hearings, but Harold McDougall, Washington bureau director, represented the organization twice during the 1997 hearings. In his first appearance before the subcommittee (May 22) McDougall said there was no documented history of discrimination against multiracials and stated that their recognition on the census—perhaps an inappropriate place for such a statement—would make it more difficult to track discrimination. The NAACP would "consider the issue in a more formal way"[68] after its annual conference that July. But by the time McDougall made his second appearance before the subcommittee, the Interagency Committee had already submitted its final recommendations to the OMB a few weeks earlier (July 9). Most significantly, the committee unanimously[69] rejected the addition of a stand-alone multiracial category, recommending instead that respondents be allowed to mark one or more races. McDougall, back before the subcommittee on July 25, said that the NAACP had discussed the matter with AMEA and other multiracial organizations and concluded that "the 'select one or more' option best suits all our purposes."[70]

The NAACP, along with other civil rights groups, accepted MOOM because it had no choice. In any case, the test results strongly suggested that the black count would be the one *least* affected by the addition of a multiracial category. The findings of the final major research effort, the RAETT, released in May 1997, mostly corroborated the results of the earlier tests. Taken together, "the results from the CPS Supplement, the NCT and the RAETT suggest that providing multiracial reporting options would not affect the percentages reporting as white or as black, but may well affect reporting in populations with higher intermarriage rates, most notably American Indians and Alaska Natives, and Asians and Pacific Islanders."[71] In turn, representatives from these groups protested, calling for further testing of the "mark all that apply" options (Jacinta Ma of the National Asian Pacific American Legal Consortium) or even explicitly opposing any change whatsoever (JoAnn Chase of the National Congress of American Indians); but the Interagency Committee passed over these petitions and the OMB followed suit soon after.

Following the Interagency Committee's recommendation, the OMB rejected a multiracial category but would allow respondents to mark as many boxes as they saw fit. Unveiling the new policy on October 30, 1997, OMB director Franklin Raines said, "We are not closing the door on the expression of multiracial heritage. We are allowing people to express their multiracial heritage in whatever way they view themselves."[72] Not all multiracial movement advocates saw it this way. Shortly after this, MOOM gave rise to a rift within the core group of multiracial activists, eventually splintering the old alliances. AMEA accepted the MOOM decision as a way to both report multiple heritages and maintain civil rights enforcement efforts. But Susan Graham of Project RACE felt that AMEA had sold out and vowed to continue the fight for a stand-alone multiracial category. Others, including Ruth and Steve White and Charles Byrd of *Interracial Voice*, reverted to the position that getting rid of racial categorization altogether was a necessary first step toward eradicating racism.

Irrespective of multiracial advocates' internal divisions, MOOM soon became the center of a new political battle, in which attention shifted to the way the Census Bureau would tabulate multiple-race responses. Although the thirty federal agencies represented on the Interagency Committee unanimously opposed the addition of a multiracial category, the committee articulated no specific suggestions as to how its proposed (and adopted) alternative could be carried out; hence, the creation of the Tabulation Working Group. The Tabulation Working Group was made up of a subset of Interagency Committee members: their job was to establish the mechanics for processing multiple race responses and to generate guidelines for federal agencies' aggregation and reporting of multiple-race data. The assignment provoked a new round of controversy about how to tackle this technically challenging and politically charged task. The situation also led to justifiable criticism of the OMB for announcing the new policy while the details still remained unsettled.

As but one indication of the difficulties involved, the Tabulation Working Group managed to produce the guidelines only a few weeks before the 2000 census was conducted. This delay was largely caused by civil rights laws' requirement that statistics plainly distinguish between those individuals who are members of minority groups and those who are not. This meant that, for the purposes of civil rights monitoring, the Tabulation Working Group had the unenviable job of devising a standard by which to reallocate multiple race responses to a single race. Multiple race responses would have to be "put back"[73] into a single box in order to produce numbers for the purposes of civil rights enforcement and comparison of 2000 data with data from earlier censuses. The latter is known as the "bridging" problem, and the Tabulation Working Group considered an extensive array of statistical possibilities to deal with it. Each would have affected the count of racial groups differently. The most seriously considered options were as follows:

Deterministic Whole Assignment—Largest Group Other Than White: This method of tabulation would have involved reassigning those who checked more than one box to the largest of the nonwhite groups she or he marked. So, a respondent reporting her or his race as black, white, and Asian would, for tabulation purposes, be counted as black. (*This would have artificially inflated the size of large minority groups.*)

Deterministic Whole Assignment—Smallest Group: This method would have assigned people selecting two or more racial groups to the group with the smallest population with respect to monoracial responses. For example, black–American Indian respondents would be counted as American Indian. (*This would have artificially inflated the size of small minority groups.*)

Deterministic Whole Assignment—Largest Group: This method would have assigned people selecting two or more racial groups to the group with the largest population with respect to monoracial responses. For example, black–American Indian respondents would be counted as black. Black-white respondents would be counted as white. (*This would have artificially inflated the size of the largest racial groups.*)

Deterministic Whole Assignment—Plurality: When respondents reported more than one race, in this method, they would have been queried about the one race they most strongly identified with. The proportion choosing each of the possibilities would have been calculated accordingly. For example, among persons who identified as white and American Indian, those who chose American Indian as their "main" race would have been assigned to the American Indian population. (*This would have served to draw attention to—yet would not have addressed—the initial complaint of multiracial groups regarding a forced choice or a privileging of one parent over the other.*)

Deterministic Fractional Assignment—Equal Fractions: This method would have assigned fractions of persons to groups according to the numbers of multiracial responses given by respondents. For instance, an individual identifying as black and white would result in 0.5 persons added to each group. (*This had the virtue of avoiding the reassignment of mixed-race responses into a monoracial group, but this method would have yielded population counts that were not whole numbers. What is the meaning of a count of 2.5 black people? What about three-fifths of a black person? Another problem, then, was that fractions invoked the bookkeeping of slavery.*)

Deterministic Fractional Assignment—Unequal Fractions: In this scenario, responses would have been tabulated through an a priori partitioning scheme. For instance, if two-thirds of the white-Asian population responded that Asian was their "main" race (that is, the race they most closely identified with) then these people would have counted toward the aggregate total of the Asian population. One-third would have counted toward the aggregate total of the white population. (*This method ran the risk of the "forced choice" problem identified earlier, but its virtue was that it rested on an empirical distribution of "main" responses for determining fractional assignments.)*[74]

In general, two problems emerged when the Tabulation Working Group tested these various methods using the CPS, NCT, and RAETT data. First, results were more or less consistent across methodologies for the white and black populations. But for American Indians and Asians, numerically small populations involving significant numbers of interracial unions, the choice of tabulation methods had a significant impact on population projections. Second, the methodologies best controlling for group size were the ones involving fractional methods. These methods had the best statistical goodness-of-fit values, but their implementation was politically impractical.

Throughout, the main concerns of civil rights groups were to (1) keep intact the data infrastructure necessary for civil rights enforcement and (2) tabulate to the minority group when an individual identified as such and also as white. OMB Bulletin No. 00–02, issued March 9, 2000, reflected these priorities. The most important aspects of the new guidelines were as follows. First, in order to distinguish those persons who selected a single race—say Asian—from those who selected Asian and another race, groups were reported in ranges from minimum to maximum sizes: this created alternate—yet official—counts of racial groups. Second, allowing people to mark more than one race resulted in a total of 57 possible multiple-race combinations. Add to that the five official single-race categories plus a sixth option, "Some Other Race," and the tally increased to 63 racial categories. Because each racial category can be divided by a question asking respondents if they are Hispanic, the constellation of race/ethnic mixtures swelled to a universe of 126 possibilities.

Third, the tabulation guidelines for MOOM stated that people who marked white and some other racial group should be tabulated as a part of the identified minority group for the purposes of civil rights enforcement.[75] Inevitably, this meant that some people classified as whites in 1990 were counted as minorities in 2000. While this procedural decision addressed the civil rights community's immediate concerns about dwindling numbers, it is otherwise difficult to justify. Also of concern is how the tabulation process undermined the principle of self-identification; that is, people were reallocated into categories they did not choose for themselves. What is more, one must contend with the awkward observation that the new allocation scheme is conceptually indistinguishable from the old one-drop rule.

"We do not want to end up at the end of the decade still thinking,"[76] Sally Katzen said confidently in 1993, yet the OMB has in fact left us with much to ponder. Although MOOM was touted as a minor reform, it is difficult to see how this move strengthens the case for race-conscious public policy. Meanwhile, the Census Bureau wants to believe that technical procedures can be divorced from politics and wants the rest of us to believe this as well. Work by Alonso and Starr; Nobles; Perlmann and Waters; Skerry; and even former bureau directors, including Barbara Bryant (appointed by a Republican president) and Kenneth Prewitt (appointed by a Democrat), show us the impossibility of such a separation.[77] Yet all of these authors stop short of a much-needed discussion about civil rights strategy. The easy conclusion about multiracial motives is not, in my view, the correct one. It is a mistake to equate the political goals of most multiracial activists with those of Newt Gingrich and company. As argued in the coming chapters, acceptance of this point provides an opening into a more viable civil rights view of multiracialism.

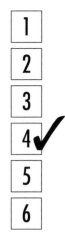

Multiracial Category Legislation in the States

Although the lion's share of attention to the multiracial movement was devoted to developments at the federal level, Ohio, Illinois, Indiana, Michigan, Maryland, and Georgia all passed multiracial category legislation between 1992 and 1998. In the same period, Florida and North Carolina added a multiracial designation by administrative mandate, and legislators introduced multiracial category bills in Minnesota, Texas, Oregon, Massachusetts, and California. Why did so many state legislatures consider, and in some cases adopt, state laws in the 1990s requiring the addition of a multiracial category on school forms, employment applications, birth and death certificates, and other official documents? This sudden explosion of activity is particularly remarkable given that, as recently as 1967, antimiscegenation laws remained on the books in sixteen states (figure 2). Less than thirty years later, almost as many states were considering some form of multiracial category legislation.

The Inadequacy of Obvious Explanations

The notion that social movements influence state legislative outcomes is not popular in studies of state politics. In a review of the literature, Paul Brace and Aubrey Jewitt report that internal factors such as party control and partisanship receive far more attention than external considerations such as the influence of social movements and interest groups. When interest groups *have* been invoked in this literature—in only 8 percent of all state politics studies from 1983 to 1999—the reference is typically to well-funded, politically savvy lobbying operations.[1] In this case, however—as at the federal level—a few grassroots activists managed to place the issue of a multiracial category onto state legislative agendas with little to no financial outlay.

Contrary to the situation at the federal level, in the states neither funding nor the composition of legislative districts was at risk. Federal and state agencies are not (either pre– or post–OMB 15) barred from collecting racial and ethnic data in more detail, provided that, when necessary, the data can be reduced to the standard, mutually exclusive categories. With little at stake materially, and reallocation again being deployed by government agencies to reconcile multiracial responses with single-race data needs, state-level multiracial category legislation seems like a symbolic gesture. The question is why this symbolic gesture took root in some contexts and not others.

In chapter 3, we saw that congressional Republicans demonstrated more enthusiasm for the addition of a multiracial category

States with interracial marriage prohibition laws that were struck down in 1967.

States that had interracial marriage prohibitions in 1952 but repealed their laws before the 1967 decision.

FIGURE 2. Interracial Marriage Bans, 1952–67. (Data from Adam Liptak, "Bans on Interracial Unions Offer Perspectives on Gay Ones," *New York Times*, March 17, 2004, A22.)

cans or Democrats in overwhelming control of the state legislatures involved, there would be reason to suspect that, against the
wishes of the opposition, the majority party could push through
undesired legislation. Yet table 4 makes it difficult to interpret
these state-level outcomes as a function of party control.

Table 4 demonstrates a slight trend toward Democratic control during the legislative sessions in which multiracial category
bills were introduced or voted upon. However, a similar trend
toward Democratic control in state legislatures prevailed across the

TABLE 4. Party Control in State Legislatures (in percentages)

Year Introduced or Voted Upon	State	House		Senate		Party of Governor
		D	R	D	R	
1992	Ohio	53.5	46.5	39.4	60.6	R
1994	Georgia	63.3	36.7	62.5	37.5	D
1995	Indiana	44.0	56.0	40.0	60.0	D
1995	Michigan[a]	48.2	50.9	42.1	57.9	R
1996	California[a]	55.0	45.0	60.0	37.5	R
1996	Illinois	50.8	49.2	47.5	52.5	R
1997	Massachusetts[a]	83.8	15.6	85.0	15.0	R
1997	Minnesota[a]	52.2	47.8	62.7	35.8	R
1997	Oregon	48.3	51.7	33.3	66.7	D
1997	Texas	54.7	45.3	48.4	51.6	R
1998	Maryland	70.9	29.1	68.1	31.9	D
Party control Average in states with multiracial category activity		57.0	43.1	53.5	46.1	
U.S. average (1990–98)		55	45	55	45	

Source: Congressional Quarterly, Inc., *Politics in America, 1994: The 103rd Congress* (Washington, DC: Congressional Quarterly Press, 1993); *Politics in America, 1996: The 104th Congress* (Washington, DC: Congressional Quarterly Press, 1995); *Politics in America, 1998: The 105th Congress* (Washington, DC: Congressional Quarterly Press, 1997). "U.S. average" data on party control are from U.S. Census Bureau, "Political Party Control of State Legislatures by Party: 1975 to 2000," *Statistical Abstract of the United States*, 121st ed. (Washington, DC: U.S. Government Printing Office, 2001).

Note: Figures reflect the partisan balance of power in each state during the legislative session in which multiracial category legislation was passed or introduced. North Carolina and Florida: administrative mandate; no vote or legislative sponsor.

[a]Michigan House, Massachusetts House, California Senate, and Minnesota Senate percentages do not sum to 100 due to vacant seats.

country during these years. Party control is not a promising means of understanding these dynamics, since Democrats controlled a majority of seats in states with multiracial category legislative activity and roughly the same majority of seats in state legislatures overall.

In any case, chapter 3 suggested that, had H.R. 830 (the "Tiger Woods Bill") come to a vote in Congress, Republicans would have been its most likely supporters. We might reasonably expect to find a similar partisan pattern at the state level. However, table 5 is at odds with this line of reasoning.

Table 5 brings two important facts to light: First, far more Democrats (nine) sponsored multiracial category bills than Repub-

TABLE 5. Bill Sponsorship and Roll-Call Votes

State	Party of Bill Sponsor	House Vote	Senate Vote	Party of Governor
Ohio (1992: passed)	D (Czarcinski)	90 to 7	19 to 12	R
Georgia (1994: passed)	D (Abernathy)	139 to 16	52 to 0	D
Indiana (1995: passed)	R (Server)	99 to 0	47 to 0	D
Michigan (1995: passed)	R (Voorhees)	62 to 41	34 to 2	R
Illinois (1996: passed)	D (Carroll)	115 to 0	53 to 0	R
California (1996: introduced)	D (Campbell)	No vote		R
Minnesota (1997: introduced)	D (Betzold)	No vote		R
Oregon (1997: introduced)	D (Beyer)	No vote		D
Massachusetts (1997: introduced)	D (Keating)	No vote		R
Texas (1997: introduced)	D (Ellis)	No vote		R
Maryland[a] (1998: passed)	D (Healey)	46 to 0 / 45 to 0	124 to 10[b] / 128 to 2[c]	D

Note: The North Carolina and Florida Departments of Education adopted multiracial designations on student enrollment forms by administrative mandate under Governors James Hunt (D) in 1994 and Jeb Bush (R) in 1995.

[a]Maryland governor Glendening (D) vetoed H.B. 215 in 1995 but signed H.B. 253 in 1998.

[b]H.B. 215 (1995).

[c]H.B. 253 (1998).

licans (two). Second, with the exceptions of the Michigan House
and the Ohio Senate, these bills passed with strong consensus. Both
facts make it impossible to attribute the same strategic motives to
Republicans at the state level as I did to their congressional counterparts in chapter 3. Thus, we rule out the most obvious explanations for the proliferation of state-level multiracial category legislation: conventional cleavages between Democrats and Republicans,
or blacks and whites, cannot account for it.

State Lobbying Efforts

School is often the place where parents first face official questions
about their children's racial identity. As part of the broader OMB
review process described in chapter 3, the National Center for Education Statistics and the Office for Civil Rights in the Department
of Education conducted two surveys to determine how schools collect and report data on their students. One survey, at the school
level, was conducted in 1995; the other, at the state level, in 1997.
The sampling frame for the former, *Racial and Ethnic Classifications
Used by Public Schools*, included over seventy-nine thousand public
elementary and secondary schools.[2] A stratified sample of one thousand schools—five hundred elementary and five hundred secondary—was selected for the survey. A considerable share of
schools (41 percent) reported that the standard federal categories
inaccurately described their students. Urban and urban fringe
schools with large enrollments were most likely to report such
problems. Yet of the schools within this group that could estimate
the number of students for whom the standard options were inadequate, the vast majority (84 percent) reported that the "inaccuracy
applied to less than 5 percent of their total student population."[3]

The other research effort in this vein—the *State Survey on
Racial and Ethnic Classifications*, which was conducted by phone with
representatives from forty-nine states and the District of Columbia
(Hawaii did not respond)—found that complaints from parents and
school districts were the main reasons for states' decisions to mod-
ify or consider modifying the standard categories. In 1997, thirty-
one states reported receiving requests over the prior five years to
add a multiracial category, while fifteen states reported receiving

requests to eliminate the collection of data on race and ethnicity altogether.[4]

Ohio was the first state to pass multiracial category legislation, in 1992; it applied to school forms only. As far as I can tell, *one* activist, Chris Ashe—a white woman, the parent of a multiracial child, and the cofounder of Project RACE—petitioned the state legislature to make the change. As shown in figure 1, only two adult-based multiracial organizations were active in Ohio during the height of movement activity. Nancy Shanks, the leader of Rainbow Families of Toledo, reported that her group of about fifty members spent approximately 80 percent of its time on social activities, versus 20 percent on educational endeavors, and was not involved in the state's multiracial category effort. Sylvia Billups of South Euclid reported seventy-five adult members in the Heights Multicultural Group and estimated that her organization spent about half of its time on social activities (plus 40 percent on education and 10 percent on public affairs). Billups told me that she was "not interested in political activity" and that a "multiracial category would not get us anywhere."[5]

In 1994, Georgia became the second state to mandate the addition of a multiracial category—in this case, on all state forms. Susan Graham, a resident of the Atlanta suburb of Marietta, single-handedly took charge of the campaign. In a personal interview at her home in 1998, Graham told me that she disagreed with AMEA on strategy from the beginning. "A better way to get to the federal government," she said she had told Carlos Fernández, Edwin Darden, and other AMEA leaders early on, would be to go "school by school, state by state."[6] Graham attempted to do just that. She had a hand in all of the state efforts; no other activist was so committed to this cause. She tried to get the IFA, the other Georgia multiracial organization, involved, but this suburban Atlanta group (and one of my case studies) was not interested. Chapter 5 describes the aftermath of her failed effort to persuade the IFA to picket the NAACP.

The *State Survey on Racial and Ethnic Classifications* notes specifically that a multiracial identifier was added in Ohio and Georgia in response to parents' requests. In contrast, the situation in Indiana was unclear even to some administrators there. In that state, the survey reports, "the change came about as a result of a change in the state code, but the respondent [from the Indiana Department of Education] did not know why the code had been changed and personally saw no need for change."[7] I found no evidence of activism in Indiana (the third state to implement a multiracial designator); nor, as reflected in figure 1, did I find any active multiracial groups in that state.

In contrast, Michigan, the fourth state to add a multiracial option (applicable to all state forms), became a veritable battleground. Kimberly Crafton, acting on behalf of her children and others like them, led the successful campaign. Having heard about the addition of a category in neighboring Ohio, Crafton wrote to her federal and state representatives but received no response. "I knew I could not tackle this project alone," she recounted to me in 1998.[8] Having heard of Susan Graham through the popular magazine *New People*, Crafton contacted Graham, who, in turn, put her in touch with like-minded activists Karen Minard of the Detroit area and Ed Mosely of Grand Rapids. Working together, Crafton, Minard, and Mosely eventually received an encouraging response from Mosely's state representative, Harold Voorhees (R-77th). Representative Voorhees agreed to sponsor multiracial legislation in Michigan as a way to reflect the diverse makeup of today's society by allowing people of mixed ancestry to express pride in "both" of their heritages.[9] In a telephone interview, he reinforced the point: "government must treat people in a manner that won't diminish people's self-esteem."[10] Opponents, led by state legislator Ed Vaughn, who is black, believed that the new option would in effect drive a wedge into the black community. Quoted in *Jet* magazine, Vaughn said: "I can see all kinds of Negroes who don't want to be black jumping off the ship."[11] State senator Henry Stallings, vice-chair of the Legislative Black Caucus, concurred with Vaughn: "In my opinion, it creates a caste system that will ultimately cause divisions among African people."[12]

Crafton and the other activists were supported by one of the state's two multiracial organizations (both were defunct by the time I conducted my fieldwork in 1997–98). Juanita Summers of Bloomfield Hills, founder of a metro Detroit support group for multiracial people, promoted the change and told a reporter: "I don't even believe there's that much opposition. I think the force that wants the multiracial category is far greater."[13] Pam D'Souza, founder of the also defunct Interracial Families in Troy, was more circumspect. "It's good because it's an admission that mixtures do exist and pure races are essentially nonexistent," she said, "but who knows what the ramifications will be to other political and racial groups?"[14] Although the multiracial proposal generated more controversy in Michigan than in any other state, Republican governor John Engler signed the change into law in 1995.

Michelle Erickson told me in a 1998 interview at her home in Naperville, Illinois, that she had not heard about these other cases before she began her crusade to change the system in her state. Attempting to secure a place for her son in the Walt Disney Magnet School six years prior, Erickson, who is white, had difficulty filling out the form for her son, whose father is black. She improvised by drawing another box on the form, labeling it "other" and checking it. Later informed by the school that she could not create her own categories and that she would have to check one box, "I said what do you mean he can't be both? He *is* both." The school in effect replied, "Sorry, you have to pick one or the other."[15] Reluctantly, she chose to designate her son as black. She wrote to complain to the principal, who never responded. She contacted the media and her alderman, Bernard Stone. "He [Stone] sent it to the state senator [Howard Carroll] and he put it into a bill."[16] Eventually, someone referred her to Susan Graham, and "Susan wrote up [an] amendment"[17] that would have barred the OMB from collapsing the data. The amendment was ultimately dropped from the bill.

Michelle Erickson's son was subsequently denied admittance to the school and even to the computer-generated waiting list for "his racial group." The letter informing Erickson that her son had not been admitted ended by thanking her for her "support of Walt Disney Magnet School, where children encounter integrated educational excellence."[18] Outraged, Erickson enrolled her son in a private school where racial designations were not requested. "I did not want to make my child choose between black and white and alienate either his mother or father," she explained to me.[19] A torrent of correspondence ensued. Alderman Stone wrote to Ted Kimbrough, the general superintendent of the Chicago Public Schools, on her behalf.[20] Kimbrough wrote back that, while he was sympathetic to Erickson's dilemma, "Until such a change in reporting is made at the state and national level, we must continue to use the categorization required by law."[21] Meanwhile, Erickson remained in contact with Howard Carroll, her state senator, who raised the issue with Sidney Yates (D-9th), their representative in Congress. Yates promised to bring the matter to the attention of his colleagues on the Health and Human Services Subcommittee when Congress reconvened in January 1993.[22] In June of that year, Yates also wrote to Secretary of Commerce Ron Brown on Erickson's behalf.[23] Around the same time, Erickson also contacted her U.S. senator, Carol Moseley-Braun, who replied in writing that "as an African-American mother of a biracial son, I can appreciate your discomfort. . . . I would like to see the racial classification section of the application form be deleted altogether."[24] Moseley-Braun proceeded to raise the issue with Secretary of Education Richard Riley, urging the department to do just that. Erickson also explained the situation in writing to her other U.S. senator, Paul Simon, as well as to Florence Cox, president of the Chicago Board of Education, and even to advice columnist Ann Landers. By 1995, Erickson was calling the multiracial category a "bipartisan civil rights issue."[25] The roll-call vote makes it difficult to advance a compelling alternative interpretation: the bill passed the Illinois House and Senate unanimously and was signed into law by Republican governor George Voinovich. In 1996, Illinois became the fifth state to add a multiracial designator in almost as many years.

It only took a "few vocal parents"[26] to get the attention of Maryland delegate Anne Healey (D-22nd), who, along with fifteen cosponsors, introduced House Bill 215 in 1995. It passed by comfortable margins (table 5), but Democratic governor Parris Glendening vetoed the bill on May 24, 1995, stating that it would be "inadvisable for Maryland to make changes in race categories until the OMB completed [its] review of Directive 15."[27] Sympathetic, however, to the issues raised by the bill he had vetoed, the governor signed House Bill 1080 into law less than a year later, creating the Maryland Task Force on Multiracial Designations. The thirteen-member task force was instructed in April 1996 to study the implications of adding a multiracial category to state forms and to report their findings and recommendations to the governor.[28]

One of those particularly vocal parents was Julie Kershaw, a white woman affiliated with Project RACE. In the fall of 1997, toward the end of the Maryland review, Kershaw refused to identify her six-year-old daughter as "black" or "white" when registering her at McCormick Elementary School in Baltimore County. Instead, she created a write-in category: "black and white." School officials told Kershaw that if she did not choose a race for her daughter, they would. "What ramifications am I creating for my child by picking one? I'm not willing to settle for what they are willing to give me," she told a *Baltimore Sun* reporter.[29] In the same article, Susan Graham put Kershaw's experience in a somewhat larger context: "What has happened with this child happens all day, every day, especially in August. It's just not fair for these children."[30]

The task force considered the experiences of other states, analyzed the financial impact of making changes to state forms, and solicited public input.[31] Using birth certificate data, for instance, it found that the percentage of Maryland infants born to parents of different races had increased from less than 1 percent in 1970 to 7 percent in 1995. In that year, just 5 percent of Maryland infants born to black mothers had nonblack fathers and only 6 percent of infants born to white mothers had nonwhite fathers. By comparison, 22 percent of infants born to Asian mothers had non-Asian fathers.[32] The Maryland review took just over a year and a half to complete. On December 1, 1997, the task force proposed a method for reporting more than one race in the form of a checklist, "whereby an individual may select all race categories that apply. . . . To the extent practical, agencies should be encouraged to permit more than one race to be collected on current forms."[33] Following the lead of the recent OMB decision (October 1997) Governor Glendening signed House Bill 253 into law on May 12, 1998, allowing respondents to "mark one or more" on state forms.

In each of these cases, multiracial category advocacy amounted to little more than a one-woman crusade undertaken by a white suburban mother. State legislatures accepted the bills, in most instances, without much opposition or evidence of partisanship, as reflected in tables 4 and 5. As a first step toward understanding these developments, note that all of the bill sponsors represented districts more affluent than the closest metropolitan cities and that all but one represented a suburban district.

Table 6 raises a number of interesting questions. Why is it that legislators representing comparatively wealthy suburban districts were most inclined to sponsor multiracial category legislation? Why did such support transcend racial and party lines? How do we move from bill sponsorship to a better understanding of legislative outcomes?

The answers involve minority suburbanization trends. U.S. suburbs are typically regarded as predominantly white and conser-

TABLE 6.   Bill Sponsor's District Characteristics

State	Party and Race of Bill Sponsor	Median Household Income[a] and Percentage Black in Bill Sponsor's District[b]	Median Household Income[c] and Percentage Black in Metropolitan City[d]	
Ohio	D-White Czarcinski	$56,281 2%	$25,928 51.0%	Cleveland
Georgia	D-Black Abernathy	$46,935 80%	$34,770 61.4%	Atlanta
Indiana	R-White Server	$42,819[e] 3%	$40,051 25.5%	Indianapolis
Michigan	R-White Voorhees	$44,662 11%	$29,526 81.6%	Detroit
Illinois	D-White Carroll	$62,407[f] 3%	$38,625 36.8%	Chicago
California	D-White Campbell	$66,235 2%	$36,687 11.2%	Los Angeles
Minnesota	D-White Betzold	$58,340 1%	$37,974 18.0%	Minneapolis
Oregon	D-White Beyer	— 1%	$35,850 1.3%	Eugene
Massachusetts	D-White Keating	$64,810 2%	$39,629 25.3%	Boston
Texas	D-Black Ellis	$64,434 53%	$36,616 25.3%	Houston
Maryland	D-White Healey	$57,303 41%	$30,078 64.3%	Baltimore

Note: Shaded districts are suburban districts. Florida and North Carolina are excluded because the multiracial designator was instituted by administrative mandate in these states.

[a]Median household income in bill sponsor's district (1999): Compiled by the author from information provided by the respective state legislative research offices.

[b]Percentage black in bill sponsor's district: Michael Barone; William Lilley III, and Lawrence J. DeFranco, *State Legislative Elections: Voting Patterns and Demographics* (Washington, DC, Congressional Quarterly, 1998).

[c]Median household income in metropolitan city (1999): Census 2000 Summary File 1.

[d]Percentage black (alone or in combination) in metropolitan city: Census 2000 Summary File 1.

[e]This is the averaged median household income of two counties: Vanderburgh ($36,823) and Warrick ($48,814). Together, they almost entirely contain Rep. Server's former district.

[f]Median family income. Illinois does not record median household income by state legislative district.

vative, but recent trends complicate both assumptions. Over the past few decades, middle- and working-class minorities have made an increasingly rapid departure from urban to suburban areas. By 2000, in metropolitan areas with populations above 500,000, over half (54.6 percent) of all Asian Americans, almost half (49.6 percent) of all Latinos, and nearly 40 percent of blacks (38.8 percent) lived in suburbs.[34] Note further that state legislators representing one of two types of districts dominate multiracial category bill sponsorship.

1. *District Type 1:* Comparatively wealthy suburban districts with a sizeable black middle-class presence (in Georgia, Maryland, Michigan, and Texas).[35]

2. *District Type 2:* Comparatively wealthy suburban districts with very few blacks (in Illinois, Indiana, Ohio, California, Minnesota, Massachusetts, and Oregon).

If we look closer, the patterns become clearer.

District Type 1: These districts (near Atlanta, Baltimore, Detroit, and Houston) have a black middle-class presence, and—although Detroit lags behind the other three—blacks in all four metropolitan areas moved to the suburbs at a higher rate than average between 1990 and 2000.

Blacks are not the only minority group outpacing nationwide suburbanization trends in type 1 cases (table 7). In the suburbs of Atlanta, Baltimore, Detroit, and Houston, other minority populations are also generally growing at a faster rate than in most American suburbs. The emerging picture is one in which younger-generation black legislators, along with liberal white Democrats (almost all of whom represent comparatively affluent suburban districts), were the most energetic legislative advocates. This hints at a new cleavage, one that is likely to transform black politics over time, as older black legislators retire or otherwise vacate their posts. The cleavage is fueled by differences of opinion among black elites about black interests.

Detroit is the exception among the type 1 cases. It exhibits lower levels of black suburbanization than other type 1 cases; it exhibits lower than average levels of suburbanization for at least one other minority group; and the legislative sponsor was a white Republican. It stands to reason, therefore, that Michigan was the focus of more conflict over the multiracial category issue than in any other state, as is clearly reflected in the roll-call votes (table 5). In a telephone interview, a veteran black state legislator from Michigan said:

> On the surface, it seems harmless, but there are mean-spirited people who want to scuttle black power. I fought the bill very hard. I argued that it was strictly an effort to destroy black economic power. The black representatives [in Michigan] were jumping on board until I came along. So many blacks don't want to be black. . . . Why would Abernathy [Georgia state senator Ralph David Abernathy III, sponsor of the Georgia bill] support it? Abernathy is confused. These Negroes are totally confused.[36]

For this older legislator, the new generation is confused; for Abernathy, son of the famous civil rights leader, multiracial recog-

TABLE 7. Black, Latino, and Asian Suburbanization Trends, 1990–2000

Closest City Center	Black Suburban Population Growth (1990–2000) (%)	Latino Suburban Population Growth (1990–2000) (%)	Asian Suburban Population Growth (1990–2000) (%)
Cleveland	44.0	274.2	57.3
Atlanta	97.8	403.8	166.5
Indianapolis	263.6	263.2	165.4
Detroit	46.3	42.6	90.3
Chicago	101.8	250.8	103.7
Los Angeles	2.1	28.7	25.3
Minneapolis–St. Paul	156.0	161.3	110.7
Eugene	11.5	111.3	-6.4
Boston	39.2	75.4	89.6
Houston	53.9	101.4	92.3
Baltimore	55.9	78.5	69.7
Average suburban population growth, 1990–2000 (%)	38[a]	72[a]	84[a]

Source: 1990 Census Summary Tape File 1; Census 2000 Summary File 1
[a]Lewis Mumford Center for Comparative Urban and Regional Research, *The New Ethnic Enclaves in America's Suburbs* (July 9, 2001).

nition is "just one more extension of the civil rights movement in trying to make America a place of equality."[37]

District Type 2: Type 2 districts more closely typify the common perception of suburbs as wealthier and whiter than city centers. Another shared characteristic is that bill sponsors in type 2 districts tend to be white Democrats from liberal/progressive states.[38] Both facts play a role in explaining outcomes.

Again, recall that, irrespective of district type, the material stakes involved in the multiracial category issue at the state level are low. The terms set by the federal government made multiracial category legislation largely a symbolic gesture, which helps to explain the generally low levels of partisanship and political conflict at the state level. Supportive legislators apparently viewed the issue as a low-cost way to signal to constituencies their sensitivity on racial matters.

It is useful to think of the multiracial category issue in the states as a barometer of legislative responsiveness, at least on symbolic matters, to perceived minority interests. Viewed in this context, we can incorporate key insights from the minority representation literature, which is fundamentally concerned with explaining the conditions under which elected officials promote or hinder the interests of minorities in the legislative arena. One persistent and thematic assertion of this work is that legislative responsiveness to black interests is related to a state's racial composition.

Yet two problems become immediately apparent in tying our case to the minority representation literature. First, this body of work rests on a fundamentally straightforward notion of minority interests.[39] Hence the following question: Is multiracial category legislation in the minority interest or opposed to it? Black legislators appear to be divided on this point. Second, black interests often serve as a surrogate for minority interests in the representation literature; yet it is difficult to view multiracial category legislation as relating exclusively to the interests (however defined) of one and only one group. It also seems inappropriate to deem the phenomenon a response to black-specific demands, since white women were the most visible proponents. Interestingly, however, most state legislators seemed to accept the multiracial category issue as a feel-good, cost-free measure to address the "quality-of-life interests of minorities,"[40] as Illinois bill sponsor Howard Carroll put it. The roll-call votes support this view; that is, the issue provoked more contention among minority legislators than in state legislative bodies as a whole.

Both the minority representation and social diversity literatures point to the importance of racial demographics, although they tend to understand racial composition differently. The latter approach involves a composite minority (Latino, Asian, and black) population measure. Figure 3 shows the racial and ethnic composition of these states in both ways.

David Canon, David Lublin, Robert Singh, Kenny Whitby, and other scholars of minority representation have demonstrated that blacks have little influence on the voting behavior of their representatives until they constitute a majority, or close to it.[41] Only when a district passes a very high threshold—between 40 and 50

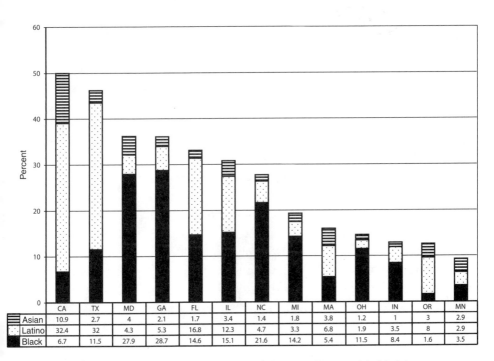

	CA	TX	MD	GA	FL	IL	NC	MI	MA	OH	IN	OR	MN
Asian	10.9	2.7	4	2.1	1.7	3.4	1.4	1.8	3.8	1.2	1	3	2.9
Latino	32.4	32	4.3	5.3	16.8	12.3	4.7	3.3	6.8	1.9	3.5	8	2.9
Black	6.7	11.5	27.9	28.7	14.6	15.1	21.6	14.2	5.4	11.5	8.4	1.6	3.5

FIGURE 3.   Percent Black, Latino, and Asian in States with Multiracial Category Activity. (Data from 2000 Census, Summary File 1.)

percent black—are congressional representatives most responsive. At this point, a representative can no longer ignore substantive black interests. I am not aware of any studies setting forth a threshold for symbolic bills in state legislatures, although it is reasonable to presume a lower cutoff point for legislative responsiveness to symbolic issues, as opposed to substantive ones.[42] Yet figure 3 shows that, even assuming a threshold half that typically thought necessary for substantive bills (say, 20 to 25 percent black), only three of the thirteen cases discussed here (Maryland, Georgia, and North Carolina) might be consistent with the idea of a statewide black threshold. Using these criteria as the gauge for responsiveness, we could perhaps explain the outcomes of interest as follows: we see multiracial category activity in Maryland, Georgia, and North Carolina because they reach a plausible threshold for legislative responsiveness to symbolic black interests. We see activity in California, Minnesota, Massachusetts, and Oregon (all under 10 percent black) because these are generally liberal/progressive states likely to pay more attention to symbolic black interests than comparatively conservative states with few blacks, such as Idaho or Montana. But there are problems with this logic. Why do we see multiracial category legislative activity in Georgia (28.7 percent black) and Maryland (27.9 percent black) but not in other states with large black populations, such as Alabama (26 percent black) and Mississippi (36.3 percent black)? At the other end of the spectrum, why do we not see legislative activity in other low black population liberal/progressive states (for example, Vermont or Wisconsin)? How do we explain the cases with black populations in between these extremes?

Most of these questions can be resolved if we focus on the *total minority population* of a state and not just its black population. Minority interests are more likely to be addressed favorably as the minority share of the population increases. This explains why we see multiracial category activity in states with large minority populations (one-third to one-half of all state residents). At the other end of the spectrum, where the minority population is small, minority interests are not paid much attention, except in more liberal/progressive states.[43] This is why we also see multiracial category activity in states with much smaller minority populations (below 20 percent). By this logic, one would expect to find the most contestation in states with neither large minority populations nor particularly liberal/progressive tendencies. The roll-call votes in Michigan and Ohio (table 5) seem to confirm this hypothesis. The only case in which this reasoning does not seem to apply is Indiana.

In states where blacks constitute the greatest part of the minority population, we go back to the question raised earlier: why do we see activity in, for example, Georgia (37.8 percent minority, of which 28.7 percent is black) and North Carolina (30.2 percent minority, of which 21.6 percent is black), but not in other states with large black populations, such as Alabama (26 percent) and Mississippi (36.3 percent)? Recall the list of southern states in which we do see legislative activity: Georgia, Florida, North Carolina, and Texas. These are states whose economies are strongly linked to international trade and services, with rapidly growing service-based urban centers and suburban middle classes. In recent years, analysts have found that the voting behavior of elected officials in these "New South" states diverges significantly from that seen in their Deep South counterparts.[44] In fact, political party scholar David Rhode argues that "since 1980, 'New South' Democrats have started to behave a lot like northern Democrats."[45] All of the southern states in which we see multiracial category legislative activity are in fact New South states.

Because there have so far been no other studies of state-level multiracial legislation, there is room here for further study and debate.[46] However, it seems reasonable to surmise at least a link between suburban development and multiracial politics (a point pressed further in chapter 5) and to note the salience of an often-overlooked relationship among constituencies, social movements, and political parties. The conventional pluralist model of U.S. politics prompts us to focus on the ways in which movements try to influence parties to achieve outcomes. But in this case, the factors necessary to sustain a pluralist line of explanation are absent. The strength of the multiracial category effort is a poor guide to movement outcomes, and multiracial category bills generally drew minimal opposition in state legislatures. The observable outcomes cannot be viewed as a victory of one party over the other.

Clearly, the relationship between movements and parties is

incomplete; what matters is the intersection of movements, parties, *and constituencies.* State legislators did not initiate or support multiracial category bills because they were strong-armed into doing so by a powerful movement, nor did they back such legislation as a way to outmaneuver the other party. Rather, legislators gauged the ways in which their responses to the multiracial category initiative would be received by their broader constituencies. In other words, the work that movements do to frame issues is potentially valuable to legislators striving to gain the support of their constituencies, even if most constituents are not active in the movement. Even limited social movements, by this logic, may mediate between larger constituencies and party politicians. The traditional notion that social movements are effective only to the degree that they mobilize supporters or exploit legislative divisions is inadequate to explain the success of multiracial category laws in the states. Rather, the multiracial movement raised an issue that was then used by state legislators in order to signal their stance on "new" versus "traditional" approaches to race and civil rights. One implication is that the influence of movements on legislatures is perhaps more pervasive than the literatures on social movements and legislative politics presume.

Another implication is that the social diversity approach set forth by race and ethnicity scholar Rodney Hero in his book *Faces of Inequality* might work differently if one considers social diversity and racial fluidity in tandem. Hero argues that the "little racial/ethnic diversity that exists in homogeneous environments [is] associated with relatively worse policy outcomes for minorities."[47] But the 2000 census shows that the highest proportion of minorities who identify with more than one race live in states that are overwhelmingly white. Perhaps, then, we should adopt a more nuanced view of homogeneity in these states, since a disproportionate share of the small minority population in these homogeneous settings is interracially married. For these reasons—along with the fact that middle-class, suburban, interracially married white women tend to serve as the public face of local multiracial advocacy—the generally accepted line of reasoning about minorities in homogeneous states might not apply.

Which elected officials, representing what kinds of constituencies, are most open to legislation reflecting more flexible notions of race? The answer varies. In the states, it is younger black elected officials and progressive white Democrats representing affluent suburban districts who seem most receptive. In Congress, it is conservative Republicans. Multiracial politics involves incongruous alliances. This leads us to the question of the activists' political commitments.

who wants it

states → younger black elected officials progressive white democrats representing affluent suburban districts

congress → conservative republicans

Political Commitments

The existing literature and conventional wisdom offer little guidance as to how multiracial activists squared their claims and efforts with civil rights imperatives. Viewed from the perspective of the grass roots, the range of options for engaging the politics of racial fluidity from the left is not as limited as one might think; however, conservatives have raced ahead to set the terms of the debate.

Grassroots Multiracial Organizations and the Enduring Black-White Divide

Recall the intermarriage patterns discussed in chapter 2: compared to Asians and Latinos, blacks are much less likely to be intermarried, and in those relatively rare cases where they are, blacks are much less likely to have a white spouse. The racial demographics of local multiracial organizations stand in stark contrast to what one would expect, given this benchmark.

- While movement spokespeople stress that multiracial identity is constitutive of people across all racial mixes, there are not many multiracially identified adults involved in the adult-based groups. Overwhelmingly, these groups are made up of monoracially identified parents who join the groups on behalf of their children.

- Multiracial organizations are almost exclusively composed of black-white couples, even though neither group drives interracial marriage trends (table 2).

- The gender and racial composition of multiracial groups mirrors Census Bureau data, indicating that the majority of all black-white interracial marriages in the United States (about two-thirds) are between black men and white women.[1]

- As in other groups of this sort (grassroots and family-focused), multiracial organizations show a gender gap. Women tend to become the leaders of these groups more often than men do.

- Most local-level organizational leaders are middle class and live in suburbs.

Consequently, it turns out that the multiracial movement at the grass roots was predominantly led by white, middle-class women living in suburbs. I did not anticipate this fact as I embarked on my research, yet it is directly relevant to our understanding of the political commitments underpinning multiracial movement claims.

As mentioned earlier, I administered both a leadership survey and a series of case study interviews with board members of multiracial organizations (fig. 1). There was considerable overlap in the questions asked in these studies; thus, when I refer to "all respondents" I am describing results compiled from both sources or a total of eighty respondents. This sum reflects responses from leaders (thirty respondents) and board members (who make up the other fifty). Again, I carried out my fieldwork at the height of movement activity, and it encompasses the universe of cases. (See appendix A for details.)

In response to an open-ended question about how these individuals identified racially, 56 percent identified as white, 22 percent as black, and 17 percent as multiracial. Only two people rejected the terms of the question altogether, responding that they belonged to the human race. Overwhelmingly, then, my respondents' understanding of multiraciality did not readily extend to themselves. According to group leaders, this pattern applied to their organizations' wider memberships. Cumulatively, these thirty leaders reported that about 52 percent of their adult members identified as white, 37 percent as black, 7 percent as multiracial, 2 percent as Latino, and 2 percent as Asian. We see little evidence of panmultiracialism here. Although group leaders lamented the fact that their organizations had not been able to attract a more diverse following, according to them almost 90 percent of their adult members identified as either black or white.

On most indicators, these group leaders and board members looked a lot like mainstream middle-class Americans, albeit more affluent, better educated, less religious, and even more suburban than average. About 81 percent of all respondents reported living in suburbs. Only 15 percent lived in urban centers, and less than 4 percent lived in rural areas. Almost half of my respondents (47.5 percent) reported annual family incomes above $60,000 per year, and another 20 percent reported family incomes between $45,000 and $60,000. Only 10 percent of all respondents reported annual family incomes below $30,000. In terms of educational attainment, half of all respondents reported having earned at least a college degree. An additional 30 percent had earned master's degrees. Clearly, multiracial group participants, mostly professionals, were notably well educated compared to most Americans; a full 80 percent of my respondents were college graduates. Only five respondents reported that their formal education ended with a high school degree, while almost as many (three) had earned a doctoral degree.

Affluent, well-educated, suburban white women are among the most politically active and civically connected Americans—but they are not typically agitating around racial issues. Unlike Americans of similar backgrounds, group members had encountered routine hostility from their families and the public—largely, in their view, because of their life-partner decisions. When asked, "Why did you join this group?" one-third of all respondents answered, "To socialize with other multiracial couples." Another one-third said, "To provide a positive environment for my children." Friendship and support for both parents and children emerge as the central factors explaining parental involvement. The majority of all respondents reported that the racial climate in their area was either "very" (37 percent) or "fairly" (46 percent) accepting of multiracial people and families. However, a whopping 96 percent also reported that they had suffered adverse treatment in public, typically consisting of rude stares, questions, and hostile comments, including a full 16 percent having been victims of attempted or actual physical violence.

Sometimes, however, the perpetrators became the victims, as in the incident reported to me by IFA board members Ed and Paula Anderson, who were driving one day in rural Georgia. A white man pulled up in the lane alongside them. For a few miles, he glared, swerved, and waved his fist menacingly. Engrossed in his assault, the bigot took his hands off the wheel and ended up driving himself off the road into a ditch.[2] More prosaic examples abound. One woman came to dread a hallmark of civic engagement: PTA meetings. The black women consistently gave her a "hard time" and she never knew "what to expect from white women."[3] Rhonda Bell reported no violent incident, but "people look and ask questions. They think I'm the babysitter."[4] As Phyllis Washington explained, "It's a lot easier to date your same race. One time we went to a restaurant with the baby and a white couple got up and moved away to another table."[5] In yet another episode, the Andersons were informed by a stranger that, "in God's eyes, it's wrong for you to be together."[6] Multiracial group members certainly did not subscribe to this biblical interpretation, nor were they particularly devout. Only 38 percent of all respondents identified with a church; within this group, Unitarians and Presbyterians predominated. Barbara Byrd (no relation to Charles Byrd) reported repeated unpleasant encounters in predominantly rural areas and "nasty stares all the time."[7] Jeff Howard reported no problems, "but then again, we don't go to places where we're going to have problems."[8] Lisa Giblin told of "constant stares and gawks."[9] A full 90 percent of respondents explained the high proportion of black-white couples in multiracial organizations by noting that this combination draws stronger reactions than does any other.

Yet, partly due to multiracial advocates' efforts, this situation may be improving. According to a poll conducted by Gallup for the American Association of Retired Persons (AARP) and the Leadership Conference on Civil Rights, by 2003 a record-high 73 percent of Americans approved of marriage between blacks and whites,[10] up sharply from less than half just ten years earlier. As shown in figure 4, the steepest increase in this acceptance, in nearly half a century of asking the question, came during the OMB review—that is, between 1994 and 1997.

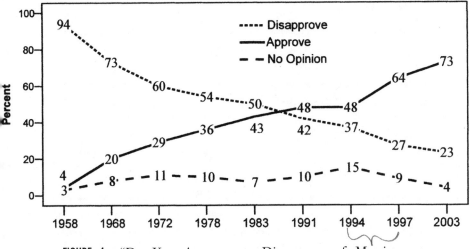

FIGURE 4. "Do You Approve or Disapprove of Marriage between Blacks and Whites?" Gallup Poll, 1958–2003 (in percentages). (Data from Gallup Organization, "Civil Rights and Race Relations," January 2004. In 1958, the question was asked of whites only.)

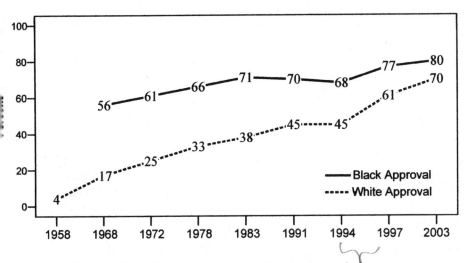

FIGURE 5. "Do You Approve or Disapprove of Marriage between Blacks and Whites?" Black and White Responses Compared. Gallup Poll, 1958–2003 (in percentages). (Data from Gallup Organization, "Civil Rights and Race Relations," January 2004. In 1958, the question was asked of whites only.)

One year after the Supreme Court finally decriminalized inter-racial marriage, nationwide approval of unions between blacks and whites hovered at 20 percent. Since then, American attitudes have undergone a transformation, plausibly hastened in recent years by sympathetic media coverage and a protracted OMB review. Yet these trends are most impressive in aggregate terms: as late as 1994, white acceptance of interracial marriage still had not attained the level of black acceptance circa 1968.

As shown in figure 5, the black-white gap closed to an all-time low of 16 percentage points by the end of the OMB review (con-ducted from 1993 to 1997). The OMB's thorough research effort brought with it prolonged media attention and public hearings held across the country. Since then, the gap has dropped to just 10 percent. This seems to be due to rising levels of white tolerance rather than a decline in acceptance among blacks.

The Split

Although most adult participants identified as white or black and were middle-class suburban dwellers, these commonalities did not give rise to political consensus. Multiracial leaders were deeply divided over the political content of multiracial identity and over whom they should welcome as allies. They were also hazy on the question of whether multiracial people could or should be at the forefront of efforts to lessen racial conflict. Disagreement over political commitments eventually split the multiracial movement in two. In 1996, a few months before the MOOM decision was announced, NAACP president Kweisi Mfume gave a radio address titled "NAACP's Views on New Multiracial Category." Arriving late to the issue, in this first major NAACP statement, Mfume said that the idea of placing a new multiracial category on the next cen-sus

> Is gathering interest in America. . . . Quite frankly [the NAACP] has some questions about [the implications]. Is the census form the correct place to make such a . . . statement about one's racial makeup? There are repercussions in the cen-

sus numbers that have a very real impact on our lives. Provisions of the Voting Rights Act are specifically directed at correcting past discrimination where African Americans were denied their Constitutional rights. With some figures showing 70 percent of African Americans fitting into a multiracial category, will we be able to identify black voters in terms of fair representation? No one should be forced to choose or reject any aspect of their heritage, but no category should be allowed to weaken others.[11]

AMEA's response, crafted by its president, Ramona Douglass, still maintained that a multiracial category would

Have zero impact on African American numbers. [Mfume] does not know our community, has failed to familiarize himself with it, yet expects us to be sensitive to people who would prefer that we either remain invisible or at least take a back seat to other communities' interests. If the same were asked of him, he would consider it both condescending and racist, as do I. When I can see that the NAACP and other traditional civil rights organizations are willing to step out from behind the safety of tired rhetoric and begin to engage in honest, direct dialogue with our interracial community leadership, then we can truly begin to talk about what our [collective] priorities should be. Until then, our priority must remain acknowledging our own community's need to be accurately and adequately represented, for the same reasons that other communities seek representation: health, education, housing, financial and employment considerations, etc.—the only difference being those other communities are being counted while we are not.[12]

By this point, AMEA had been arguing for years that a multiracial category would have no impact on civil rights enforcement. It vacillated between affirming this position and claiming those protections as its own, just as it alternated between views of race as biological (for example, the health claim) and constructed.

Things fell apart about a month before the OMB's announcement of multiracial recognition. In June 1997, movement leaders

RACE
vs
AMEA

convened in Oakland, California, to plan a coordinated response. Going into that meeting, AMEA stated that it would support the OMB decision as a way to maintain the "collection of racial data which will not adversely affect existing civil rights protections."[13] Yet AMEA and Project RACE had previously complained jointly to Katherine Wallman at OMB that such an outcome would "still render a multiracial person invisible, and merely serve to collapse [our] numbers back into the existing categories" (see chap. 3). This is what led to the split. To Project RACE, AMEA had sold out. AMEA, for its part, saw MOOM as a necessary compromise. The tendencies seen in AMEA's early documentation all resurfaced in its response to Mfume: the desire to be a showpiece for race relations, the quest for equal protections and privileges, the assertion of minimal impact on civil rights enforcement, and the recourse to legal action when all else failed.

Also consistent with long-standing sentiments, APFU denounced any desire to secure special privileges or protections for multiracial people.

> We do this not for political or financial reasons, but because we want to help families and individuals who come to us for support. . . . For groups like the NAACP, the issue may be FUNDS. For APFU, the issues are FAMILY and the raising of healthy children who are proud of their TOTAL heritage. Mr. Mfume was not even remotely concerned about the best interests of our children. It seemed that he was more concerned about voting rights and government funds. To us, color of skin should NEVER but NEVER be a prerequisite for receiving Federal help. The basis should be NEED ONLY.[14]

Government funds and, yes, even voting rights took a backseat in Ruth and Steve White's list of priorities. Susan Graham did not respond to the NAACP address, probably because she held out hope that, through the "Tiger Woods Bill" (H.R. 830), she had found a way to avoid dealing with the venerated civil rights organization altogether. (At her home in 1998, I noticed a photograph of Graham and Newt Gingrich on the living room wall, presumably taken during their brief encounter, described in chapter 3.)

The multiracial category initiative, which had served for a

number of years as the movement's rallying cry, meant different things to different people. The leaders of AMEA saw it as a means for obtaining the same protections enjoyed by other minority groups.[15] Ruth and Steve White of APFU rejected protections or privileges for multiracial people—or any other group—if racial distinctions were involved. Subscribing from the beginning to the color-blind rhetoric and sentiments associated with the right wing, they viewed the multiracial category as a stepping-stone toward the elimination of all racial categories. Susan Graham of Project RACE cared primarily about getting a multiracial category on the census; if this adversely affected civil rights enforcement efforts, so be it. In Graham's estimation, "AMEA decided that they had to get NAACP permission to be multiracial."[16] In describing these now-overt differences, Charles Byrd of *Interracial Voice* drew the dividing line between AMEA and everyone else. At the second multiracial solidarity march, held in Los Angeles on August 9, 1997, Byrd announced a new alliance:

> We decided not to align ourselves with the NAACP; an organization whose commitment to a future of racelessness through assimilation into the American mainstream is exceedingly suspect. . . . What this . . . demonstrates is that the multiracial community is no different from any other in that we have differing and competing philosophies. Some of us are content with identity-politics as usual, and others of us are ready for bold moves that challenge convention. . . . For some of us, the "check-all-that-apply" scheme proposed by the government simply is not good enough.[17]

Byrd, along with Susan Graham, joined in this short-lived agreement with Ruth and Steve White. For this group, the next logical step in civil rights was a type of assimilation far beyond that which the NAACP was likely to advocate.

The Followers

The ideological differences that had been evident from the beginning were, in the wake of the 1997 OMB decision, laid bare. I conducted my field studies of local groups in this climate. Throughout 1997 and beyond, I found that the loosely defined followers, if there at all, were not exactly following. It took considerable effort to track down Project RACE "vice president" Lucy Callahan, who admitted, "Project RACE is Susan Graham."[18] In Salinas, California, the APFU "Northern California director" told me that "there is no Salinas group. I am it."[19] It went on and on this way, as I worked through the masthead of APFU and Project RACE. Again, AMEA was the only umbrella organization with a membership. They were thus the only group who felt it necessary to "combat the cynicism and skepticism both within and out of the interracial/multiracial community concerning the need for a multiracial category."[20] Put differently, AMEA had to convince its members, whereas APFU and Project RACE had no members to convince.

As it turned out, only 40 percent of the organizational leaders in my survey and 47 percent of all respondents wanted a multiracial category on the census. Thirty-six percent of leaders (and 23 percent of respondents) preferred some version of the multiple check-off scheme instead. Ultimately, the OMB offered what many of the people in multiracial groups seem to have wanted. I came to see this over time, through interviews typically conducted at respondents' homes, although some were held in high school gymnasiums, in pizza parlors, and at group cookouts. Members, who were familiar with the recent OMB decision and the subsequent split between the umbrella groups from coverage in Internet and print media like *Interracial Voice*, *New People*, *Interrace Magazine*, *The Biracial Child*, and the *New York Times*, discussed their views on these matters at length. In April 1998, I was in Atlanta, Georgia, to interview members of the IFA. Susan Graham, who lived nearby, was simultaneously organizing a protest of the NAACP's upcoming annual meeting. To publicize the protest she distributed a flyer containing the following statement:

> The NAACP has been the driving force behind the OPPOSITION of a multiracial category on the U.S. Census and on the OMB directive about race and ethnicity, as many of you know. [The NAACP] has sanctioned "check one or more" but only if persons who do so are counted as black. This smacks of political racism. . . . What would the NAACP do if they were in our

position? They would certainly scream and yell as the opposing group. They would marshal their forces and stage an uprising. . . . We have an opportunity to stage a protest of the NAACP's racist behavior. The NAACP announced this week that their national convention will be held July 11–17 in Atlanta. Georgia is one of the states [with] a multiracial classification. The place would be ideal to hold a protest rally; also it is the home of Project RACE.[21]

I listened while IFA members considered the pros and cons of participating in what would have amounted to an Atlanta protest of the NAACP. The group came to its decision once someone asked, "How's it going to look if a bunch of white people go out, in the South, and picket the NAACP?"[22] IFA refused to participate.

After the meeting, I met with Pam Olive, IFA recording secretary, who had joined the group eleven years prior. In our first interview, Olive told me that her world changed in 1987, when she got pregnant. She wanted to elaborate on this when I checked back with her recently. Back then, she had never

Seen a child that I knew was of mixed race but that was the least of my concerns. I was born in 1952 and raised in the segregated South. Although things had changed a lot by 1987, segregation and racism still existed, as they continue to at a lesser degree now. I knew that my family and society wouldn't be supportive of my decision to keep this unplanned pregnancy. I knew I was embarking on a life-changing journey. I was going to be a single parent of a mixed race child.

[This was my first pregnancy and I] thought long and hard about whether I should bring a child into a world where it would be distrusted because of the color of its skin. Years later, when my daughter proudly told other children that "there are lots more like me," I was grateful that we had found this group [the IFA] that she so positively identified with.

. . . A co-worker once told me, in reference to another co-worker who was African American that "I don't see what her problem is. They can sit at the front of the bus now." She didn't see that inequities still exist, and I wondered if I wouldn't have if I hadn't had this child. I had seen the world through my daughter's eyes, to some extent, and what an education that has been.[23]

The experience of seeing race anew was a powerful one for the white women in my study; and women held the leadership positions by a three-to-one margin over men (sixty compared to twenty).

Figure 6, reflecting all respondents ($N = 80$), shows the predominance of white women in leadership posts overall and in the groups I surveyed and studied. Across the country, sixteen out of thirty group leaders were white women,[24] and an additional eighteen white women served on the boards of directors in my four case studies. In comparison, only one black man served as the leader of an organization, and only five additional black men served on the boards of directors in all of my case studies combined. Interestingly, in interviews with these men, I found that two had been leaders in the civil rights movement and one had been an activist, yet current-day civil rights organizations disappointed all of them.

Most group leaders, at an average age of forty-three, were too young to have participated in the civil rights movement of the 1950s and 1960s. However, Phil Savage, board member and past

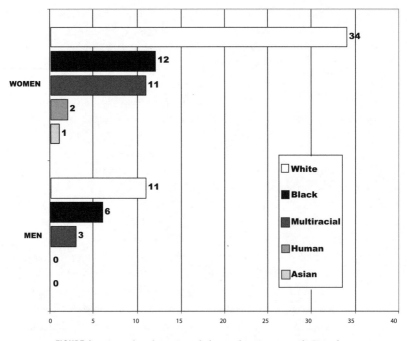

FIGURE 6. Leadership Breakdown by Race and Gender

> I was Tri-State director of the NAACP for the Eastern
> seaboard. I helped organize SNCC [Student Non-Violent
> Coordinating Committee] before the NAACP's employment
> and helped to elect [Marion] Barry as SNCC's first chairper-
> son. I'm a life member of the NAACP, but I'm ashamed of the
> NAACP for its stance on the multiracial category. Now, the
> NAACP depends on race in order to exist. . . . that's totally
> contrary to what I was taught. It distresses me to see this con-
> stant emphasis on race.[25]

Lou Steadwell, another black IFC board member, was
recruited in college to work for SNCC.

> I worked for the North End Community Action Project in
> Hartford, Connecticut. We believed in picketing and boy-
> cotting. . . . Now, well, the civil rights movement is in decline,
> both morally and politically. True, multiracial groups aren't all
> that concerned about fighting racism, but multiracialism is the
> future of this country. We [multiracial organizations] need to
> add subtlety to the civil rights position; we need to provide the
> forum for discussions about race.[26]

A third black man would "be a card-carrying member of the
NAACP," he told me, if not for the fact that "they have a huge
blind spot" when it comes to "the needs of this emerging community."[27] A fourth man, Ed Anderson (who was subjected to the
bigot's wrath in rural Georgia, as noted previously), was "disgusted
by the NAACP's response to our [multiracial] groups." A former
NAACP supporter and current IFA board member, Anderson
wished that "more black males were involved in the leadership."[28]
He thought white women were not necessarily the best spokespeople and should not serve as the predominant voice.

Edwin Darden, the only national black male leader during the
period of this study, served as AMEA's eastern regional vice president and, for a time, as president of the IFC. In a 1991 *Washington
Post* editorial, "My Black History Paradox: For Some of Us the
Price of Racial Pride Is Racial Harmony," he wrote about the bal-

ancing act of being a black person in an interracial family. Each year as Black History Month approached, "tugged by conflicting feelings of anticipation and dread," Darden saw "little desire [on the part of many blacks] to participate in an interracial society. On a personal level, that has translated into contempt and hostility toward people who dare cross the color line to form a family."[29] In one of our many conversations, I asked if he had ever participated in another social movement. His father had been a civil rights activist in New York City, he replied, but his only other foray into activism was in college: he led a student uprising to decry the poor quality of the cafeteria food. A strong Democrat and a lawyer in his early forties, Darden married a white woman in 1984; they joined IFC in 1989. Darden, like Ed Anderson, stressed the need to persuade more black men to get involved in multiracial politics. "That voice hasn't been heard, our visibility hasn't been seen," he said.[30]

While 20 percent of all respondents identified as church leaders, a much larger proportion (50 percent) reported having been involved in a prior social movement. Within that group, only three people reported their level of participation as a "one shot" thing. Nineteen reported having participated in some prior social movement "occasionally"; ten responded "frequently"; and seven replied "constantly." The plurality (35 percent) had been involved in the antiwar movement. After those who protested the Vietnam War, the other movements mentioned by respondents included civil rights (17.5 percent), women's rights (15 percent), and environmental issues (5 percent). The rest had participated in an array of other campaigns (gay rights, homeless rights, anti-Klan, and animal rights) typically cast as liberal causes. Overall, grassroots members subscribed to progressive movements and tended to discuss their endeavors as part of a larger whole, extended now to include the cause of multiracial recognition. For instance, Linda Ricks, IFA newsletter editor, met her husband, Dwayne, at a union meeting in 1979. Before they met, Linda had protested the Vietnam War at the University of Georgia, while Dwayne had been active in Atlanta's antiwar movement. Together, they demonstrated for the Equal Rights Amendment, for divestment in South Africa to end apartheid, and against a nuclear power plant near Barnwell, South Carolina. She said she would be willing to participate in a multiracial demonstration because "it is important that kids can identify with all of who they are." IFA "played a role in getting 'multiracial' added to the forms in Georgia," she told me. "Members of the IFA also carried a banner at some of the Martin Luther King Jr. Peoples' Marches in Atlanta and at the Hosea Williams march in Forsyth County."[31]

Yet many white women implied or stated outright that race had been little more than a passing thought until they married a black man and had children. Bridget Bielinski, the BFN newsletter editor,

> grew up in Glenview [Illinois], it was an all white environment. My education since being in an interracial relationship has been phenomenal. . . . race is a fiction. . . . I'm sensitive to the whole argument of the white mother who doesn't want her kids to be black [but] that's not what this is about. It's about providing a situation in which it's okay for your kid to identify with their full heritage.[32]

Bielinski favored the addition of a multiracial category to the census, although she also saw a need for "constant vigilance against discrimination." She did not think the two desires were at odds.[33] Julie Bolen, IFA secretary, saw "no basis for racial categories in general," but, she said, "people are not ready to let [race] go."[34] One group leader went so far as to say, "people have an obligation to marry outside their race. I am pro-*Bulworth*"[35] (referring to a popular movie promoting miscegenation as the solution to America's racial strife).

While I cannot generalize beyond my data, certain notions recurred along racial and gender lines. White women appeared to be more optimistic that multiracial families and individuals, through their positive example, could disrupt patterns of American racial polarization. These women's racial center of gravity came from the difficulties they and their children had suffered as interracial families. This was among the strongest themes emerging from my fieldwork. Barbara Byrd said, "It's about our children's identities. . . . it is important to show that interracial relationships are just as strong as monoracial relationships. Especially now, with the NAACP position, it is important to be more active."[36] Byrd said it was about the children, while acknowledging that multiracial organizations also functioned as a refuge for parents. Stacey Bell, corresponding secretary of I-Pride, was not "driven by the political side; it is just important that my kids have a choice."[37] Nancy Conner, BFN membership chairperson, said, "it's wrong to force people to deny part of themselves." She preferred the multiple check-off option. While she would not go as far as to picket the NAACP over tabulation, as Susan Graham had urged IFA members to do in Atlanta a few months earlier, she would "telephone, send faxes and write letters."[38]

Among the most politically minded group leaders were Pat Barner, president of the Interracial Connection in Norfolk, Virginia, and Kevin Barber, leader of the Multiracial Family Circle in Kansas City, Missouri. Barner, a white woman, had unsuccessfully tried to steer her group in a more political direction. "Until we try to do like Georgia," she told me, "our school system is not going to change."[39] Barber, the lone multiracial male at the helm of a local organization, felt that "a lot of issues should be brought out nationally. We could do that." Kevin Barber was, like Pat Barner, frustrated by his group's lack of political enthusiasm. He simply could not understand their reluctance to act, particularly since "the black man and white woman have suffered the most discrimination." Especially "pissed off that [black Congresswoman] Maxine Waters was against [the multiracial category effort]," he searched for like-minded activists. Barber went to the Latino side of town to recruit members, but "they [didn't] want to hear it." He tried the gay and lesbian community center, but the three white lesbians he met there "wanted to just chit chat. Like AA [Alcoholics Anonymous] or something. I'm into advocacy!"[40] People like Pat Barner and Kevin Barber were rare at the local level. On average, local leaders reported that their groups spent 17 percent of their time on public affairs, 25 percent on educational activities, and 53 percent on social activities, whereas they saw the optimal distribution as being 23, 30, and 40 percent, respectively.[41]

The black women seemed circumspect about the possibility of societal transformation through their relationships. Emma Tarleton, founder of the IFC, started the organization because she was interracially married. Back in 1984, she told me, hers was the "only such family in the area. Where would my daughter see a family like mine validated?"[42] Tarleton, like the other eleven black women in local leadership positions whom I talked to, made a point of explaining how—her affirming experiences in multiracial organizations notwithstanding—she continued to experience and regard racism as an ongoing, corrosive force in American society. Gloria Keegan, a black woman and IFA co-secretary, said,

> Instead of attacking [the race problem in our country] we bandaid it. . . . there's some of that in the multiracial movement as well. [But] civil rights groups are [even more] confused. They can't deal with gay issues, gender issues, multiracial issues, religion, especially here in the Bible belt . . . but what are these Republicans getting out of this? That makes me nervous.[43]

Gene Foard, a black IFA board member, echoed Keegan's concerns. Although feeling shut out from black institutions, Foard hardly saw that as reason to turn to conservative Republicans as allies. "Distressed" by civil rights opposition to multiracial recognition, she nevertheless could not bring herself to oppose the NAACP completely.[44] Lucille Hallisy, a black "card-carrying liberal," was in Memphis and "marched when the Rev. Martin Luther King Jr. was shot." Years later, she joined BFN and became the publicity director. She wanted to "walk into a place where you didn't have to explain," and she refused to take an anti-NAACP posture. They may "need new ways of accomplishing stuff," she said, "but they've done too many good things to be picketed."[45]

Generalizations

Without making sweeping claims based on a modest data set, it may be possible to draw a few generalizations. First, my respondents felt they had something worth sharing with the world. Second, multiracial advocates expressed a cumulative and collective disappointment in civil rights institutions generally and in the NAACP particularly. Third, in AMEA's affiliate groups, there was a clear readiness to talk about the first two issues, even as people differed along racial and gender lines in *how* they discussed these matters. In *Interrace* magazine, in the *AMEA Networking News*, at multiracial cookouts and conferences, and in congressional testimonies, I found a thematic if ill-defined assertion that interracial love and the acknowledgment of multiracial people could, if recognized, help American society move beyond an impasse. Although the black women and men I interviewed were more cautious about making this claim, my respondents all believed to varying degrees that the grip of racial polarization in American life could somehow be lessened through the example of multiracial individuals and families. This served as a common basis for moral conviction, even if individuals and groups disagreed on the details.

Four years after Arthur Fletcher testified that he could see a whole host of light-skinned black Americans running for the door the minute they had another choice, his successor as chair of the U.S. Commission on Civil Rights, Mary Frances Berry, said that "[a multiracial category] might make some people feel better, but it won't change American racism one bit."[46] According to Jesse Jackson, the multiracial movement was a "diversion, designed to undermine affirmative action."[47] *Ebony* even went so far as to ask in 1995 if this was a "plot to create a 'colored' buffer race in America."[48] A year later, *Emerge*, a now-defunct magazine targeting upscale blacks, declared in an article title, "Multiracial Grouping Undermines Black Clout."[49] The message from black leaders and the black press was that these people were racial defectors who wanted to be white or, at the least, to escape blackness. Members at the grass roots felt they bore the brunt of these accusations. Black recrimination seemed to come from all sides; but in multiracial circles the NAACP became shorthand for the opposition. A reluctant standard-bearer for the resistance (as discussed in the next chapter, there was no one else to do it), the NAACP warily avoided the issue to the extent practicable. When the organization did enter the fray, its carefully crafted, lawyerly statements hardly matched the invective expressed elsewhere. Yet the NAACP came to epitomize multiracial advocates' frustration nonetheless. The white women leading many of the multiracial groups viewed the NAACP's position as a demoralizing rejection of their and their children's realities. Black respondents were further disappointed at what they saw as a bankrupt civil rights agenda. I return to these issues in the next chapter.

At first simply relieved to encounter members willing to talk about these matters so feelingly with someone they did not know

escape
blackness

personally, over time I came to recognize this willingness to talk as a force of its own. Many white respondents seemed stunned by the treatment to which they found themselves subjected as members of interracial families. They seemed not to have thought much about race until relatively late in life. Surely, late is better than never, and legal scholar Randall Kennedy may have been right when he said: "few situations are more likely to mobilize the racially privileged individual to move against racial wrongs than witnessing such wrongs inflicted on one's mother-in-law, father-in-law, spouse, or child."[50] This is at once a statement about newfound experience of racial discrimination and about a sense of entitlement. Affluent, well-educated, suburban white women, considered from this perspective, seem less-improbable activists.

Feelings of rejection may explain why people were drawn to these groups in the first place; but it is beyond the scope of this study to draw sweeping conclusions about such matters. American attitudes toward black-white interracial marriage have clearly improved over time (figs. 4 and 5), but it would seem that the white partners in these marriages remain more susceptible to severe familial estrangement. Indeed, many of the white women in my study had been effectively disowned by someone in their family, and even those on good terms with their relatives conveyed the sense that things had changed. In one way or another, most seem to have experienced a shift in standing, and more than a few probably hoped to confer the privileges of nonblack status on their children via multiracial recognition. But this is a complex dynamic, and part of what makes it so is the impossibility of disentangling the needs of parents from those of their children. It is unclear, therefore, where to shine the spotlight when trying to evaluate the multiracial campaign's central concern. It could be that self-esteem, the fallback position of the multiracial movement in the 1990s, was a bigger worry for the parents than for their children.[51] Either way, the facts suggest that interracial family life is at least as challenging for parents as it is for children. While the legitimacy of multiracial claims is far from sacrosanct, dismissal on grounds of false consciousness or negligible suffering is inappropriate.

Nor should we simply wave off the self-esteem claim as trivial. Self-esteem was, after all, a primary rationale of the Supreme Court in *Brown v. Board of Education*. The evils of segregation disfigured us all, as W. E. B. Du Bois, James Baldwin, Lillian Smith, and others explained well before 1954. In "From Racial Liberalism to Racial Literacy: *Brown v. Board of Education* and the Interest-Divergence Dilemma," Lani Guinier reminds us once more that blacks were not the only ones with psychological problems stemming from segregation, yet the debate about self-esteem in *Brown* ran in only one direction. That *Brown* largely treated self-esteem as a "black" problem may have restigmatized blacks, Guinier contends. This move also positioned the "peculiarly American race 'problem' as a psychological and interpersonal challenge rather than a structural problem rooted in our economic and political system," Guinier writes.[52] The point is this: The idea that racism will give way one person at a time or that love will somehow conquer all—while most plausible to the white women in my study—is suspect so long as it lacks an accompanying vocabulary of racial and class privilege. Consider *Brown:* fifty years later, segregation in education—as in many other spheres of American life—persists far beyond what even the casual observer can credibly chalk up to mere coincidence.

This leads to an intriguing question about Derrick Bell's interest-convergence principle, which Guinier understands as a central tool for determining when the cause of racial equality is championed or evaded. Bell's concise formula holds that "The interest of blacks in achieving racial equality will be accommodated only when it converges with the interests of whites."[53] What are we to make of this idea in a multiracial context? Again, we run into the problem of how to evaluate whether multiracial recognition is a step in the direction of blacks' achieving racial equality.

But we need not trouble ourselves with the fine points of black interests here. The interests of whites, in this formulation, drive the process. Given its propinquity to the needs of white women, the self-esteem claim, whatever else it may be, is not politically trivial if we expect the requests and desires of whites to be met before others, per Bell. Interestingly, the story told in chapters 3 and 4 does not contradict this explanation of varied federal and state outcomes. More provocatively stated, the needs of white women played a starring, if unsung, role in the demise of single-race categories at the turn of the century.[54]

The preponderance of black-white couples in multiracial organizations, the race-gender breakdown of these couples, and a gendered division of labor combine to explain why relatively affluent, suburban white women took the lead. This in turn may help us understand why fighting racism was not a priority in the multiracial groups I studied. While interracial families and multiracial activists were able and willing to announce their presence in ways that had few precedents in American society, these activists were also conflicted and inconsistent in their political commitments, which facilitated the appropriation of their cause from the right.

[handwritten margin note: fighting racism not a priority]

By March 31, 2000, Americans had received their 2000 census forms. On that day, in a strong statement of political commitment, C-SPAN covered a remarkable awards ceremony at which Ruth and Steve White of APFU bestowed their annual "Racial Harmony Hall of Fame" award on Ward Connerly—of Proposition 209 (anti-affirmative action) fame—at a Dupont Circle hotel. Notably, this was originally supposed to be a "multiracial leadership roundtable," at which the various factions would come together to iron out their differences. When informed that Connerly, a controversial advocate of color-blind public policy, would receive an award at the event, AMEA called for a boycott. Before C-SPAN arrived, Steve White introduced the small group of multiracial activists[55] to Edward Blum, chair of the conservative Campaign for a Color-Blind America, who said:

> My organization has been behind many of the recent court cases challenging the constitutionality of the Voting Rights Act. I've been following the multiracial movement and the tremendous progress made by this group. For those who haven't yet sent in their census form, you don't have to pick anything. Leave it blank. [This is what] Ward [Connerly] intends to advocate to America. . . . JUST DON'T ANSWER THE RACE QUESTION.[56]

Although Yvette Hollis, black co-editor of *New People* magazine, raised the after-the-fact concern of "fragmenting the minority community if you create a multiracial category," everyone else quickly rejected this argument.[57] "Civil rights people are just protecting their own jobs," remarked her (white) husband, Dan, the other half of *New People*'s editorial staff.

Nathan Douglas, one of a handful of Project RACE supporters—and a man who described himself to me in our first meeting as a "recovering redneck"[58]—added, "As one who's faced down the NAACP, I agree with Dan."[59] (I suspect that Douglas was referring to an incident at the National Multicultural Institute Conference in Washington on May 30, 1998. At that otherwise decorous event, I saw him jump to his feet with a poster-sized photograph of his multiracial child and scream wildly at Harold McDougall of the NAACP, who was sitting on a panel with Susan Graham. The moderator, Clarence Page, looked stunned.) Blum, of the Campaign for a Color-Blind America, coolly brought the discussion around to a larger principle: "civil rights advocates are against us . . . because the data in the census is used to continue an entire regime of racial preferences."[60] Steve White said, "We have a system that deserves to collapse under its own weight. Affirmative action is the real institutional racism."[61] His wife, Ruth, agreed: "What Ward stands for, we stand for!"[62]

C-SPAN and Connerly came in, and the cameras began to roll. Ruth White introduced the honoree: "We want to become a color-blind society and move our country in that direction. The man who deserves this award—not just anyone can get it—is Ward Connerly."[63] Connerly rose and took the podium. "We're going through a gut-wrenching debate on race in this country," he said, "though it [race] almost doesn't exist. Many people think we need to use race to get beyond race, but I disagree. The multiracial movement is stepping outside of the box."[64] After the taping, Connerly dashed to a cab; he had to get across town to debate Carol Moseley-Braun. The roundtable attendees lingered to reaffirm their view that the new objective should be to get rid of racial categories altogether. In my survey, only 13 percent of leaders and 22 percent of all respondents agreed with this proposition, though none even in this minority expressed their views in quite the same terms heard that day.

> *Nathan Douglas:* "AMEA sees the civil rights model as the preferred model. Their intention is to create a new minority: multiracial."

Charles Byrd: "With all the goodies, benefits, and set-asides."

Steve White: "Another group crying to the government for special treatment."

Ruth White: "I don't want anybody to get anything based on the color of their skin. If it came to that, just do without."[65]

There is a clear difference between the multiracial movement that I had found throughout the country and the movement televised live on C-SPAN that day. The people at the grass roots did not share the ideological convictions of these supposed representatives. The overwhelming majority of surveyed members identified themselves as either strong (26 percent) or moderate (41 percent) Democrats and declared themselves either strongly (32 percent) or moderately (37 percent) in favor of affirmative action. However, as shown in table 8, members were all over the map in terms of strategic alliances.

Defying straightforward interpretation, although no respondent identified as a strong Republican, more than half (56 percent) felt that the multiracial movement should welcome the support of that party to further the cause. I was surprised to find that many of those who were willing to accept Republican backing also identified themselves as strong or moderate Democrats. Even more perplexing, although black respondents identified overwhelmingly with the Democratic Party, half of the blacks in my study were accepting of Republican intervention in multiracial politics. Fifty-seven percent of white respondents concurred. This would be an interesting question to put to a wider sample.

Fifteen of all eighteen blacks identified themselves as either strong or moderate Democrats, but twelve of the eighteen also characterized civil rights organizations as conservative. An additional three said they did not know where to place civil rights groups on a liberal-conservative continuum. Only two saw civil rights organizations as moderate, and one saw them as liberal. I suspect that their disappointment contributed to their willingness to turn to Republicans for support, even though, overwhelmingly, they did not identify with that party. Some individuals, such as Kevin Barber (the lone local group leader to identify as multiracial), seemed more alienated from black Democrats and civil rights organizations than enthusiastic about Republicans. For some white women, such as Bridget Bielinski, Republican interest raised no red flags. These women did not seem to suspect that their powerful GOP allies had probably surfaced not because they cared more about the self-esteem of multiracial children than did Democrats but because they were intent upon undermining civil rights enforcement efforts.

I found contradiction and nuance in multiracial organizations.

TABLE 8. Should the Multiracial Community Welcome Republican Support?[a]

	Welcome Republican Support	Be Wary of Republican Support	Don't Know
White			
Strong Democrat	8	4	
Moderate Democrat	7	9	1
Independent	1	2	1
Moderate Republican	5		
Libertarian	1		
No party ID	4	2	
Subtotal	*26*	*17*	*2*
Black			
Strong Democrat	4	5	
Moderate Democrat	3	3	1
Independent	1		
Moderate Republican	1		
Libertarian			
No party ID			
Subtotal	*9*	*8*	*1*
Multiracial			
Strong Democrat	1	1	
Moderate Democrat	2	2	
Independent	3	1	
Moderate Republican	2		
Libertarian	1		
No party ID	1		
Subtotal	*10*	*4*	
Total	45	29	3

Note: No respondents identified as strong Republicans.

[a]Not included in the table: one moderate Asian Democrat; two Democrats of the human race: one strong, one moderate. All three were wary of Republican support.

Powerful people had taken strong positions on either side of a cause orchestrated by a handful of disorganized movement leaders, who did not even clarify their motives to each other until after they had already acrimoniously split. In the local groups that I studied, participants differed along racial and gender lines in their hopes and expectations for the multiracial movement. It was against this backdrop that influential people eager to dismantle race-conscious public policies worked to appropriate the multiracial identity movement. Given the company that activists seemed to keep, Harold McDougall of the NAACP wanted proponents of a multiracial category to substantiate how their efforts were actually assisting in the struggle against racism. The advocates have yet to put forth a well-thought-out answer. Still, there are precious few venues in the United States in which black and white people socialize on as regular and as comfortable a basis as they do at multiracial cookouts. These gatherings, both unusual and uplifting, may be signs of progress. Under these circumstances, even if one supports the pragmatic policy stance of the NAACP and its allies, it is hard to feel good about doing so. It would be heartbreaking to conclude that multiracial identification is a de facto setback for civil rights.

Growing Racial Diversity and the Civil Rights Future

Civil rights opposition to a multiracial category turned, in the first instance, on the fact that mutually exclusive racial statistics make institutional racism easier to document and thus harder to perpetrate. Multiracial advocates, however, saw compulsory single-race categories as an outdated response to a growing multiracial reality and maintained that their recognition would come at no adverse civil rights cost. The OMB decision of 1997 appeared to validate both of the latter claims. Multiracial activists wanted to convey to Americans that the recognition of racial mixture was the next logical step in civil rights. Yet it is difficult to view this as a credible answer to a deeper set of questions about the future direction of civil rights advocacy. For one thing, the multiracial movement has emphasized the right to determine one's own identities (at the level of the individual), while its antiracism agenda (at a structural level) has been limited to vague declarations that multiracial recognition could somehow help to reduce racial strife. Nevertheless, racial debates are likely to proceed differently because of the 2000 census. The turning point traces back to the efforts of a handful of activists who challenged the government on race and won a form of recognition applicable and available to all.

This book began with the assertion that the seemingly trivial decision to allow people to identify with multiple racial heritages, without adding a multiracial category, would introduce new questions and controversies into an already volatile debate on race-conscious public policy. Group leaders and board members across the country, whatever their attitude toward a multiracial category, asserted that multiracial recognition could help to alleviate America's tenacious race problems. I heard this moral claim made more consistently than any other. Thus, even those unconcerned with government per se professed indignation over their perceived treatment by minority institutions. Unexpectedly, I found that white, liberal, and suburban-based middle-class women (married to black men) held the leadership roles in most multiracial organizations. These white women helped to set an optimistic tone for multiracial activism; many believed that American racial polarization could be overcome by their example. Most of these women were looking for community—not for a census designation. Movement spokespeople reversed these priorities somewhat, although they parted ways after the OMB decision of 1997. Weak to begin with, and increasingly divided among themselves, movement leaders have enabled—sometimes actively—opportunistic conservatives to fill the void.

The New Context

Stakeholders had to wait until incredibly late in the process for the OMB's final verdict on tabulation guidelines for multiple race responses. The "fairly speedy" process promised by Sally Katzen in 1993, at the beginning of the OMB review, turned out differently. When the tabulation decision was finally announced, just weeks before the March 2000 census mailing, civil rights advocates had no choice but to accept the arrangement. As Martha Riche, bureau director from 1994 to 1998, confirmed to me, they had few options. Explaining the experience of black civil rights representatives, she said, "[they] seemed the least comfortable but the . . . process created a logic that they would have had a hard time escaping by the time they saw where things were heading."[1] Nonetheless, the guidelines satisfied rights groups' most pressing concerns: numbers would not be "drained" from any minority group, and MOOM did not appear to make the prospect of demonstrating racial discrimination more difficult. As explained by Hilary Shelton, NAACP Washington bureau chief, one of civil rights advocates' two primary concerns was to secure a "historic arc," whereby "the compilation of multi-check offs find their way back to a historic [minority] category."[2] This was accomplished. The new policy dictated that responses combining one minority race and white would be allocated to the minority race for civil rights purposes. The second bedrock civil rights concern involved the extent to which a multiracial option might obscure the documentation of patterns of discrimination and inequality. But again, this did not appear to pose enforcement difficulties, primarily because so few Americans were expected to identify with more than one race.

About seven million people reported more than one race in 2000. Table 9 includes only those combinations comprising more than 100,000 people; together, these combinations made up 93

TABLE 9. Top Combinations of Two or More Race Reporting, 2000

Combination	Number	Percentage of Multiple Race Population	Percentage of U.S. Population	90% Confidence Interval
Total	7,270,926[a]	100	2.58	2.58–2.59
White *and* Some Other Race	2,322,356	31.9	0.83	0.82–0.83
White *and* American Indian and Alaska Native	1,254,289	17.3	0.45	0.44–0.45
White *and* Asian	862,032	11.9	0.31	0.30–0.31
White *and* Black	791,801	10.9	0.28[b]	
Black *and* Some Other Race	462,703	6.4	0.16	0.16–0.17
Asian *and* Some Other Race	280,600	3.9	0.10[b]	
Black *and* American Indian and Alaska Native	206,941	2.8	0.07[b]	
Asian *and* Native Hawaiian and Other Pacific Islander	138,556	1.9	0.05[b]	
White *and* Black and American Indian and Alaska Native	116,897	1.6	0.04[b]	
White *and* Native Hawaiian and Other Pacific Islander	111,993	1.5	0.04[b]	
American Indian and Alaska Native *and* Some Other Race	108,576	1.5	0.04[b]	
Black *and* Asian	106,842	1.5	0.04[b]	
All other combinations[c]	507,340	7.0	0.18[b]	

Source: Nicholas A. Jones, "We the People of More than One Race in the United States," *Census 2000 Special Reports,* April 2005; Census 2000 Summary File 4.

[a]Initially reported at 6.8 million (2.4 percent of the total U.S. population) from short form data reported in Summary File 1; the bureau recently revised this upward using Summary File 4 data (based on long form data) to 7.2 million. The percentages do not sum to 100.0 due to rounding.

[b]Confidence interval rounds to the percentage shown.

[c]"All other combinations" represents the remaining 45 combinations of people who reported more than one race; none of the remaining combinations numbered more than 100,000 people.

[handwritten margin notes: "biggest", "white and 'some other race'"]

percent of the "Two or More Races" population. Note that about 70 percent of all multiple-race responses included "white" as one of the reported races. Thus, instead of diluting the minority count, MOOM slightly increased the tally. Note also that the largest race combination, "White and Some Other Race," represented about one-third of the total multiple race population (see later discussion), while "White and Black" responses, by comparison, made up only about 11 percent. Another way to understand civil rights advocates' acquiescence on tabulation, then, is to recognize that the most prominent and powerful partners in the civil rights coalition were the least directly affected by this change. Latinos already enjoyed most of the functional freedom of MOOM, along with a favorable tabulation calculus whereby a respondent marking more than one box—as long as Hispanic was one of them—would still count as Hispanic. A senior MALDEF spokesperson explained, "When [the multiracial category proposal] came up we could have said 'it's not our issue.' But because we work in coalition [with other civil rights organizations] we took a position that would preserve the needs of our coalition partners."[3] In contrast, some black elites seemed to worry about mass desertion from black identification, but this did not happen.

Following are some of the most important issues raised by the new situation.

Maximum and Minimum Counts. Multiple-race reporting, while low nationwide, was far from evenly distributed across racial groups. As shown in figure 7, the percentage of blacks who checked both black and something else (4.8) was relatively low.[4] I suspect that some blacks would have viewed higher numbers as an indication of black flight; but, as it turned out, only whites were more likely to identify with just one race. Put differently, whites seem far more securely affixed to traditional views of singular racial identification than anyone else, including blacks, who nonetheless occupy the same end of the spectrum. The problems identified by the Tabulation Working Group relating to small populations (chap. 3) shine through in these data. The difference between minimum and maximum counts is significant for Asians (almost a 14 percent differential), considerable for American Indians/Alaska Natives (nearly 40 percent), and astronomical for the newly recognized group of Native Hawaiians/Other Pacific Islanders (over 50

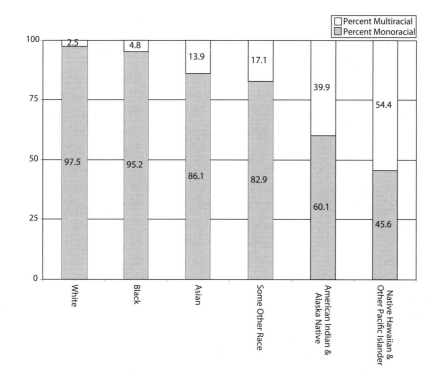

FIGURE 7. Minimum Count of Census Race Groups as Percentage of Maximum Count, 2000

	White	Black	Asian	Some Other Race	American Indian & Alaska Native	Native Hawaiian & Other Pacific
Percentage of total U.S. population, alone or in combination	77.1	12.9	4.2	6.6	1.5	0.3
Number of total U.S. population, alone or in combination	216,930,975	36,419,434	11,898,828	18,521,486	4,119,301	874,414
Alone	211,460,626	34,658,190	10,242,998	15,359,073	2,475,956	398,835
In combination	5,470,349	1,761,244	1,655,830	3,162,413	1,643,345	475,579

Source: U.S. Census Bureau 2000, Summary File 1.

Note: Short form data indicated that 6.8 million Americans reported more than one race in 2000. "Percentage multiracial" is the proportion that the "more than one race" (multiracial) population represented of the total count of each racial group. This double counts persons who appear in more than one racial category, resulting in totals of more than 100 percent.

percent). The ability of researchers and other interested parties to easily compare the racial counts under the new OMB guidelines with alternatives considered but not adopted by the bureau creates "enormous potential for public scrutiny and debate about any tabulation procedure," write Joel Perlmann and Mary Waters.[5] What is the denominator?

Program Eligibility. The collection of data on Americans who marked more than one race serves no statutory purpose. Yet the very existence of the data naturally leads one to conclude that it refers to meaningful multiracial populations. This would imply, for instance, that the black-white population is measurably different from blacks or whites who identify monoracially. A 2005 bureau report, "We the People of More Than One Race in the United States," documents such variation. Memorably titled, this 2000 census special report shows, for instance, that median family income in 1999 for all American families was $50,046. Median income for white *and* Asian families was $52,413. For white *and* black families the comparable figure was $34,196.[6] The data provoke a number of questions. Are we to believe that the 63 (or 126) possible categories are on equal footing with the 6 stand-alone categories? Is someone who marks white and a minority race on a form eligible for the same programs and protections as someone who identifies only as a member of a minority group? What if it can be shown that that same person had, in the past, identified only as white? Although confidentiality rules prevent such analyses of individuals' census responses, racial categories used by the government reach deeply into the private sector. The government backs away from such questions, and they remain unanswered.

Whites Counted as Minorities. The new tabulation rules meant that, inevitably, some of the people who were classified as white by the bureau in 1990 were counted as minorities in 2000. This quelled civil rights advocates' most immediate worries about dwindling numbers. However, the inflation of the minority count is otherwise difficult to justify. Further, survey data suggest that, upon reinterview, many multiracials would identify differently.[7]

One-Drop Redux. MOOM violates the live-by-the-sword principle of self-identification instated by the bureau in 1970: multiple-race individuals said they were X and then were reclassified as Y. This pushed Susan Graham of Project RACE to the extraordinary length of attempting to organize a multiracial protest of the NAACP during its 1998 annual meeting. MOOM, the difference in circumstances and intent notwithstanding, reconstitutes the one-drop rule.

Multiracial advocates received something akin to symbolic recognition in 1997, since federal-level multiple-race data serve no statutory purpose and those identifying as multiracial on state forms (chap. 4) are recollapsed into OMB's standard racial and ethnic categories whenever necessary for the purposes of federal reporting. Yet the implications remain unclear, and the circumstances invite further challenge. Joshua Goldstein and Ann Morning make an apt point: "in the past, classification systems had been formalized in response to legislation, but now the enforcement and monitoring of laws had to respond to a change in the statistical system."[8] Where the MOOM option breaks down the binary race formulation, tabulation must put it back together. Roderick Harrison, an analyst at the Joint Center for Political and Economic Studies and a former Tabulation Working Group member—who was "removed," he says, "so that the Census Bureau could 'speak with one voice'"[9]—worries that the data on small populations put the entire system at risk because of its "dubious validity or meaning."[10] Minimum and maximum differentials of this magnitude, Harrison opines, could give way to wider misgivings about the idea of race writ large. He also suspects that the new data will generate litigation "owing to a few challenges in places where 'civil rights' and single-race counts or characteristics are sufficiently different for courts to rule against the procedures issued in the civil rights guidance."[11] As a practical matter, this may seem far-fetched,[12] but it would only take one court case, Harrison notes ominously.

Related Trends Magnify These Issues

Increasing numbers of Americans, beyond the "multiracials" thus far discussed, view race in terms that tax the systems set up by those who would count them. Identifying with none of the standard racial options, close to seven million people marked "Other Race" on the 1980 census. Almost ten million did so in 1990. In 2000, as shown in table 10, over fifteen million Americans—about one in twenty—selected the (renamed) designator "Some Other Race." The segment of the American population identifying in this fashion has more than doubled over the past two decades. This makes "some other" the fastest growing race.

This spells more trouble for the ever-besieged Census Bureau.[13] Fifteen million people, to put this in perspective, exceeds the total Asian, American Indian and Alaska Native, and Native Hawaiian and Other Pacific Islander populations combined. Who are these fifteen million Americans of "some other" race?

Recall that the Census Bureau treats race and ethnicity as separate concepts. The result is two separate questions on the (short) form sent to all households. The question "Is Person 1 Spanish/Hispanic/Latino?" came first in 2000, followed by the companion question: "What is Person 1's race? Mark one or more races to indicate what this person considers himself/herself to be." Table 11 reports Latino racial reporting in the census since 1980.

Latinos can be of any race, and as table 11 shows, about half of all Latinos (49.9 percent) identified racially as white in 2000.[14] By comparison, just 2.7 percent identified racially as black. The rest, considered by the bureau to be Hispanic ethnically *and* racially (hence the redundancy of "Hispanic Hispanic" in table 11), identified as "Hispanic" in response to the question on ethnicity and mostly as "Some Other" in response to the race question, often writing in a term like "Mexican" on the line provided for explanation. (See appendix B for a reproduction of the race and ethnicity questions used in 2000.) Thus, Latino racial reporting is, and has been, fundamentally bifurcated. Consider the state of affairs: originally intended as a catchall, residual category,[15] "Some Other

TABLE 10. "Other Race" Reporting, 1960–2000 (in millions)

Year	Other Race
1960	0.2
1970	0.7
1980	6.8
1990	9.8
2000[a]	15.3

Source: U.S. Census Bureau of the Census 2001 Summary File 1.
[a]Renamed "Some Other Race."

Race" now encompasses about half of the Latino population.
Looking at it the other way around, <u>over 95 percent of the fifteen
million Americans of "some other" race are Latinos.</u>[16]

Arguably, identification with "Some Other Race" tells us more
about how people do *not* identify racially than how they do. The
Census Bureau leaves considerable room for interpretation, and
there is abundant debate about how to read these trends. The discussion is at once academic and practical: the content of Latino
racial identity has everything to do with the extent to which Latinos identify as minorities, the future of black-brown coalitions, and
other interesting topics. The point is that the Hispanic category,
from the start, was a conceptual departure from the rest of the
American classification system. As the Latino population has
grown, this arrangement has become increasingly unwieldy, at least
for those who do the counting.

MOOM was sold as a symbolic response to a different demographic trend. Under the circumstances, however, one wonders
whether perhaps it is not multiracials but Latinos who are leading
the way in the binary breakdown.[17] The evidence seems to point in
this direction, since one combination—"Some Other Race and
White"—accounts for about one-third of the multiracial population
as measured in 2000, and this represents the plurality of multiple
race responses overall (table 9). Maybe some of these people saw
themselves as multiracial in the sense described in this book, but

TABLE 11. Racial Composition of the Latino Population, 1980–2000

	1980	1990	2000	Growth 1980–1990 (%)	Growth 1990–2000 (%)
White Hispanic	9,397,240 (63.7%)	11,776,701 (53.9%)	17,601,942 (49.9%)	25.3	49.5
Hispanic Hispanic	4,979,240 (33.7%)	9,426,634 (44.2%)	16,700,055 (47.4%)	89.3	77.2
Black Hispanic	388,240 (2.6%)	633,516 (2.9%)	939,471 (2.7%)	63.2	48.3
Total Hispanic	14,764,720 (100%)	21,836,851 (100%)	35,241,468 (100%)	47.9	61.4

Source: John R. Logan, *How Race Counts for Hispanic Americans* (Albany, NY: Lewis Mumford Center for Comparative Urban and Regional Research, 2003).

more likely they were rejecting the terms of American-style racial classification from a different perspective. Note also that states with large Hispanic populations—California, New York, and Texas—accounted for about 40 percent of total multiracial responses in 2000. In California, home to one in eight Americans, multiracial births are growing at a faster rate than monoracial Asian or black births.[18] This fast-growing, youthful population is concentrated in states with an already large and complex minority presence.

Bringing Multiracial Politics into the Civil Rights Fold

The uncertainties go well beyond the technical. A society long hostile to acknowledging racial mixture will somehow have to come to terms with a growing population of self-identified multiracial individuals and others who are difficult to place conceptually and ascriptively in the old familiar race hierarchy. The existing terms, stipulated by MOOM, preserve the single-race imperatives of civil rights enforcement but seem to rest on a less than solid foundation. Looking forward, multiracialism is likely to grow in significance: it is symbolically powerful, it evidently holds appeal across the political spectrum, it offers an institutional foothold to other aspiring racial groups—and it will leave its imprint on future successful bids.[19] All of this means that civil rights institutions must contend with racial mixture now and in the future. I reject the pervasive and troubling notion that multiracialism is necessarily a civil rights setback. Yet, so long as there is a vacuum from the left, the political advantage of these developments will probably accrue to the right.

One way to make sense of growing racial diversity is to conclude that categorizing by race is impossible. Even worse, it divides us. We cannot move beyond race, so goes the argument, if we are constantly reminding people of it. If not for chronic disparities in the distribution of well-being and a gaping racial divide even in Americans' awareness of the differential, foregoing the collection of racial data might seem the principled, if not the realistic, thing to do. Yes, racial counting is by definition an imprecise endeavor, but the alternative is continued racial disparity without even a paper trail. Therefore, weighing the ethical reasons for compiling racial data against the inherent elusiveness of the enterprise, I come down on the side of data collection. The data itself will tell us if racial disparities diminish to the point that we do not need to collect more data.[20]

I can live with this tautology but find it much more difficult to come to terms with the prospect that multiracial identification is necessarily a civil rights liability. While multiracialism may be but a step from the color blindness of the right, at the same time it is not so far from principled color consciousness on the left either. After all, as I have shown throughout, the multiracial idea can support competing ideological agendas. My research unearthed little evidence that the people at the grass roots were right-wing sympathizers. If, instead, right-wing elites seeking to undermine civil rights gains appropriated the multiracial movement, then we should be clear about the distinction and the implications. This alternate account leaves open the possibility that multiracial politics could be brought into the fold from the left. This, I argue, is politically worthwhile, possible, and enormously desirable.

What Makes a Left Multiracialism Politically Worthwhile?

My findings demonstrate that the elected officials most open to the idea of multiraciality over the past decade have been conservative Republicans in Congress and state legislators (mostly Democrats) representing affluent, suburban districts. Apparently, multiracial politics involves unconventional political alliances: the idea holds some appeal across the ideological spectrum and involves increasing numbers of whites. In response to a question asked after a 1995 speech, President Clinton stated that the proposal to add a multiracial box on the census "makes sense,"[21] though he said he had not heard about it before. Within a few years, Newt Gingrich was the most prominent backer of the idea. Republicans—and conservatives more widely—have exhibited keen interest in multiracialism as a means of capitalizing on the prevailing confusion about race. They have tried to use multiracialism to undermine civil rights enforcement while seeming progressive in doing so. Meanwhile, those on the left, if paying attention at all, have trivialized multiracial advocacy. But focusing on the inconsistencies in multiracial thought or concentrating on the fact that the number of involved activists was small does little to explain the government's obliging response. Multiracial recognition was validated from both sides of the partisan divide in the 1990s, I contend, because Democrats wanted multiracial recognition *without* adverse civil rights consequences, while Republicans wanted multiracial recognition *with* adverse civil rights consequences.

Conservative members of Congress with poor civil rights records supported the multiracial category effort and even introduced alternate measures to institutionalize it irrespective of OMB action on the matter. In accepting APFU's "Racial Harmony Hall of Fame" award, Ward Connerly told the television viewing audience that racial categorization was both illogical and counterproductive if our collective goal was to diminish racial polarization. Close on the heels of these remarks came a remarkable vote on the idea of the social construction of race. With a few exemptions, California's Proposition 54 (also known as the "racial privacy" initiative) would have barred the state from collecting racial and ethnic data on grounds that it is unreasonable to do so if we are ever to move "beyond" race. Backed by none other than Ward Connerly, the 2003 initiative took the effort to subvert race-conscious public policy to a different strategic level. In Proposition 209, conservatives attacked race-conscious public policies; in Proposition 54, they attacked the idea of race itself. Proposition 54's backers readily exploited the new data. "Surely, the government doesn't believe 58 new races have emerged since 1970," chided a Web site promoting racial privacy. "The new race classifications were invented by different groups trying to get in on America's racial spoils system."[22] This characterization of the multiracial movement's goals encapsulates the Right's intent to undercut racial data collection as a way of dismantling race-conscious public policy. With these aims, the right wing, to repeat, has brazenly taken the lead in defining for Americans what "multiracial" *is*.

Meanwhile, the NAACP, figurehead of the opposition, labored to avoid similar accusations, while still opposing multiracial demands. Other civil rights groups had their own reasons for remaining on the sidelines. The resulting void made possible the proliferation of stock stories—for instance, that the multiracial movement was a right-wing plot or that it was simply about white women who wanted their children to be white—that came to be understood as emblematic of civil rights resistance. These narratives are reductionist, but more to the point, they are also politically misleading. Recall the message of chapter 4 about constituencies. Most state legislators apparently did not consider the multiracial idea a duplicitous menace. Instead, they seem to have approached it as a symbolic gesture toward all minorities.[23] Perhaps they sincerely cared about the self-esteem of multiracial children; maybe they saw it as racial sensitivity on the cheap. Either way, constituent sanction was improbable, which brings me to another reason why constructive engagement with multiracialism from the left is politically worthwhile.

Until recently, debates about the social construction of race tended to be dominated by lawyers and academics. This set the terms for a discussion deeper than it has been wide, but in a countervailing trend, the multiracial movement and Proposition 54 helped to introduce the idea of race-as-construct into the popular arena. This represents at least a partial circumvention of elites, putatively bringing the debates over the social construction of race closer to the people. Granted, we have not seen much in the way of popular participation in either case, but one telling difference is that the enthusiasts of racial privacy evidently wanted it that way. Discussing the genesis of the privacy initiative, Edward Blum—chair of the Campaign for a Color-Blind America—laid out a strategy that relied on low voter turnout in a primary election.[24] Not incidentally, Proposition 54 funding hardly came from the grass roots; it traced back to a handful of wealthy backers, whose identities were only disclosed after California Common Cause filed a civil suit against the campaign for violations of the Political Reform Act.[25] That Proposition 54 was defeated tells us something about the state of popular thinking about racial categories in America—but given the extraordinary circumstances, it tells us less than we need to know. Had the vote taken place when originally scheduled—in a March 2004 primary instead of alongside the dramatic recall of Democratic governor Gray Davis—it probably would have been closer than 36 percent to 64 percent.[26] In the end, Proposition 54 opponents stressed the adverse consequences of privatized health data in what Butch Wing, the California state coordinator for Jesse Jackson's Rainbow Push Coalition, called a "perfect storm."[27] In other words, an improbable but propitious convergence of events contributed to the defeat of the initiative.

[handwritten margin note: helped bring race as a social construct into public arena]

In contrast to the proponents of racial privacy, multiracial advocates at least perceived some benefit in citizen participation, even if they did not muster much of it. The media came to the rescue more than once, and a prolonged OMB review meant prolonged attention to the multiracial cause. Thus, in recent years, multiracialism gained attention and popular legitimacy through consideration in the *New York Times,* in *Newsweek,* on *Oprah,* and even in the voting booth. According to a poll conducted in 2001, two-thirds of Americans agreed that it would be "good for the country" if more people thought of themselves as multiracial rather than as belonging to a single race.[28] Interracial dating, marriage, and race as a social construction all seem to be moving closer to popular acceptance. The OMB review and subsequent press coverage, as suggested in figures 4 and 5, seem to have influenced this trend appreciably.

Of course, racial mixture is nothing new; wider acceptance of it is the novelty. Think of it this way: more Americans have someone in their family of a different race, and admit it, than ever before. Both the multiracial movement and Proposition 54 were born in California, an outlier (or harbinger) among the states. Future research will undoubtedly help to explain why racial privacy initiatives did or did not spread to other states. Either way, the idea of race-as-construct now extends far beyond where it did even a decade ago, and civil rights disengagement comes at some cost. Conservatives are likely to expand their interest in multiracial trends. And small as the multiracial movement's base is, the profile of the typical multiracial activist seems to overlap significantly with that of the most participatory Americans. A vacuum from the left has allowed the conservative right to seize the advantage in the growing debate about racial fluidity, at precisely the moment when the notion of racial mixture seems to be reaching more Americans than ever before.

What Makes a Left Multiracialism Possible?

Color blindness in theory is at odds with this study of multiracialism on the ground. In the color-blind story, there is no accounting for the reality that multiracial organizations are a response to racial difficulties. People joined these groups in order to shield themselves and their children from intolerance, which, they said, came from all sides. The pressure of this intolerance was much greater for black-white families, according to my respondents, who were attuned to the difficulties of bigotry in very personal ways. If American society were really prepared to move beyond race, then the multiracial movement described here would not exist as such. Nor would the debate surrounding multiracial recognition have been as fierce; nor would so few (white and black) Americans have marked more than one box when given the opportunity. Nor, in another telling sign, would the relatively few Americans who *did* choose more than one race have overwhelmingly picked *only two* (93 percent).[29] Again, "race-as-construct" is not to be confused with "post-race."

Recall that my respondents identified predominantly as strong or moderate Democrats who favored race-conscious public policy. Those involved in prior social movements identified with progressive causes. They did not express strong preferences for a multiracial census category or for any particular policy along these lines. In my estimation, the multiracial agenda that exists is malleable. Further research is needed on the matter, especially since a new generation of multiracial activists is emerging on college campuses. But it is plausible that multiracial activists' alienation from civil rights institutions might explain their acceptance of Republican support for the cause. In any case, recall Ward Connerly's critique of the multiracial category effort: "The new race classifications were invented by different groups trying to get in on America's racial spoils system." If so, the multiracial advocates to whom Connerly referred wanted something different from him. By this logic, in fact, multiracial groups were not trying to dismantle race-conscious public policy at all; rather, they wanted a piece of the pie. Or at least in part. In reality, multiracial advocates wanted many things, of which a piece of the pie was just one.

Since the 1997 decision, AMEA has repeatedly sought to make clear that the right-wing color-blind agenda is not its agenda.[30] The others, paper organizations with just a few charismatic personalities running the show, seem to have folded up shop. In a follow-up discussion about Proposition 54, a black AMEA board member was contrite: "we naively thought we were all on the same side, we all want to get to the point where race doesn't matter. . . .

I'm not sure we didn't get outsmarted."[31] Again, the college-based groups probably represent the next phase in multiracial politics, and they seem to be left-leaning.[32] Certainly, there is something to build upon here within a civil rights framework.

What Makes a Left Multiracialism Appealing?

The civil rights movement brilliantly exposed the immorality of segregation and insisted upon full equality for all Americans. Against this backdrop, opposition to multiracial recognition from the champions of freedom, integration, and interracial cooperation seemed out of place. The introduction of multiracial issues into the civil rights fold would allow for civil rights consistency, which is enormously appealing. John Conyers and a few other black elites seemed to reach this same, principled conclusion: bringing multiracial concerns under the civil rights tent would be more consonant with civil rights values.

Civil Rights Resistance

Civil rights advocates found MOOM tolerable because it served as a technical absorption of multiracialism (that is, no loss of minority numbers). Thus, in the new arrangement, multiracial persons are technically already under that civil rights tent. My prescription is to extend this welcome beyond the mechanical inclusion imposed by the tabulation guidelines. Were civil rights advocates to offer the symbolic goods that the OMB recently extended to multiracial people, this would align more closely with recognized civil rights principles and, at the same time, could help to deflect the right-wing advance. Civil rights advocates have no room to maneuver on one end of the spectrum: racial data is necessary for compliance monitoring. At the other end, however, there is perhaps room to move and space worth moving into. While a symbolic civil rights welcome would be woefully inadequate according to some multiracial activists, a similar reception was all that was on offer from the OMB. In any event, my research strongly suggests that many multiracial individuals and families would probably not view symbolic outreach as insignificant. Again, even among those unconcerned with government forms, much of the resentment felt by multiracial activists traced back to their perceived treatment at the hands of minority institutions.

Yet even a symbolic step would probably be difficult to take. For lurking just beyond civil rights advocates' concerns about basic policy issues are deeper suspicions about the racial loyalties of multiracial people. Indeed, resistance to multiracialism has revolved around not one but two centers of gravity: civil rights enforcement and group abandonment. The latter qualm has played out quite differently for different groups. While black institutions insinuated that multiracial people were racial defectors, Latino groups could not take this same tack for a variety of reasons and, indeed, did not. Refraining from the more personal attacks heard from the black civil rights community, Latino civil rights groups—along with Asian and American Indian organizations—nonetheless opposed the multiracial category census addition in 2000. That Hispanic, Asian, and American Indian groups stood against multiracial recognition at all seems somewhat tenuous considering intermarriage rates approaching 30 percent or higher in these groups (table 2). Looking forward, advocates for these groups are likely to find it difficult to resist the idea and reality of racial mixture and even harder to take an adversarial stance toward it.

The stakes are high for blacks, and there are no easy answers. While the contemporary politics of racial fluidity are not rooted exclusively in the interests or experiences of one community—to think that any one group "owns" the debate over multiracialism is illogical and demonstrably untrue—blacks' connection to it has been more harrowing than most. Preoccupation with interracial contact, always with sex a paramount concern, was used in one way or another by whites to justify the degraded position of blacks in American life for centuries. White anxieties about interracial sex figured prominently in the distinction between political and social equality—separate as the fingers on the hand[33]—and the repeal of the remaining intermarriage bans, again, came markedly late in the civil rights trajectory. Although we tend to recall it primarily in relation to punitive measures against interracial contact in most areas of public life, Jim Crow was particularly lethal when it came to private, intimate association. No other racial or ethnic group has a history as tightly bound to state-sanctioned and state-enforced racial separation.

Thus, for many blacks who would look back, the topic of racial mixture is fraught with trouble and woe. For some who would peer into the possible future, though, growing racial fluidity seems unlikely to lift all boats. Instead, if today's panethnics are tomorrow's whites, then racial fluidity could be leading to an exit from minority identification for a growing number of Latinos and Asians. This would leave blacks, among other things, with a diminishing pool of allies. The possibility that a black-nonblack divide is emerging to supplant the black-white one is a big idea with a dual message: racial diversity is growing but alongside an enduring black-white color line, which still "permeates white relationships with virtually all other groups in this country."[34] Even the multiracial advocacy groups in my study are structured around this bifurcation.

While most black leaders were opposed to a multiracial category, there were notable exceptions. Ralph Abernathy III, John Conyers, Carol Moseley-Braun, and a few other blacks of influence seemed to signal that blacks could simultaneously lay claim to multiracial identity. Arthur Fletcher's successor at the U.S. Commission on Civil Rights, Mary Frances Berry, also confirmed this idea, if indirectly. In hearings held by the commission in 2002, "Briefing on the Consequences of Government Race Data Bans on Civil Rights," Berry asked expert testifiers:

> Do you have any idea why only 2.4 percent [of the U.S. population] checked that off? And why didn't, if there's this great trend toward everybody being multiracial—for example, in my own case, as in the case of many African Americans, I could have checked off Indian if I had wanted to, because I'm Caucasian, Black, and Indian, to my knowledge, to my personal knowledge. So why was it only 2.4 if . . . people are so puzzled about what race they are?[35]

Berry, situating herself among the 70 percent of blacks identified by Mfume as multiracial, apparently views herself as such in a technical (and thus less meaningful) sense; she opposed the original stand-alone multiracial category proposal in part because politically she is black. Akin to Lani Guinier and Gerald Torres's assertion in *The Miner's Canary*, this positions black racial group membership and legitimacy not as a matter of racial purity; rather, the salient qualifications have to do with political and cultural allegiances. The point is this: the revelation of multiple origins need not have anything to do with group abandonment.

Black resistance to multiracialism is complex. It is historically informed and rooted in protecting the legal interests of black constituencies, it goes well beyond that to stirring questions of racial loyalty, and it is not all resistance. As Americans in general, and blacks in particular, sort out how to feel about multiracialism they should consider a few things. It is a mistake to presume that just 2 percent of the population is implicated. Growing racial diversity, arguably the balancing act at the center of American racial politics today, elevates the significance of the multiracial idea far beyond its measured proportions. In earlier chapters I pressed this point primarily on conceptual grounds, but considered here more narrowly as a demographic trend, it is clear that the self-identified multiple-race population is growing rapidly—in some places at a faster rate than the black population—and the "Some Other Race" trajectory adds to the effect. As Roderick Harrison cautions, we disregard another part of the story, multiple-race identification as a proportion of each group's total tally, at significant analytic cost. Race, as we have known it, may be ingrained for whites and blacks, but the color line seems to be less sharply drawn for everyone else.

Next, it is a losing proposition to refuse to grapple with multiracialism seriously and on its own terms—that is, without some regard to its meaning for the people who claim it. While the modern-day federal categorization system is supposed to monitor and facilitate action against discrimination, not to validate identity, multiracial identity claims are not without power. There are many inconsistencies in multiracialism, yet to focus on just the contradictions, to dismiss the whole issue as irrelevant, or to label all multiracial advocates as right-wing apologists is to ignore important political realities and possibilities. I do not claim that bringing multiracialism into the civil rights fold will be a magic bullet; rather, I am saying it would be better to be in than out. The American understanding of "multiracial" is being shaped right now, in extraordinary and unparalleled ways. Avoidance from the left provided an opportunity for conservatives to frame multiraciality in terms not even resonant with its initial champions. An antagonistic relationship to the idea and reality of racial fluidity is detrimental to the interests of civil rights institutions and may further estrange people from them.

Some are already gone. In defiance of the OMB decision of 1997, Charles Byrd advised *Interracial Voice* readers to "Check White! *Check Anything But Black!* Check Every Box on the Form! Don't Return a Census Form At All! Check Hispanic! Check American Indian!"[36] Why check "anything but black" given the allegedly color-blind ethos to which Byrd subscribes? Multiracial advocates have occasionally shown disregard for the primary rationale behind collecting racial data and have looked coldly upon the difficult predicament of civil rights proponents. Yet if some people do not want to be black—one interpretation of this tirade—then perhaps blacks should let them go.

The boundaries of blackness, long defined by whites yet never under their full control, are perhaps most closely monitored now by blacks themselves. It is one thing if whites see black homogeneity where there is none. Blacks have never had the luxury of embracing their complexities, racial or otherwise, with the reasonable expectation that whites would accept, respect, or even discern such nuance. It is another thing altogether if blacks (being more alert to the complexities of black life) are complicit in the containment of their own and each other's identities. The politics of national black organizations, operating within a racial framework stressing homogeneity, do not discourage this practice. Indeed, via community campaigns to "just mark black"[37] on the 2000 census, and in other ways earlier described, black institutions legitimate and sanction the gatekeeping mechanisms at work elsewhere in black life. The implication is that some people cannot be trusted to express their racial identities without "real" black instruction and critique.

Far from a trivial distraction, multiracialism brings us to matters of tremendous importance for American politics generally and for black politics in particular. Read as a means of maneuvering toward whiteness, multiracialism offers little for blacks to celebrate. Read as part of a wider failure of black elites to navigate difference within black communities, multiracialism leads to the inescapable conclusion that racial identity, blackness included, is manifestly composite. The matter of choice and freedom in racial identification is far too loaded for the civil rights community to ignore or perhaps even to resist—even more so since the OMB, an unlikely trailblazer, has already made the leap. In-kind affirmation from black elites arguably would do no more to destabilize black identity than does the current strategy, which rejects the support of multiracial people in combating racial alienation. If abandonment is part of the problem, then blacks need to ask themselves who is abandoning whom; it is not always so clear. Even presuming the inevitable—that some will exit—whether they bemoan these departures or not, blacks cannot be better off by having attempted to block the door.

Appendix A

This book documents a series of political developments about which only scant information was available in the existing literature. Most of the material presented in this book necessarily comes from primary sources. In addition, I was present at many of the turning points in the life of the multiracial movement and so was able to observe as the various actors expressed their ideas publicly, to me personally, and to each other. I draw upon my observations from many multiracial events across the country from 1996 to 2003 and the following primary information sources:

- an original survey and questionnaire administered to the universe of group leaders ($N = 30$) and the board members of four local affiliate groups ($N = 50$);

- two-month stays in each local affiliate's city to conduct interviews, attend group meetings and social events, and compile documentation including organizational newsletters, meeting minutes, written correspondence, conference proceedings, and so forth; and

- interviews with civil rights advocates, legislators, and Census Bureau officials.

I also relied upon congressional hearings and state legislative records, along with census data and related bureau documentation.

Leadership Survey

Although comprising only thirty interviews, my leadership survey is comprehensive in that it covers what I believe to be the entire universe of adult-based group leaders in the United States near the height of movement activity. Starting out with a list of sixty-three organizations that I compiled from out-of-date directories available on the Internet, incomplete lists provided to me by movement activists, and published directories of American associations and nonprofit organizations, I was able by late 1997 to verify through verbal or written communication with prior group leaders and members that twenty-three of these groups had disbanded. That left forty groups. Within this remaining population, I determined that a group had disbanded if (a) it was impossible to reach a representative after repeated efforts over several months via phone, electronic mail, or regular mail; and when (b) none of the proximate active group leaders had knowledge of the group's existence. This situation applied in ten of the forty remaining groups, leaving a roll of thirty active organizations nationwide.

I administered the leadership survey to all thirty group leaders. This involved a mix of in-person (thirteen) and telephone (seventeen) interviews. To ensure a high response rate, I avoided the mail-out, mail-back method. All of those group leaders interviewed by phone were expecting my call and had a hard copy of the survey in front of them as we talked and I recorded their answers. The disadvantage is that people often furnish different answers depending on the interview context, and I employed diverse methods (in-person and telephone) to solicit this information. The advantage is that I achieved a 100 percent response rate. What is more, I was able to gather much more information using these methods than respondents tend to provide (if they bother to respond at all) via mail-out, mail-back surveys. I followed the same procedure with in-person interviews. That is, I furnished each respondent with a copy of the survey and recorded his or her answers on a separate copy as we went through it together. To further promote participation, I created a "dissertation newsletter" and sent out four issues over one and a half years (1998–2000) to keep all participants and other interested parties invested in and linked to my study.

In content, via a combined multiple choice/open-ended format, the leadership survey focused on two different sets of issues. First, I asked group leaders about their socioeconomic status, personal hopes, political motivations, partisanship, prior social movement involvement, and other individual characteristics. Next, I asked about the groups they led. The latter set of questions focused on organizational capacity and political activity. The survey was designed to take about one hour to complete; most interviews ran about twice that time on the phone and even longer in person.

In a related effort, I spent ten consecutive months (1997–98) studying the four most politically oriented multiracial groups across the country (criteria described in the next section). This fieldwork resulted in an additional fifty case study interviews with the board members of the following groups: Interracial/Intercultural-Pride (San Francisco/Berkeley), the Biracial Family Network (Chicago), the Interracial Family Alliance (Atlanta), and the Interracial Family Circle (Washington, D.C.). I had initially hoped to conduct a random sample of interviews with rank-and-file members, but some group leaders refused to release their full membership lists to me for privacy reasons. Thus, formal case study interviews were restricted to the board members (secretaries, treasurers, newsletter editors, and so forth) of each group. Even so, I found many opportunities to interact with the rank-and-file members of these organizations, as I attended all functions held by the respective groups during my approximate two-month stay in each city.

Case Study Selection Criteria

All of my case studies were AMEA affiliates, because Project RACE and APFU did not have affiliate groups. I chose among AMEA affiliates based on geographical variation and the fact that most "national" leaders started out in a few of these groups. My initial rationale for selecting groups from different parts of the country was that I expected the racial composition of the groups to vary depending on region; however, this turned out not to be the case. Within these geographical constraints (I would pick one group from each region), I focused on the most politically oriented organizations for case study analysis, using three proxies to gauge political involvement. First, as mentioned earlier, I chose local groups that had produced "national" leaders. Second, I focused on groups with relatively large memberships (at least one hundred adult members), both as an indicator of political capacity and because I expected to conduct formal interviews with a sample of rank-and-file members. Furthermore, preliminary research showed that large groups (usually including a secretarial board position) were the only ones keeping organizational records and consistently publishing newsletters. Third, I took into consideration what I learned from the activists themselves about which groups were at the forefront of the political effort.

The data reflect the results of structured interviews with group leaders and board members only. However, I was regularly exposed to rank-and-file participants' views and circumstances in person (noted previously) and on paper, since many of these people contributed short articles for publication in their organizations' newsletters. I reviewed all internal documentation provided to me by the groups. In all four cases, I obtained and read meeting minutes and back issues of newsletters; in a few instances, I was able to augment this wealth of information with internal correspondence and financial records.

Case Study Questionnaire

I interviewed all of the board members in person, following the procedure described previously for the leadership survey. These interviews, in most cases, were completed at board members' homes. In content, the case study questionnaire (a combined multiple choice/open-ended format) overlapped considerably with the leadership survey. Thus, I asked board members many of the same questions about their socioeconomic status, personal hopes, political motivation, partisanship, prior social movement involvement, and other individual characteristics. The questionnaire was designed to take about forty-five minutes to complete; most interviews ran at least twice that time. Together, the leadership survey ($N = 30$) and case study questionnaire ($N = 50$) add to eighty total responses. I draw from the cumulative responses of both leaders and board members on overlapping questions when I refer to "all respondents."

I conducted a number of in-person and telephone interviews with state legislators, civil rights representatives, and individuals affiliated with the Census Bureau. I could not rely upon a standard questionnaire in these cases, since developments were unfolding as I conducted my research. Thus, I asked each respondent a series of tailor-made questions to fill factual gaps and to solicit their individual and institutional opinions of multiracial category initiatives in the context of current events.

Appendix B

Reproduction of the Census 2000 Questions on Ethnicity and Race

➜ **NOTE: Please answer BOTH Questions 7 and 8.**

7. **Is Person 1 Spanish/Hispanic/Latino?** *Mark* ☒ *the* **"No"** *box if* **not** *Spanish/Hispanic/Latino.*

☐ **No,** not Spanish/Hispanic/Latino ☐ Yes, Puerto Rican
☐ Yes, Mexican, Mexican Am., Chicano ☐ Yes, Cuban
☐ Yes, other Spanish/Hispanic/Latino — *Print group.* ⬎

8. **What is Person 1's race?** *Mark* ☒ **one or more races** to *indicate what this person considers himself/herself to be.*

☐ White
☐ Black, African Am., or Negro
☐ American Indian or Alaska Native — *Print name of enrolled or principal tribe.* ⬎

☐ Asian Indian ☐ Japanese ☐ Native Hawaiian
☐ Chinese ☐ Korean ☐ Guamanian or Chamorro
☐ Filipino ☐ Vietnamese ☐ Samoan
☐ Other Asian — *Print race.* ⬎ ☐ Other Pacific Islander — *Print race.* ⬎

☐ Some other race — *Print race.* ⬎

Source: U.S Census Bureau, Census 2000 Questionnaire.

Appendix C

Multiracial Organizations, 1997–98

The following table reports the data collected on adult-based groups ($N = 30$) as depicted in figure 1.

Acronym	Group Name	Year Formed	City	State	Umbrella Affiliated?	Adult Group Members	Group Time Spent on the Following Activities (%)				
							Public Affairs	Social	Educational	Religious	Other
4-C	Cross-Cultural Couples & Children	1997	Plainsboro	NJ	No	30	25	60	15	0	0
AMEA	Association of Multiethnic Americans	1988	San Francisco	CA	Umbrella Organization	400	50	20	30	0	0
APFU-LA	A Place For Us	1984	Gardena	CA	Umbrella Organization	200	30	30	30	10	0
APFU-Little Rock	A Place For Us	1993	Little Rock	AR	Yes	30	10	40	10	40	0
BFN	Biracial Family Network	1980	Chicago	IL	Yes	100	20	30	30	0	20
CHP	Creole Heritage Preservation	1975	Natchitoches	LA	No	300	25	25	25	0	0
GIFT-NC	Getting Interracial Families Together	1997	Greenville	NC	No	25	20	50	15	15	0

GIFT-NJ	Getting Interracial Families Together	1994	Montclair	NJ	No	140	10	80	10	0	0
HMC	Heights Multicultural Group	1993	South Euclid	OH	No	75	10	50	40	0	0
HONEY	Honor Our New Ethnic Youth	1983	Eugene	OR	Yes	30	10	65	20	5	0
I-Pride	Interracial/Intercultural Pride	1979	Berkeley	CA	Yes	200	40	40	20	0	0
IC	Interracial Connection	1982	Norfolk	VA	Yes	25	0	90	10	0	0
ICB	Interracial Club of Buffalo	1983	Buffalo	NY	Yes	50	0	80	20	0	0
IFA-Atlanta	Interracial Family Alliance	1983	Atlanta	GA	Yes	150	35	35	30	0	0
IFA-Dallas/Ft. Worth	Interracial Family Alliance	1990	Dallas	TX	No	100	5	45	45	5	0
IFA-Houston	Interracial Family Alliance	1982	Houston	TX	Yes	45	0	90	10	0	0

(continues)

Acronym	Group Name	Year Formed	City	State	Umbrella Affiliated?	Adult Group Members	Group Time Spent on the Following Activities (%)				
							Public Affairs	Social	Educational	Religious	Other
IFC-DC	Interracial Family Circle of Washington DC	1984	Washington	DC	Yes	150	40	55	5	0	0
IFN	Interracial Family Network	1989	Evanston	IL	No	175	0	95	5	0	0
IR LIFE	InterRacial Life	1996	East Brunswick	NJ	No	20	25	50	25	0	0
MACT	Men of All Colors Together	1980	San Francisco	CA	No	60	5	25	25	0	45
MASC	Multiracial Americans of Southern California	1987	Los Angeles	CA	Yes	500	30	40	30	0	0
MFC	Multiracial Family Circle	1991	Kansas City	MO	No	150	0	50	50	0	0
MFOP	Multiracial Families of Oak Park	1993	Oak Park	IL	No	50	5	70	25	0	0

MFSG	Multiracial Family Support Group	1995	Somerset	NJ	No	10	10	70	20	0	0
MOSAIC	Multiethnics of Southern Arizona in Celebration	1997	Tucson	AZ	Yes	30	0	50	50	0	0
MOXCHA	MOXCHA	1994	Edmonton	Alberta	Yes	11	5	10	80	0	5
NEAMF	New England Alliance of Multiracial Families	1992	West Newton	MA	No	200	10	75	15	0	0
Project RACE	Project Reclassify All Children Equally	1992	Roswell	GA	Umbrella Organization	100	75	5	20	0	0
RFT	Rainbow Families of Toledo	1983	Toledo	OH	No	50	0	80	20	0	0
UNITY	UNITY Multiracial Social Group	1994	Orange Park	FL	Yes	30	5	70	20	0	5

Notes

CHAPTER 1

1. Alan Patureau, "Principal Called Mixed-Race Pupil a Mistake," *Atlanta Journal Constitution*, March 10, 1994, A3. Also reported in *AMEA Networking News* 4, no. 5 (fall 1993): 1.

2. Press Release, *AMEA Networking News* 5, no. 1 (winter-spring 1994): 3.

3. Charles Byrd, "Multiracial Solidarity March on the Mall in Washington, D.C., July 20 1996!" www.webcom.com/~intvoice/ (accessed July 1, 1996).

4. Kweisi Mfume, "NAACP's Views on New Multiracial Category," www.naacp.org (accessed November 15, 1996).

5. Newt Gingrich, "Open Letter to Franklin Raines," July 1, 1997, www.speakernews.house.gov (accessed July 12, 1997).

6. Mae M. Cheng, "Census Not Just Numbers: Outgoing Leader Says 2000 Survey Redefines Race," *Newsday*, January 30, 2001, A15.

7. The Census Bureau tried to count mulattos, quadroons, and octoroons (intermittently from 1850 to 1920) but with an entirely different purpose in mind, namely, to scientifically "prove" the racial inferiority of blacks. See, for instance, Melissa Nobles, *Shades of Citizenship: Race and the Census in Modern Politics* (Palo Alto: Stanford University Press, 2000).

8. Paul Starr, "Social Categories and Claims in the Liberal State," *Social Research* 59, no. 2 (1992): 263.

9. Kenneth Prewitt, "Public Statistics and Democratic Politics," in *The Politics of Numbers*, ed. William Alonso and Paul Starr (New York: Russell Sage Foundation, 1987), 261–74.

10. I could not study both adult- and college-based groups because I did not have research assistance in the mid-1990s. There were more multiracial conferences, meetings, pancollegiate summits, and so forth, taking place across the country than I could have possibly covered alone had I attempted to do both. Further, my process for ensuring a high response rate was labor intensive (see appendix A), and I had to make choices. I decided to focus on the groups that seemed to be at the forefront of the census battle.

11. See, for instance, James McBride, *The Color of Water: A Black Man's Tribute to His White Mother* (New York: Riverhead Books, 1996); Maria P. P. Root, ed., *Racially Mixed People in America* (Newbury Park, CA: Sage, 1992); Lise Funderburg, *Black, White, Other: Biracial Americans Talk about Race and*

145

Identity (New York: William Morrow, 1994); and Shirlee Taylor Haizlip, *The Sweeter the Juice* (New York: Simon & Schuster, 1994).

12. Nobles, *Shades of Citizenship*, 142, 137.

13. Joel Perlmann and Mary C. Waters, "Introduction," *The New Race Question: How the Census Counts Multiracial Individuals* (New York: Russell Sage Foundation, 2002), 17.

CHAPTER 2

1. Carlos A. Fernández, "Government Classification of Multiracial/Multiethnic People," in *The Multiracial Experience: Racial Borders as the New Frontier*, ed. Maria P. P. Root (Thousand Oaks, CA: Sage, 1996), 23.

2. AMEA, Mission Statement. http://www.ameasite.org (accessed August 27, 2002).

3. Project RACE, Mission Statement, http://www.projectrace.com/about projectrace/ (accessed August 27, 2002).

4. APFU, Mission Statement, 1.

5. Nancy G. Brown and Ramona E. Douglass, "Making the Invisible Visible: The Growth of Community Network Organizations," in *The Multiracial Experience*, 338. Initial plans for a political action committee were vetted in the *AMEA Networking News:* "[It is] the only effective means for influencing real legislative and regulatory reform regarding official classifications. Letter writing campaigns and informational letters to legislators cannot substitute for the real thing. . . . In order to be in contention we must have an entity devoted exclusively to lobbying lawmakers. [Since] most, if not all policies setting forth racial and ethnic classifications are determined at the federal level . . . members of AMEA's Washington affiliate, the IFC [Interracial Family Circle] would be involved with this, because of their obvious strategic proximity." *AMEA Networking News* 1, no. 4 (fall 1990): 2.

6. Carlos Fernández, "Message from the President," *Mélange* 1, no. 1 (September 1989): 1 (later renamed *AMEA Networking News*).

7. For instance, in her book *Diminished Democracy: From Membership to Management in American Civic Life* (Norman: University of Oklahoma Press, 2003), political scientist Theda Skocpol chronicles the rise of top-heavy, professionally managed groups including the mailing-list assemblages of check writers targeted through direct mail that activist and scholar Marshall Ganz has labeled "bodyless heads" (163).

8. Members of Congress voiced opposition (including Augustus Hawkins, Mervyn Dymally, Edward Roybal, Patricia Schroeder, Ted Weiss, Matthew Martinez, Robert Garcia, Don Edwards, and John Conyers) as did influential actors in a number of the federal agencies (including the Civil Rights Division of the Department of Justice, the Department of Health and Human Services, the EEOC, and the Office of Personnel Management). House Subcommittee on Census, Statistics, and Postal Personnel, Committee on Post Office and Civil Service, *Hearings on the Review of Federal Measurements of Race and Ethnicity*, testimony by Sally Katzen on July 29, 1993, 103d Cong., 1st sess., April 14, June 30, July 29, and November 3, 1993, 215.

9. AMEA, "President's Report to the Board of Directors," September 22, 1989, 2.

10. However, in 1989, Mahin Root, a multiracial teenager, tried to register at a public high school in Greensboro, North Carolina. The school required specification of race on a school form, and she left it blank. Although pressured by the school to choose a race for administrative purposes, she replied that it would be against her religious faith (Bahai) to do so. Eventually, the Office of Civil Rights in the Department of Education got involved, as it requires all public school systems to submit racial data on their students. The Roots eventually allowed the school system to consider their daughter black. "No Place for Mankind," *Time*, September 4, 1989, 17.

11. *The Peacemaker* (April 1988): 3.

12. F. James Davis, *Who Is Black? One Nation's Definition* (University Park: Pennsylvania State University Press, 1991), 13.

13. APFU, "For the Good of America," 1989, flyer.

14. Steve Hawk, "Activists Rally around Family of Beaten Girl," *Orange County Register*, September 2, 1990, Metro 3.

15. APFU, Press Release, 1990.

16. *Peacemaker* (fall 1989); my emphasis.

17. Susan Graham, in-person interview, April 16, 1998.

18. Most of the national spokespeople emerged from these groups (Carlos Fernández was first a member of I-Pride, Ramona Douglass of BFN, and Edwin Darden of IFC). See appendix A for details.

19. John McCarthy and Mayer N. Zald, *The Trend of Social Movements in America: Professionalism and Resource Mobilization* (Morristown, NJ: General Learning Corporation, 1973). Also see John McCarthy and Mayer N. Zald, "Resource Mobilization and Social Movements: A Partial Theory," *American Journal of Sociology* 82 (1977): 1212–41.

20. Authors' calculation, based on primary research.

21. This is surely a low estimate because it excludes the student groups. By 2000, there were approximately 30 student groups on college campuses. Interestingly, the push for a multiracial category did not start, nor was it primarily sustained, on college campuses. In recent years, however, the college groups have become more vocal and increasingly central to the debate.

22. Memo from Ramona Douglass to Carlos Fernández, July 1995.

23. Doug McAdam, *Political Process and the Development of Black Insurgency, 1930–1970* (Chicago: University of Chicago Press, 1982).

24. Sidney G. Tarrow, *Power in Movement* (New York: Cambridge University Press, 1994), 81.

25. Peter Skerry, *Counting on the Census? Race, Group Identity, and the Evasion of Politics* (Washington, DC: Brookings Institution Press, 2000), 4.

26. Harvey M. Choldin, *Looking for the Last Percent: The Controversy over Census Undercounts* (New Brunswick, NJ: Rutgers University Press, 1994), 30.

27. Ibid., 32.

28. Margo J. Anderson and Stephen E. Feinberg, *Who Counts? The Politics of Census-Taking in Contemporary America* (New York: Russell Sage Foundation, 1999), 42.

29. William Petersen, "Politics and the Measurement of Ethnicity," in *The*

Politics of Numbers, ed. William Alonso and Paul Starr (New York: Russell Sage Foundation, 1987), 232.

30. Anderson and Feinberg, *Who Counts?* 51.

31. Ibid., 53.

32. "1990 Census," *Encyclopedia of the U.S. Census,* ed. Margo J. Anderson (Washington, DC: Congressional Quarterly Press, 2000), 158.

33. Skerry, *Counting on the Census?* 23.

34. Barbara Everitt Bryant and William Dunn, *Moving Power and Money: The Politics of Census Taking* (Ithaca, NY: New Strategist Publications, 1995).

35. Bryant and Dunn, *Moving Power and Money,* 158–59. Also see Skerry, *Counting on the Census?* 23.

36. Bryant and Dunn, *Moving Power and Money,* 158–59.

37. Choldin, *Looking for the Last Percent,* 137.

38. Ibid., 143.

39. Skerry, *Counting on the Census?* 25.

40. Martha Riche, personal e-mail to author, January 4, 2004.

41. U.S. Executive Office of the President, Office of Management and Budget, "Standards for the Classification of Federal Data on Race and Ethnicity," *Federal Register* 60, no. 166 (August 28, 1995): 44674.

42. TerriAnn Lowenthal, in-person interview, July 13, 1999. Lowenthal now serves on AMEA's advisory board.

43. Jan Carpenter Tucker, in-person interview, September 16, 1998.

44. Sharon Lee, "Racial Classifications in the U.S. Census: 1890–1990," *Ethnic and Racial Studies* 16, no. 1 (1993): 83.

45. Project on Race and Ethnic Measurement in Federal Statistics, working group, New School for Social Research, New York, November 11, 2002.

46. Margo Anderson, "Counting by Race: The Antebellum Legacy," in *The New Race Question,* 270.

47. Ibid.

48. Ibid., 280.

49. Rachel Moran, *Interracial Intimacy: The Regulation of Race and Romance* (Chicago: University of Chicago Press, 2001), 19.

50. Randall Kennedy, *Interracial Intimacies: Sex, Marriage, Identity, and Adoption* (New York: Pantheon Books, 2003), 22–23; emphasis in original. See also Moran, *Interracial Intimacy;* Gunnar Myrdal, *An American Dilemma: The Negro Problem and Modern Democracy* (New York: Harper and Brothers, 1944); Paul Spickard, *Mixed Blood: Intermarriage and Ethnic Identity in Twentieth-Century America* (Madison: University of Wisconsin Press, 1989); Werner Sollors, ed., *Interracialism: Black-White Intermarriage in American History, Literature, and Law* (New York: Oxford University Press, 2000).

51. Moran, *Interracial Intimacy,* 80.

52. Harvey Fireside, *Separate and Unequal: Homer Plessy and the Supreme Court Decision that Legalized Racism* (New York: Carroll & Graf, 2004), 1.

53. Ibid., 323.

54. Choldin, *Looking for the Last Percent,* 27.

55. Ibid., 41.

56. Joseph B. Kadane and Caroline Mitchell, "Statistics in Proof of Employment Discrimination Cases," in *Legacies of the 1964 Civil Rights Act,* ed. Bernard Grofman (Charlottesville: University Press of Virginia, 2000).

57. Daryl Lindsey, "The Stakes Are a Bit Higher for Us: The NAACP's Washington Bureau Chief Takes the Census Bureau to Task for Its New Multiracial Categories," *Salon*, February 16, 2000, http://www.salon.com/news/feature/2000/02/16/naacp (accessed November 2, 2003).

58. Nathaniel Persily, "The Legal Implications of a Multiracial Census," in *The New Race Question*. For an opposing viewpoint, see Roderick Harrison, "Inadequacies of Multiple-Response Race Data," in the same volume.

59. Analysts predict exponential growth in the coming years. See Nicholas A. Jones, "We the People of More Than One Race in the United States," *Census 2000 Special Reports*, April 2005, http://www.census.gov/prod/2005pubs/censr-22.pdf (accessed May 1, 2005). Also see Barry Edmonston, Sharon M. Lee, and Jeffrey S. Passel, "Recent Trends in Intermarriage and Immigration and Their Effects on the Future Racial Composition of the U.S. Population," in *The New Race Question*, 227–55.

60. Bruce M. Clark and Robert Timothy Reagan, "Redistricting Litigation: An Overview of Legal, Statistical, and Case-Management Issues," *Federal Judicial Center*, 2002, http://www.fjc.gov/newweb/jnetweb.nsf/autoframe?open form&url_r=pages/556&url_l=index (accessed November 16, 2003), 10, n. 9.

61. See Susan McManus and Lawrence Morehouse, "Redistricting in the Multiracial Twenty-First Century: Changing Demographic and Socioeconomic Conditions Pose Important New Challenges," in *Race and Representation*, ed. Georgia Persons (New Brunswick, NJ: Transaction, 1997). Also see Suzanne Dovi, "Preferable Descriptive Representatives: Will Just Any Woman, Black, or Latino Do?" *American Political Science Review* 96, no. 4 (December 2002): 729–43.

62. See Haynes Walton Jr., *When the Marching Stopped: The Politics of Civil Rights Regulatory Agencies* (Albany: State University of New York Press, 1988). Also see John Skrentny, *The Minority Rights Revolution* (Cambridge: Belknap Press of Harvard University Press, 2002).

63. Executive Office of the President, Office of Management and Budget, "Exhibit F (Revised May 12, 1977): Race and Ethnic Standards for Federal Statistics and Administrative Reporting." *Circular No. A-46: Standards and Guidelines for Federal Statistics*, May 3, 1974, 3–4.

64. OMB Bulletin No. 00–02, "Guidance on Aggregation and Allocation of Data on Race for Use in Civil Rights Monitoring and Enforcement," March 9, 2000, http://whitehouse.gov/OMB/bulletins/b00–02.html (accessed December 2005).

65. Skerry, *Counting on the Census?* 38.

66. Reynolds Farley, "Racial Identities in 2000: The Response to the Multiple-Response Option," in *The New Race Question*, 41.

67. Helen Samhan, executive director of the Arab American Institute, Project on Race and Ethnic Measurement in Federal Statistics, working group meeting, New York, November 11, 2002.

68. Conference of Americans of Germanic Heritage, "Statement of the Conference of Americans of Germanic Heritage with Respect to OMB 15," presented at OMB Public Hearings, San Francisco, CA, July 14, 1994, http://www.germanic.org/omb15stm.htm (accessed June 19, 2003).

69. See, for instance, Felix M. Padilla, *Latino Ethnic Consciousness: The Case of Mexican Americans and Puerto Ricans in Chicago* (Notre Dame, IN: University of

Notre Dame Press, 1985); Suzanne Oboler, *Ethnic Labels, Latino Lives: Identity and the Politics of (Re)Presentation in the United States* (Minneapolis: University of Minnesota Press, 1995); Yen Le Espiritu, *Asian American Panethnicity: Bridging Institutions and Identities* (Philadelphia: Temple University Press, 1992); Pei-te Lien, *The Making of Asian America through Political Participation* (Philadelphia: Temple University Press, 2001); Skrentny, *The Minority Rights Revolution.*

70. Paul Ong and David Lee, "Changing of the Guard? The Emerging Immigrant Majority in Asian American Politics," in *Asian Americans and Politics: Perspectives, Experiences, Prospects,* ed. Gordon Chang (Palo Alto: Stanford University Press, 2001). Also see David Lopez and Yen Espiritu, "Panethnicity in the United States: A Theoretical Framework," *Ethnic and Racial Studies* 13, no. 2 (1990): 198–224.

71. U.S. Department of Commerce, U.S. Bureau of the Census, "Interracial Married Couples: 1960 to Present," Internet release date, July 27, 1998, www.census.gov/population/socdemo/ms-la/tabms-3.txt (accessed April 2002).

72. Joshua R. Goldstein, "Kinship Networks that Cross Racial Lines: The Exception or the Rule?" *Demography* 36, no. 3 (August 1999): 406.

73. Frank D. Bean and Gillian Stevens, *America's Newcomers and the Dynamics of Diversity* (New York: Russell Sage Foundation, 2003), 195.

74. Ibid., 192.

75. See George Yancey, *Who Is White? Latinos, Asians, and the New Black/Nonblack Divide* (Boulder, CO: Lynne Rienner, 2003).

76. As late as 1991, F. James Davis predicted that the one-drop rule would remain uncontested for the foreseeable future, but by the end of that decade the rule had been challenged. Similarly, most observers would have found preposterous the idea of a vote on the idea of race as construct, until it happened in 2003 (see chap. 6).

77. Lopez and Espiritu, "Panethnicity in the United States," 203.

78. See, for instance, David R. Harris and Jeremiah Joseph Sim, "An Empirical Look at the Social Construction of Race: The Case of Multiracial Adolescents," *Research Report* 00–452 (Ann Arbor: Population Studies Center, University of Michigan, 2000); Haizlip, *The Sweeter the Juice*; Gregory Howard Williams, *Life on the Color Line: The True Story of a White Boy Who Discovered He Was Black* (New York: Plume Books, 1996).

79. See, for instance, Jennifer Lee and Frank Bean, "America's Changing Color Lines: Immigration, Race/Ethnicity and Multiracial Identification," *Annual Review of Sociology* 30 (2004): 221–42.

80. U.S. Department of Commerce, U.S. Bureau of the Census, "Profile of the Foreign-Born Population in the United States: 2000," *Current Population Reports,* Series P23–206 (Washington, DC: U.S. Government Printing Office, 2001).

81. Ramona Douglass, in-person interview, June 14, 1998.

82. APFU, "Unity Under the Stars: 1998 Racial Harmony Hall of Fame Inductee's Award Banquet." Photocopy, 1998.

83. The awards were given posthumously in the cases of Abernathy and Loving. Later awardees include filmmaker Edward James Olmos and entertainer Montel Williams.

84. NBC helped to cover expenses for the 1997 inductee's award banquet. In 1998, corporate contributions came from the Walt Disney Company along with the Milkin Family Foundation and the Herb and Vitamin Center.

85. APFU Memo, July 1995.

86. But see G. Reginald Daniel, *More than Black? Multiracial Identity and the New Racial Order* (Philadelphia: Temple University Press, 2002), who points out that a few groups emerged between the 1890s and 1950s—the Manasseh Societies, the Penguin Club, Club Miscegenation—though they were, by necessity, mostly clandestine operations. In my fieldwork, I found that the leaders of contemporary support groups were generally unaware of the existence of these earlier organizations.

87. Susan Graham, in-person interview, April 6, 1998.

88. "We are changing race as we know it," she added. Ramona Douglass, in-person interview, June 14, 1998.

CHAPTER 3

1. The EEOC was chaired at that time by Clarence Thomas. Thanks to Jim Reische for this observation.

2. U.S. Congress, House, Subcommittee on Census, Statistics, and Postal Personnel, Committee on Post Office and Civil Service, *Hearings on the Review of Federal Measurement of Race and Ethnicity*, testimony by Sally Katzen, July 29, 1993, 103d Cong., 1st sess., April 14, June 30, July 29, and November 3, 1993, 215.

3. Project on Race and Ethnic Measurement in Federal Statistics, working group meeting, New York, March 24, 2004.

4. Other subcommittee members included Thomas Petri (R-WI) and Albert Wynn (D-MD).

5. U.S. Congress, House, Subcommittee on Census, Statistics, and Postal Personnel, Committee on Post Office and Civil Service, *Hearings on the Review of Federal Measurement of Race and Ethnicity*, opening statement by Thomas Sawyer, April 14, 1993, 103d Cong., 1st sess., April 14, June 30, July 29, and November 3, 1993, 128.

6. House Subcommittee, testimony by Sally Katzen, July 29, 1993, 214.

7. Ibid., 226.

8. See, for instance, Rainer Spencer, *Spurious Issues: Race and Multiracial Identity Politics in the United States* (Boulder, CO: Westview Press, 1999); Nobles, *Shades of Citizenship*; Skerry, *Counting on the Census?*; Perlmann and Waters, *The New Race Question*.

9. House Subcommittee, testimony by Sally Katzen, July 29, 1993, 228.

10. House Subcommittee, testimony by Harry Scarr, April 14, 1993, 3.

11. House Subcommittee, testimony by Billy Tidwell, July 29, 1993, 234.

12. House Subcommittee, testimony by Sonia Pérez, June 30, 1993, 172.

13. House Subcommittee, testimony by Stephen Carbo, June 30, 1993, 179.

14. Ibid., 189.

15. Jeffrey S. Passel, "The Growing American Indian Population, 1960–1990: Beyond Demography," *Population Research and Policy Review* 16, no. 1–2 (1997): 12.

16. House Subcommittee, testimony by Rachel Joseph, July 29, 1993, 236.

17. House Subcommittee, testimony by Arthur Fletcher, November 3, 1993, 273.

18. *AMEA Networking News* 4, no. 5 (fall 1993): 4.

19. House Subcommittee, testimony by Carlos Fernández, June 30, 1993, 127.

20. Ibid.

21. House Subcommittee, testimony by Susan Graham, June 30, 1993, 108.

22. House Subcommittee, testimony by Carlos Fernández, June 30, 1993, 128. He explained further: "whenever the question calls for 'racial' classification, the category 'multiracial' should be included. Whenever a question calls for 'ethnic' classification, the category 'multiethnic' should be included. Whenever racial and ethnic information is sought in a combined format, the category 'multiracial/multiethnic' should be included."

23. Ibid.

24. Ibid.

25. U.S. Congress, House Subcommittee on Census, Statistics, and Postal Personnel, Committee on Post Office and Civil Service, *Hearings on the Review of Federal Measurement of Race and Ethnicity*, opening statement by Thomas Sawyer on July 29, 1993, 197.

26. House Subcommittee, testimony by Daniel Akaka, July 29, 1993, 199.

27. Elizabeth M. Grieco, "The Native Hawaiian and Other Pacific Islander Population: 2000," *Census 2000 Brief,* December 2001, http://www.census.gov/prod/2001pubs/c2kbr01–14.pdf (accessed December 2005).

28. House Subcommittee, testimony by Norman Mineta, July 29, 1993, 208.

29. House Subcommittee, testimony by Barney Frank, July 29, 1993, 211.

30. House Subcommittee, question from Thomas Petri, June 30, 1993, 192.

31. House Subcommittee, response from Stephen Carbo, June 30, 1993, 193.

32. House Subcommittee, question from Thomas Petri, June 30, 1993, 194.

33. U.S. Congress, House, Subcommittee on Census, Statistics, and Postal Personnel, Committee on Post Office and Civil Service, *A Bill to Amend the Paperwork Reduction Act*, 104th Cong., 2d sess., H.R. 3920, *Congressional Record* 142, no. 114, daily ed., July 30, 1996: H8982.

34. Petri later withdrew support from H.R. 830, and there was no vote.

35. National Research Council, Committee on National Statistics, Workshop on Race and Ethnicity Classification: An Assessment of the Federal Standard for Race and Ethnicity Classification, Washington, DC, 1994.

36. In addition, the National Center for Educational Statistics and the Office of Civil Rights in the Department of Education jointly conducted two comprehensive surveys of racial classification issues in public schools; both are discussed in chapter 4.

37. *AMEA Networking News* 4, no. 5 (fall 1993): 4.

38. "Coalition Statement on Proposed Modification of OMB Directive No. 15," 1994, photocopy, 1.

39. AMEA and Project RACE, response to "Coalition Statement," 1994, 1.

40. Carlos Fernández, "The Wedowee Case: What Happened and What It Means for Us," *AMEA Networking News* 5, no. 1 (winter–spring 1994): 2.

41. U.S. Executive Office of the President, Office of Management and Budget, "Standards for the Classification of Federal Data on Race and Ethnicity," *Federal Register* 60, no. 166 (August 28, 1995): 44674.

42. AMEA and Project RACE, Joint Statement "Regarding the Mandate of the 2000 Census to Count All Americans," sent to Katherine Wallman, September 29, 1995.

43. Constance F. Citro, "Advisory Committees," in *Encyclopedia of the U.S. Census*, 15.

44. Further, per Harvey Choldin, "census officials have never claimed that these [advisory] committees were composed of experts; rather, they acknowledge them to be part of a classic strategy of cooptation." In Peter Skerry, *Counting on the Census?* 38.

45. The nine-member Undercount Steering Committee assembled to advise Bryant voted seven to two in favor of adjustment. She agreed with the majority. "It was my judgment (with studies to back me up) that if you correct errors at a higher level, you improve things at the lower level." Bryant and Dunn, *Moving Power and Money*, 156.

46. Byrd felt that, although the umbrella groups had achieved significant success, "not much effort . . . has been expended to disseminate news of the movement to mixed-race individuals on a grassroots level, and if the multiracial initiative fails, it will be because the government simply did not take our arguments or our numbers seriously." Charles Michael Byrd, "Why the Multiracial Community Must March on July 20!" http://www.intvoice.com.

47. Ibid. http://www.intvoice.com (accessed June 1996); emphasis in original.

48. Ramona Douglass, "Solidarity March," on-line posting, Interracial Individuals Listserv, July 25, 1995, http://soyokaze.biosci.ohio-state.edu/~jei/ii (accessed August 1995).

49. Clarence Page, "Biracial People Feel 'Boxed In' by Census Form," *Chicago Tribune*, July 28, 1996, B3.

50. Department of Labor, Bureau of Labor Statistics, *A Test of Methods for Collecting Racial and Ethnic Information: May 1995*, USDL 95–428 (Washington, DC, 1995), 2–3.

51. U.S. Department of Commerce, U.S. Bureau of the Census, "Findings on Questions on Race and Hispanic Origin Tested in the 1996 National Content Survey," Population Division Working Paper No. 16 (Washington, DC: U.S. Government Printing Office, 1996).

52. Ramona Douglass, "Letters to the Editor," *Interracial Voice*, February 1997, http://www.intvoice.com (accessed March 1997).

53. Ramona Douglass, "Upcoming Hearings" memorandum to Nancy Brown and Faye Mandell, March 16, 1997.

54. Ramona Douglass, "Beyond the 2000 Census: Community as Team," speech delivered at the University of Michigan, Ann Arbor, April 5, 1997.

55. In order to "acknowledge the rights of multiracial people to identify truthfully and accurately, without hurting minority groups that need accurate reporting of race and ethnic data for civil rights purposes." JACL, "JACL Policy Position on the Multiracial Category," July 9, 1997, http://www.jacl.org (accessed July 1997).

56. Libertarian Party, Press Release, July 10, 1997, photocopy.

57. Charles Byrd, "Interracial Voice Interviews Congressman Thomas Petri," April 23, 1997, http://www.intvoice.com (accessed May 1997).

58. Ibid.

59. Susan Graham, "Multiracial Life after Newt," November 9, 1998, http://www. projectrace.home.mindspring.com/director.html (accessed November, 22 1998).

60. Newt Gingrich, "Open Letter to Franklin Raines." July 1, 1997, http://www.speakernews.house.gov (accessed July 12, 1997).

61. U.S. Congress, House, Subcommittee on Government Management, Information, and Technology, Committee on Government Reform and Oversight, *Hearings on Federal Measures of Race and Ethnicity and the Implications for the 2000 Census*, testimony by Newt Gingrich, July 25, 1997, 105th Cong., 1st sess., April 23, May 22, and July 25, 1997, 662.

62. Rick Christie, "Gingrich Lists His Action Plan for Racial Gulf," *Atlanta Journal-Constitution*, June 19, 1997, A3. Also see Steven A. Holmes, "Gingrich Outlines Plan on Race Relations," *New York Times*, June 19, 1997, B12.

63. House Subcommittee, testimony by Thomas Sawyer, April 23, 1997, 221.

64. Ibid., 220.

65. House Subcommittee, testimony by Thomas Petri, April 23, 1997, 223.

66. House Subcommittee, testimony by Carrie Meek, April 23, 1997, 231–32.

67. House Subcommittee, testimony by John Conyers, July 25, 1997, 535; emphasis in original.

68. House Subcommittee, testimony by Harold McDougall, May 22, 1997, 309.

69. But per Roderick Harrison, now a researcher at the Joint Center for Political and Economic Studies, this consensus was achieved only with his removal from the committee. See chap. 6.

70. House Subcommittee, testimony by Harold McDougall, July 25, 1997, 585.

71. U.S. Department of Commerce, Bureau of the Census, "Results of the 1996 Race and Ethnic Targeted Test," Population Division Working Paper no. 18 (Washington, DC, 1997). RAETT, in contrast to the CPS and NCT efforts, was designed with small populations in mind.

72. Faye Fiore, "Multiple Race Choices to be Allowed on 2000 Census," *Los Angeles Times*, October 30, 1997. A1.

73. Joshua R. Goldstein and Ann J. Morning, "Back in the Box: The Dilemma of Using Multiple-Race Data for Single-Race Laws," in *The New Race Question*, 119–36.

74. Executive Office of the President, Office of Management and Budget, Tabulation Working Group of the Interagency Committee for the Review of Standards for Data on Race and Ethnicity, "Provisional Guidance on the Implementation of the 1997 Standards for Federal Data on Race and Ethnicity," appendix C, *Federal Register*, December 15, 2000.

75. Should a person marking two or more minority races become involved in a civil rights enforcement case, the individual would be allocated to the race that she or he believes the discrimination was based on. Alternately, should the

enforcement action require assessing disparate impact or a discriminatory pattern, the rule is to "analyze the patterns based on alternative allocations to each of the minority groups." Executive Office of the President of the United States, Office of Management and Budget, "To the Heads of Executive Departments and Establishments, Subject: Guidance on Aggregation and Allocation of Data on Race for Use in Civil Rights Monitoring and Enforcement," Bulletin 00–02, March 9, 2000, Washington, DC.

76. House Subcommittee, testimony by Sally Katzen, July 29, 1993, 226.

77. See, for instance, William Alonso and Paul Starr, eds., *The Politics of Numbers* (New York: Russell Sage Foundation, 1987); Melissa Nobles, *Shades of Citizenship: Race and the Census in Modern Politics* (Palo Alto: Stanford University Press, 2000); Joel Perlmann and Mary Waters, eds., *The New Race Question: How The Census Counts Multiracials* (New York: Russell Sage Foundation, 2002); Peter Skerry, *Counting on the Census? Race, Group Identity, and the Evasion of Politics* (Washington, DC: Brookings Institution Press, 2000); Kenneth Prewitt, "Race in the 2000 Census: A Turning Point," in Perlmann and Waters, *The New Race Question;* and Barbara Everitt Bryant and William Dunn, *Moving Power and Money: The Politics of Census Taking* (Ithaca, NY: New Strategist Publications, 1995).

CHAPTER 4

1. According to Paul Brace and Aubrey Jewett, "Field Essay: The State of the State Politics Research," *Political Research Quarterly* 48, no. 3 (September 1995): 643–82, quoted in Rodney Hero, *Faces of Inequality* (New York: Oxford University Press, 1998), 26.

2. This survey excluded special education, vocational, and alternative/other schools; schools outside the fifty states and the District of Columbia; and schools whose highest grade was less than first grade. Nancy Carey and Elizabeth Farris, *Racial and Ethnic Classifications Used by Public Schools,* NCES 96–092, Judi Carpenter, project officer (U.S. Department of Education, National Center for Education Statistics, Washington, DC, 1996).

3. Ibid., iii.

4. Some of the states receiving requests for a multiracial category also received requests to eliminate the collection of race and ethnic data. Nancy Carey, Cassandra Rowand, and Elizabeth Farris, *State Survey on Racial and Ethnic Classifications,* NCES 98–034, Shelley Burns, project officer (U.S. Department of Education, National Center for Education Statistics, Washington, DC, 1998), table 8, 12.

5. Sylvia Billups, telephone interview, February 19, 1998.

6. Susan Graham, in-person interview, April 16, 1998.

7. U.S. Department of Education, National Center for Education Statistics, *State Survey on Racial and Ethnic Classifications,* 16.

8. Kimberly Crafton, e-mail to author, August 31, 1998.

9. Supportive legislators seemed to think of multiracial people in terms of a melding of two (distinct) heritages and multiracial activists presented their case as such.

10. Harold Voorhees, telephone interview, December 4, 1998.

11. "Black Lawmakers Oppose Michigan Bill that Makes New Multiracial Class," *Jet*, June 19, 1995, 46.

12. Ibid.

13. Elizabeth Atkins Bowman, "Multiracial Category Sparks Controversy: Some Glad There's a Move to Get Item on Documents; Others Call It 'Racist,' a Throwback to Days of Slavery," *Detroit News*, April 13, 1995, C2.

14. Kenneth Cole, "Multiracial Box on Job, School Forms Riles Critics," *Detroit News*, June 28, 1995, 3D–6D.

15. Michelle Erickson, in-person interview, July 30, 1998.

16. Ibid.

17. Ibid.

18. Raphael Guajardo, principal of the Walt Disney Magnet School, "Walt Disney Magnet School Notification," letter to Michelle Erickson, April 13, 1992. Erickson kindly supplied me with copies of related documentation.

19. Michelle Erickson, in-person interview, July 30, 1998.

20. Bernard Stone, "Questionnaire Redesign," letter to Ted Kimbrough, May 11, 1992.

21. Ted Kimbrough, "Racial/Ethnic Section of the Options for Knowledge Form," letter to Bernard Stone, June 1, 1992.

22. Sidney Yates, letter to Michelle Erickson, November 2, 1992.

23. Sidney Yates, "Michelle Erickson, My Constituent," letter to Ronald Brown, June 4, 1993.

24. Carol Moseley-Braun, "Racial Classifications in the Chicago Public School System," letter to Michelle Erickson, March 3, 1993.

25. Michelle Erickson, "SB-406," letter to Dan Cronin, May 3, 1995.

26. Isabelle Horon, telephone interview, June 23, 2004.

27. Maryland Task Force on Multiracial Designations, *Executive Summary*, http://www.mdarchives.state.md.us/msa/mdmanual/26excom/defunct/html/25mult.html (accessed June 26, 2004).

28. The law stipulated the members of the task force, including chairwoman Dr. Isabelle L. Horon, director of the Maryland Vital Statistics Administration (and an adoptive parent of a multiracial child); a number of appointed and elected state officials; a high school principal; a demographer; a genealogist; and Shegoftah N. Queen, another parent. Queen was not affiliated with a multiracial organization.

29. Mary Maushard, "School Labels Difficult for Multiracial Children," *Baltimore Sun*, August 5, 1997, B1.

30. Ibid.

31. The task force determined that the costs involved in making such a change would be minimal and that the total number of state forms requiring modification along these lines would range from eight hundred to one thousand. Five poorly attended public hearings were held throughout the state in September and October 1997. Only fifteen persons provided testimony. According to Isabelle Horon, chairwoman of the task force, "nobody from the civil rights community came; the only people who showed up were parents." Telephone interview, June 23, 2004.

32. Further, the task force determined that 55 percent of infants born to

American Indian mothers had non–American Indian fathers. Maryland Task
Force on Multiracial Designations, *Executive Summary*.

33. Ibid.

34. William F. Frey, "Melting Pot Suburbs: A Census 2000 Study of Suburban Diversity," *Brookings Institution Census 2000 Series* (June 2001): 1–17.

35. Since Barone classifies state senator Rodney Ellis's district as "rural," it does not fit comfortably into this typology. I group it with "District Type 1" cases since it is characterized by a sizeable black middle class.

36. Anonymous, telephone interview, December 3, 1998.

37. Susan Laccetti, "Bill Would Add 'Multiracial' Category to Forms Seeking Race," *Atlanta Journal-Constitution*, March 24, 1994, B2. Also see David A. Bositis, *Diverging Generations: The Transformation of African American Policy Views* (Washington, DC: Joint Center for Political and Economic Studies, 2001).

38. See Robert S. Erikson, Gerald C. Wright, and John P. McIver, *Statehouse Democracy: Public Opinion and Policy in the American States* (New York: Cambridge University Press, 1993).

39. See, for example, Carol M. Swain, *Black Faces, Black Interests: The Representation of African-Americans in Congress* (Cambridge: Harvard University Press, 1993); and David Canon, *Race, Redistricting, and Representation: The Unintended Consequences of Black Majority Districts* (Chicago: University of Chicago Press, 1999).

40. Howard Carroll, telephone interview, November 17, 1998. Why it was a minority issue, per se, Carroll did not say.

41. Canon, *Race, Redistricting and Representation;* David Lublin, *The Paradox of Representation: Racial Gerrymandering and Minority Interests in Congress* (Princeton: Princeton University Press, 1997); Robert Singh, *The Congressional Black Caucus: Racial Politics in the U.S. Congress* (Thousand Oaks, CA: Sage, 1998); and Kenny Whitby, *The Color of Representation: Congressional Behavior and Black Interests* (Ann Arbor: University of Michigan Press, 1997).

42. For more on race and symbolism in Congress, see Katherine Tate, *Black Faces in the Mirror: African Americans and Their Representatives in the U.S. Congress* (Princeton: Princeton University Press, 2003), especially chap. 5.

43. See Erikson, Wright, and McIver, *Statehouse Democracy.*

44. See, for example, Kenny J. Whitby and Franklin D. Gilliam Jr., "A Longitudinal Analysis of Competing Explanations for the Transformation of Southern Congressional Politics," *Journal of Politics* 53 (1991): 504–18; and Charles S. Bullock and Mark J. Rozell, eds., *The New Politics of the Old South: An Introduction to Southern Politics* (Lanham, MD: Rowman & Littlefield, 1998).

45. David Rhode, *Parties and Leaders in the Post-Reform House* (Chicago: University of Chicago Press, 1991), 56.

46. For instance, it could be argued that Texas and California are bifurcated cases, while the others are heterogeneous (Hero, *Faces of Inequality*). In fact, there is some evidence to support that view in the case of California. In that state, A.B. No. 3371 passed in the Assembly (forty-one to thirty-one) and died in the Senate. Unlike the debate in any other state, the opposition argued that the "bill would cause significant problems [for the Department of Fair Housing

and Employment] with respect to their investigation of discrimination complaints and with respect to their ability to monitor state contractors' hiring prac-
tices." California State Assembly, *Third Reading*, April 24, 1996, http://www
.leginfo.ca.gov (accessed November 22, 1996).

47. Hero, *Faces of Inequality*, 88.

CHAPTER 5

1. Black-white marriages by gender in the United States from 1980 to 1998
break down as follows: black male–white female marriages represented 70 percent
of the total; white male–black female marriages represented 30 percent of the
total. U.S. Department of Commerce, U.S. Bureau of the Census, "Marital Status
and Living Arrangements," *Current Population Reports*, Series P-20-514 (Washington, DC: U.S. Government Printing Office, 1998). Also see U.S. Department
of Commerce, U.S. Bureau of the Census, "Interracial Married Couples: 1960 to
Present," Internet release date, July 27, 1998, www.census.gov/population/
socdemo/race/intereactab2.txt (accessed April 2002).

2. Ed and Paula Anderson, in-person interview, May 6, 1998. At their
request, I interviewed the Andersons together.

3. Anonymous, in-person interview, March 29, 1998.

4. Rhonda Bell, in-person interview, July 16, 1998.

5. Phyllis Washington, in-person interview, April 30, 1998.

6. Ed and Paula Anderson, in-person interview, May 6, 1998.

7. Barbara Byrd, in-person interview, April 16, 1998.

8. Jeff Howard, in-person interview, April 8, 1998.

9. Lisa Giblin, in-person interview, March 26, 1999.

10. Similarly, a 2003 Pew Research Center poll reported that 77 percent of
Americans agreed with the statement "I think it's all right for blacks and whites
to date each other." The Pew Research Center for the People and the Press,
"The 2004 Political Landscape: Evenly Divided and Increasingly Polarized,"
November 5, 2003, http://people-press.org/reports/display.php3?ReportID
=196.

11. Mfume, "NAACP's Views."

12. Ramona Douglass, "AMEA Response to Mfume," *Interracial Voice*,
November 1997, http://www.intvoice.com (accessed October 3, 1997).

13. Susan Graham, Third Multiracial Leadership Summit, statement, June
7, 1997. Graham initially lent lukewarm support for this move but recanted during the course of the June 7, 1997, meeting. A few weeks later, Carlos Fernández sent a letter to Thomas Petri declaring that a multiracial category "1)
DOES NOTHING to challenge the infamous one-drop rule, which is at the
core of this country's failure to recognize multiracial/multiethnic people; 2)
Poses a possible threat to the legitimate interests of the various minority communities in the U.S., *and thereby to the interests of the individuals in our community
who are also members of these various communities;* and 3) [Would threaten] the
continuity and integrity of racial and ethnic statistics. *Only the inclusion of multiple check-offs averts any possible adverse effects, and not incidentally, does not unneces-
sarily alienate people of goodwill in the civil rights community whose backing for any*

proposal to count multiracial/ethnic people we believe is essential if it is to gain bipartisan support and have any reasonable chance of succeeding." Carlos Fernández, "Multiracial Designation," letter to Tom Petri, July 29, 1997; my emphasis.

14. Ruth and Steve White, "APFU Response to Mfume," *Interracial Voice*, http://www.intvoice.com (accessed October 3, 1997); emphasis in original.

15. At one level, this positions multiracialism as analogous to the experience of blacks. However, since the other four corners of the ethnoracial pentagon (David Hollinger, *Postethnic America: Beyond Multiculturalism* [New York: Basic Books, 1995]) are implicated, the black analogy (Skrentny, *The Minority Rights Revolution*) takes us only so far.

16. Susan Graham, in-person interview, April 6, 1998.

17. Charles Byrd, speech given at Multiracial Solidarity March II, Los Angeles, August 9,1997.

18. Lucy Callahan, in-person interview, May 6, 1998.

19. Anonymous, in-person interview, June 12, 1998.

20. AMEA, President's Report, November, 1994.

21. Susan Graham, "A Real Protest," flyer distributed in the Atlanta metro area, April 1998; emphasis in original.

22. Interracial Family Alliance meeting, Atlanta, May 2, 1998.

23. Pam Olive, e-mail to author, May 30, 2005.

24. The other fourteen group leaders included four white men, two black men, one multiracial man, two black women, and five multiracial women.

25. Phil Savage, in-person interview, June 22, 1998.

26. Lou Steadwell, in-person interview, May 31, 1998.

27. Anonymous, telephone interview, May 28, 1998.

28. Ed Anderson, in-person interview, May 6, 1998.

29. Edwin Darden, "My Black History Paradox: For Some of Us, the Price of Racial Pride Is Racial Harmony," *Washington Post*, February 24, 1991, B5.

30. Edwin Darden, telephone interview, June 26, 2003.

31. Linda Ricks, in-person interview, April 10, 1998.

32. Bridget Bielinski, in-person interview, July 17, 1998.

33. Irene Rottenberg, telephone interview, February 11, 1999.

34. Julie Bolen, in-person interview, April 14, 1998.

35. Anonymous, telephone interview, June 28, 2003.

36. Barbara Byrd, in-person interview, April 16, 1998.

37. Stacey Bell, in-person interview, February 15, 1998.

38. Nancy Conner, in-person interview, May 29, 1998.

39. Pat Barner, telephone interview, March 7, 1999.

40. Kevin Barber, telephone interview, February 3, 1999.

41. Author's calculation from leadership survey.

42. Emma Tarleton, in-person interview, May 22, 1998.

43. Gloria Keegan, in-person interview, April 24, 1998.

44. Gene Foard, in-person interview, April 15, 1998.

45. Lucille Hallisy, in-person interview, July 16, 1998.

46. Mary Frances Berry, interview on "Our Voices," *Bev Smith Show*, May 24, 1997.

47. Jerelyn Eddings and Kenneth T. Walsh, "Counting a 'New' Type of American," *U.S. News and World Report*, July 14, 1997, A22.

48. Lynn Norment, "Am I Black, White, or in Between?" *Ebony*, August 1995, 108–12.

49. Spencer, *Spurious Issues*, 137.

50. Randall Kennedy, "How Are We Doing with *Loving?*" in *Mixed Race America and the Law: A Reader*, ed. Kevin R. Johnson (New York: New York University Press, 2003), 66.

51. Candy Mills, a black woman married to a white man (who together started *Interrace* magazine in 1989), suggested as much to a *New York Times* reporter in *Interrace*'s seventh year of publication. See Linda Matthews, "More than Identity Rides on a New Racial Category," *New York Times*, July 6, 1996, A1.

52. Lani Guinier, "From Racial Liberalism to Racial Literacy: *Brown v. Board of Education* and the Interest-Divergence Dilemma," *Journal of American History* 91, no. 1 (June 2004): 96.

53. Ibid., 94.

54. Note also that a number of white women of influence in the OMB (including Sally Katzen, Suzann Evinger, and Katherine Wallman) facilitated the change.

55. Adhering to the boycott, no AMEA members attended. From the multiracial activist community, only those affiliated with Project RACE (Nathan Douglas, James Landrith, and William X. Nelson), APFU (Valerie Wilkins, Ruth and Steve White, Rita Frazier), *New People* magazine (Dan and Yvette Hollis), and *Interracial Voice* (Charles Byrd) were present.

56. Edward Blum, Leadership Roundtable, Washington, DC, March 31, 2000; my emphasis. As discussed in chapter 6, Blum and the Campaign for a Color-Blind America worked closely with Ward Connerly in California on Proposition 209 (the anti–affirmative action initiative), and they also collaborated on Proposition 54 (the initiative that would have banned the collection of racial data). Note that if a respondent leaves the race question blank, the Census Bureau "imputes" a race for that individual based on the racial composition of the neighborhood.

57. Yvette Hollis, Leadership Roundtable, March 31, 2000.

58. Nathan Douglas, in-person interview, June 28, 1998.

59. Nathan Douglas, Leadership Roundtable, March 31, 2000.

60. Edward Blum, Leadership Roundtable, March 31, 2000.

61. Steve White, Leadership Roundtable, March 31, 2000.

62. Ruth White, Leadership Roundtable, March 31, 2000.

63. Ruth White, "Racial Classifications on Census Forms," C-SPAN News Conference, March 31, 2000.

64. Ward Connerly, "Racial Classifications on Census Forms," C-SPAN News Conference, March 31, 2000.

65. After C-SPAN finished recording the show, the Leadership Roundtable discussion resumed.

CHAPTER 6

1. Martha Riche, e-mail to author, January 4, 2004. Her successor, Kenneth Prewitt, confirmed that the attention of black civil rights advocates throughout the debate surrounding the 2000 census was mostly devoted to the

undercount. Project on Race and Ethnic Measurement in Federal Statistics, working group meeting, 2004.

2. Lindsey, "The Stakes Are a Bit Higher."

3. Anonymous, Project on Race and Ethnic Measurement in Federal Statistics, working group meeting, 2002.

4. Yet it was high by a different standard. After extensive testing (chap. 3) the bureau expected that only about 2 or 3 percent of previously identified blacks would choose more than one race in 2000. As shown in figure 7, that figure was almost 5 percent. See Eric Schmitt, "Multiracial Identification Might Affect Programs," *New York Times*, March 14, 2001.

5. Perlmann and Waters, "Introduction," *The New Race Question*, 15.

6. U.S. Department of Commerce, U.S. Bureau of the Census, "We the People," see fig. 13.

7. Harris and Sim, "An Empirical Look."

8. Goldstein and Morning, "Back in the Box," 121.

9. Harrison, "Inadequacies of Multiple-Response Race Data," 137.

10. Ibid., 139.

11. Ibid., 145–46.

12. See Persily, "The Legal Implications."

13. See Rachel L. Swarns, "Other Race Stays on the Books," *New York Times*, November 23, 2004, A19; and Ian Haney López, "The Birth of a 'Latino Race,'" *Los Angeles Times*, December 29, 2004, B11. Also see Clara Rodriguez, *Changing Race: Latinos, the Census, and the History of Ethnicity in the United States* (New York: New York University Press, 2000), and Suzane Oboler, *Ethnic Labels, Latino Lives, Identity and the Politics of (Re)presentation in the United States* (Minneapolis: University of Minnesota Press, 1995).

14. Interestingly, in the reverse, this means that about 7 percent of the white population in 2000 was also Hispanic. See Elizabeth M. Grieco, "The White Population: 2000," *Census 2000 Brief*, August 2001, http://www.census.gov/prod/2001pubs/c2kbr01–4.pdf (accessed January 5, 2003).

15. See Rodriguez, *Changing Race*.

16. Elizabeth M. Grieco and Rachel C. Cassidy, "Overview of Race and Hispanic Origin," *Census 2000 Brief*, March 2001, see tables 10 and 11, http://www.census.gov/prod/2001pubs/c2kbr01–1.pdf.

17. All of this could mean that Latinos are undermining the old familiar black-white dichotomy, but, on the other hand, such patterns in Latino racial identification (table 11) may also serve to reinforce and deepen that divide. See, for instance, Silvio Torres-Saillant, "Inventing the Race: Latinos and the Ethnoracial Pentagon," *Latino Studies* 1, vol. 1 (March 2003): 121–51.

18. Sonya Tafoya, "Mixed Race and Ethnicity in California," in *The New Race Question*, 105.

19. To clarify the latter statement, consider how the two major changes in racial data collection in 2000 interact. The new "Native Hawaiian Other Pacific Islander" category is arguably of dubious analytic value since alternate ways of counting this population lead to widely disparate tallies (and probably descriptive characteristics) of this population (see fig. 7).

20. I thank Christopher Edley Jr. for this observation.

21. Bill Clinton, "Remarks by the President to the American Society of Newspaper Editors," Dallas, Texas, April 7, 1995.

22. American Civil Rights Institute, "Proposition 54," May 17, 2002, http://www.racialprivacy.org/facts_myths.htm (accessed January 23, 2003).

23. Otherwise interpreted, whites are not implicated and blacks are not the only ones implicated.

24. Edward Blum, Project on Race and Ethnic Measurement in Federal Statistics, working group meeting, New York, November 11, 2002.

25. Common Cause, *California Common Cause Complaint*, July 9, 2002, http://www.commoncause.org (accessed November 9, 2003).

26. Los Angeles Times, "Exit Poll," www.latimes.com/timespoll (accessed November 18, 2003).

27. Butch Wing, "The Coalition that Kicked Proposition 54 out of the California Door," lecture presented at the John F. Kennedy School of Government, Harvard University, March 9, 2004.

28. Gallup Organization, CNN, and *USA Today*, "Gallup/CNN/USA Today Poll," March 9–11, 2001.

29. Nicholas A. Jones and Amy Symens Smith, "The Two or More Races Population: 2000," *Census 2000 Brief*, November 2001, http://www.census.gov/prod/2001pubs/c2kbr01-6.pdf (accessed May 25, 2005).

30. First, in 1997, AMEA changed its mission statement. Now it reads: "to educate and advocate on behalf of multiethnic individuals and families by collaborating with others to eradicate all forms of discrimination," http://www.ameasite.org (accessed August 27, 2002). Second, in response to the C-SPAN show discussed in chapter 5, AMEA leaders finally undertook a series of frank, internal discussions about their political commitments. I was privy to some of these exchanges. In the end, Ramona Douglass reaffirmed to me her conviction that "[AMEA is] a new civil rights group." She continued: "For the Record Kim and For Your Research: Susan [Graham] made it clear that she would side with whomever was willing to side with our issues even at the expense of other minority community interests. As a minority female whose family was a part of the Civil Rights Movement of the 1960s, I perceived that stance as a disaster to us and to the future healing of America. Who will benefit from the illusion of a race-free society? Who will suffer? These are the questions I would pose to our community leaders and their constituents." Personal correspondence, April 4, 2000. Douglass later articulated similar concerns in a televised debate with Ward Connerly. "Strength in Numbers," on *Uncommon Knowledge*, Stanford University Television, filmed on February 22, 2002, http://www.uncommonknowledge.org/01-02/638.html (transcript accessed May 2005). Most recently, AMEA opposed a proposal to add a multiracial category in the University of California system. See Michelle Locke, "UC Regent Ward Connerly Pushes for Multiracial Category," *San Jose Mercury News*, March 17, 2004, http://www.mercurynews.com/mld/mercurynews/news/local/states/california/the_valley/8210470.htm (accessed May 25, 2005).

31. Anonymous, telephone interview, June 26, 2003.

32. I base this impression on my observations at a number of multiracial student conferences and from various interactions over the years with multiracial student activists at the University of California, Berkeley (Hapa Issues Forum), Dartmouth College (MOSAIC), Harvard University (Hapa Harvard), and Wellesley College (Fusion). I have also discussed these issues at length with

Matt Kelley. Among the younger AMEA board members, Kelley started a multiracial student group as a nineteen-year-old freshman at Wesleyan University in 1998. In that same year, he launched *MAVIN* magazine, dedicated to the "mixed race experience." In 2000, *MAVIN* magazine became the 501(c) (3) nonprofit MAVIN Foundation (http://www.mavin.net/index.html), and its activities are frequently covered in the national media. See, for instance, Mireya Navarro, "When You Contain Multitudes," *New York Times*, April 24, 2005, 9–1.

33. In Booker T. Washington's 1895 speech known as the "Atlanta Compromise," he famously said, "In all things that are purely social we can be as separate as the fingers, yet one as the hand in all things essential to mutual progress." Louis R. Harlan, ed., *The Booker T. Washington Papers*, vol. 3 (Urbana: University of Illinois Press, 1974).

34. Paula McClain and Steven Tauber, "Racial Minority Group Relations in a Multiracial Society," in *Governing American Cities: Inter-Ethnic Coalitions, Competition, and Conflict*, ed. Michael Jones-Correa (New York: Russell Sage Foundation, 2001), 111.

35. Mary Francis Berry, "Briefing on the Consequences of Government Race Data Bans on Civil Rights." *U.S. Commission on Civil Rights Hearings*, May 17, 2002, http://usccr.gov/pubs/racedata/trans.html (accessed January 3, 2003).

36. Charles Michael Byrd, "Census 2000 Protest: Check American Indian!" *Interracial Voice*, January 1, 1998, http://www.webcom.com/~intvoice/protest.html.

37. Diane Jean Schemo, "Despite Options on Census, Many to Check 'Black' Only," *New York Times*, February 12, 2000, A1.

Bibliography

INTERVIEWS

Anderson, Ed, and Paula Anderson. In-person interview. May 6, 1998.
Barber, Kevin. Telephone interview. February 3, 1999.
Barner, Pat. Telephone interview. March 7, 1999.
Bell, Rhonda. In-person interview. July 16, 1998.
Bell, Stacey. In-person interview. February 15, 1998.
Bielinski, Bridget. In-person interview. July 17, 1998.
Billups, Sylvia. Telephone interview. February 19, 1998.
Bolen, Julie. In-person interview. April 14, 1998.
Byrd, Barbara. In-person interview. April 16, 1998.
Callahan, Lucy. In-person interview. May 6, 1998.
Carpenter Tucker, Jan. In-person interview. September 16, 1998.
Carroll, Howard. Telephone interview. November 17, 1998.
Conner, Nancy. In-person interview. May 29, 1998.
Darden, Edwin. Telephone interview. June 26, 2003.
———. Telephone interview. May 28, 1998.
Douglas, Nathan. In-person interview. June 28, 1998.
Douglass, Ramona. In-person interview. June 14, 1998.
Erickson, Michelle. In-person interview. July 30, 1998.
Foard, Gene. In-person interview. April 15, 1998.
Giblin, Lisa. In-person interview. March 26, 1999.
Graham, Susan. In-person interview. April 6 and 16, 1998.
Hallisy, Lucille. In-person interview. July 16, 1998.
Horon, Isabelle. Telephone interview. June 23, 2004.
Howard, Jeff. In-person interview. April 8, 1998.
Keegan, Gloria. In-person interview. April 24, 1998.
Lowenthal, TerriAnn. In-person interview. July 13, 1999.
McGee, Judi. 1998. In-person interview. June 12, 1998.
Olive, Pam. In-person interview. May 2, 1998.
Ricks, Linda. In-person interview. April 10, 1998.
Rottenberg, Irene. Telephone interview. February 11, 1999.
Savage, Phil. In-person interview. June 22, 1998.
Seiler, Noreen. In-person interview. May 29, 1998.

Steadwell, Lou. In-person interview. May 31, 1998.
Tarleton, Emma. In-person interview. May 22, 1998.
Vaughn, Ed. Telephone interview. December 3, 1998.
Voorhees, Harold. Telephone interview. December 4, 1998.
Washington, Phyllis. In-person interview. April 30, 1998.
White, Ruth. In-person interview. September 20, 1998.

REFERENCES

Alba, Richard D. *Ethnic Identity: The Transformation of Ethnicity in the Lives of Americans of European Ancestry.* New Haven: Yale University Press, 1990.
Alba, Richard D., and Reid M. Golden. "Patterns of Ethnic Marriage in the United States." *Social Forces* 65 (1986): 202–23.
Alonso, William, and Paul Starr, eds. *The Politics of Numbers.* New York: Russell Sage Foundation, 1987.
AMEA. Mission Statement. http://www.ameasite.org (accessed August 27, 2002).
———. President's Report. November 1994.
———. President's Report to the Board of Directors. September 22, 1989, 2.
———. Press Release. *Networking News* 5, no. 1 (winter-spring, 1994): 3.
———. *Networking News* 4, no. 5 (fall 1993).
———. *Networking News* 1, no. 4 (fall 1990).
AMEA and Project RACE. Joint Statement "Regarding the Mandate of the 2000 Census to Count All Americans." Sent to Katherine Wallman, September 29, 1995.
———. Response to "Coalition Statement on Proposed Modification of OMB Directive No. 15." October 22, 1994, Photocopy, 1.
American Civil Rights Institute. "Proposition 54." http://www.racialprivacy.org/facts_myths.htm (accessed January 23, 2003).
Anderson, Benedict R. *Imagined Communities: Reflections on the Origin and Spread of Nationalism.* New York: Verso, 1991.
Anderson, Margo. *The American Census: A Social History.* New Haven: Yale University Press, 1988.
———. "Counting by Race: The Antebellum Legacy." In *The New Race Question: How the Census Counts Multiracial Individuals,* ed. Joel Perlmann and Mary Waters. New York: Russell Sage Foundation, 2002.
———, ed. *Encyclopedia of the U.S. Census.* Washington, DC: Congressional Quarterly Press, 2000.
Anderson, Margo, and Stephen E. Feinberg. *Who Counts? The Politics of Census-Taking in Contemporary America.* New York: Russell Sage Foundation, 1999.
APFU. "For the Good of America." 1989. Flyer.
———. Memo. July 1995.
———. Mission Statement. http://www.aplaceforusnational.com (accessed April 1998).
———. *The Peacemaker* (fall 1989).
———. *The Peacemaker* (April 1988): 3.
———. Press Release. September 5, 1990.

———. "Unity Under the Stars: 1998 Racial Harmony Hall of Fame Inductee's Award Banquet." Photocopy, 1998.

Banton, Michael. "Categorical and Statistical Discrimination." *Ethnic and Racial Studies* 3 (1983): 269–83.

Barone, Michael, William Lilley III, and Lawrence J. Defranco. *State Legislative Elections: Voting Patterns and Demographics.* Washington, DC: Congressional Quarterly, 1998.

Bates, Karen G. "Color Complexity." *Emerge*, June 1993, 38–39.

Baumgartner, Frank R., and Bryan D. Jones. *Agendas and Instability in American Politics.* Chicago: University of Chicago Press, 1993.

Bean, Frank D., and Gillian Stevens. *America's Newcomers and the Dynamics of Diversity.* New York: Russell Sage Foundation, 2003.

Bell, Derrick A. *Race, Racism, and American Law.* 5th ed. New York: Aspen, 2004.

Berry, Mary Frances. "Briefing on the Consequences of Government Race Data Bans on Civil Rights." *U.S. Commission on Civil Rights Hearings.* http://usccr .gov/pubs/racedata/trans.html (accessed January 3, 2003).

———. Interview on "Our Voices." *Bev Smith Show*, May 24, 1997.

"Black Lawmakers Oppose Michigan Bill that Makes New Multiracial Class," *Jet*, June 19, 1995, 46.

Blum, Edward. Leadership Roundtable. Washington, DC, March 31, 2000.

———. Project on Race and Ethnic Measurement in Federal Statistics. Working group meeting, New School for Social Research, New York, November 11, 2002.

Bonilla-Silva, Eduardo. *White Supremacy and Racism in the Post-Civil Rights Era.* Boulder, CO: Lynne Rienner, 2001.

Bositis, David A. *Diverging Generations: The Transformation of African American Policy Views.* Washington, DC: Joint Center for Political and Economic Studies, 2001.

Bowman, Elizabeth Atkins. "Multiracial Category Sparks Controversy: Some Glad There's a Move to Get Item on Documents; Others Call It 'Racist,' a Throwback to Days of Slavery." *Detroit News*, April 13, 1995, 2C.

Brace, Paul, and Aubrey Jewett. "Field Essay: The State of the State Politics Research." *Political Research Quarterly* 48, no. 3 (September 1995): 643–82.

Brown, Nancy G., and Ramona Douglass. "Making the Invisible Visible: The Growth of Community Network Organizations." In *The Multiracial Experience: Racial Borders as the New Frontier*, ed. Maria P. P. Root. Thousand Oaks, CA: Sage Publications, 1996.

Bryant, Barbara Everitt, and William Dunn. *Moving Power and Money: The Politics of Census Taking.* Ithaca, NY: New Strategist Publications, 1995.

Bullock, Charles S., and Susan A. MacManus. "Policy Responsiveness to the Black Electorate: Programmatic Versus Symbolic Representation." *American Political Quarterly* 19 (1981): 357–68.

Bullock, Charles S., and Mark J. Rozell, eds. *The New Politics of the Old South: An Introduction to Southern Politics.* Lanham, MD: Rowman & Littlefield, 1998.

Byrd, Charles Michael. "Census 2000 Protest: Check American Indian!" *Interracial Voice*, January 1, 1998, http://www.webcom.com/~intvoice/ protest.html.

————. "Interracial Voice Interviews Congressman Thomas Petri." *Interracial Voice*, April 1997, http://www.webcom.com/~intvoice/interv5.html.

————. "Multiracial Solidarity March on the Mall in Washington, D.C., July 20, 1996!" *Interracial Voice*, July 1996, http://www.webcom.com/~intvoice.

————. "The Political Realignment: A Jihad against Race Consciousness." *Interracial Voice*, September–October 2000, http://www.webcom/intvoice/jihad.html.

————. Speech given at Multiracial Solidarity March II. Los Angeles, August 9, 1997.

————. "Why the Multiracial Community Must March on July 20!" *Interracial Voice*, June 1996, http://www.webcom.com/~intvoice.

California State Assembly. *Third Reading*. http://www.leginfo.ca.gov (accessed November 22, 1996).

Cameron, Charles, David Epstein, and Sharyn O'Halloran. "Do Majority-Minority Districts Maximize Substantive Black Representation in Congress?" *American Political Science Review* 90 (1996): 794–812.

Canon, David. "Electoral Systems and the Representation of Minority Interests in Legislatures." *Legislative Studies Quarterly* 24 (1999): 331–83.

————. *Race, Redistricting, and Representation: The Unintended Consequences of Black Majority Districts*. Chicago: University of Chicago Press, 1999.

Carey, Nancy, and Elizabeth Farris. *Racial and Ethnic Classifications Used by Public Schools*. NCES 96–092, Judi Carpenter, project officer. U.S. Department of Education, National Center for Education Statistics, Washington, DC, 1996.

Carey, Nancy, Cassandra Rowand, and Elizabeth Farris. *State Survey on Racial and Ethnic Classifications*, NCES 98–034, Shelly Burns, project officer. U.S. Department of Education, National Center for Education Statistics, Washington, DC, 1998.

Chang, Gordon H., ed. *Asian Americans and Politics: Perspectives, Experiences, Prospects*. Stanford, CA: Stanford University Press, 2001.

Cheng, Mae M. "Census Not Just Numbers: Outgoing Leader Says 2000 Survey Redefines Race." *Newsday*, January 30, 2001, A15.

Choldin, Harvey M. *Looking for the Last Percent: The Controversy over Census Undercounts*. New Brunswick, NJ: Rutgers University Press, 1994.

Christie, Rick. "Gingrich Lists His Action Plan for Racial Gulf." *Atlanta Journal-Constitution*, June 19, 1997, A3.

Citro, Constance F. "Advisory Committees." In *Encyclopedia of the U.S. Census*, ed. Margo J. Anderson. Washington, DC: Congressional Quarterly Press, 2000.

Clark, Bruce M., and Robert Timothy Reagan. "Redistricting Litigation: An Overview of Legal, Statistical, and Case-Management Issues." *Federal Judicial Center*, 2002. http://www.fjc.gov/newweb/jnetweb.nsf/autoframe?open form&url_r=pages/556&url_l=index (accessed November 16, 2003).

"Coalition Statement on Proposed Modification of OMB Directive No. 15." October 2, 1994. Photocopy, 1.

Cohen, Cathy. *The Boundaries of Blackness: AIDS and the Breakdown of Black Politics*. Chicago: University of Chicago Press, 1999.

Cohen, Patricia Cline. *A Calculating People: The Spread of Numeracy in Early America*. Chicago: University of Chicago Press, 1982.

Cohen, Richard. "A New Breed for Black Caucus." *National Journal* 26 (1987): 2432–33.

Cohn, D'Vera. "A Racial Tug of War over Census: New Option Fosters Group Competition." *Washington Post*, March 3, 2000, B1.

Cole, Kenneth. "Multiracial Box on Job, School Forms Riles Critics." *Detroit News*, June 28, 1995, 3D–6D.

Colker, Ruth. *Hybrid: Bisexuals, Multiracials and Other Misfits under American Law*. New York: New York University Press, 1996.

Common Cause. *California Common Cause Complaint*. July 9, 2002. http://www.commoncause.org (accessed November 9, 2003).

Conference of Americans of Germanic Heritage. "Statement of the Conference of Americans of Germanic Heritage with Respect to OMB 15." Presented at OMB Public Hearings, San Francisco, July 14, 1994. http://www.germanic.org/omb15stm.htm (accessed June 19, 2003).

Congressional Quarterly, Inc. *Politics in America, 1994: The 103rd Congress*. Washington, DC: Congressional Quarterly Press, 1993.

———. *Politics in America, 1996: The 104th Congress*. Washington, DC: Congressional Quarterly Press, 1995.

———. *Politics in America, 1998: The 105th Congress*. Washington, DC: Congressional Quarterly Press, 1997.

Connerly, Ward. *Creating Equal: My Fight against Race Preferences*. San Francisco: Encounter Books, 2000.

———. "Racial Classifications on Census Forms." C-SPAN News Conference, March 31, 2000.

Cose, Ellis. *Colorblind: Seeing Beyond Race in a Race-Obsessed World*. New York: HarperCollins, 1997.

DaCosta, Kimberly M. "Multiracial Identity: From Personal Problem to Public Issue." In *New Faces in a Changing America: Multiracial Identity in the 21st Century*, ed. Loretta Winters and Herman DeBose. Thousand Oaks, CA: Sage Publications, 2003.

Dalmage, Heather M. *Tripping on the Color Line: Black-White Multiracial Families in a Racially Divided World*. New Brunswick, NJ: Rutgers University Press, 2000.

———, ed. *The Politics of Multiracialism*. Albany: State University of New York Press, 2004.

Daniel, G. Reginald. *More than Black? Multiracial Identity and the New Racial Order*. Philadelphia: Temple University Press, 2002.

Darden, Edwin. "My Black History Paradox: For Some of Us, the Price of Racial Pride Is Racial Harmony." *Washington Post*, February 24, 1991, B5.

Davis, F. James. *Who Is Black? One Nation's Definition*. University Park: Pennsylvania State University Press, 1991.

Dawson, Michael C. *Behind the Mule: Race and Class in African-American Politics*. Princeton: Princeton University Press, 1994.

———. *Black Visions: The Roots of Contemporary African-American Political Ideologies*. Chicago: University of Chicago Press, 2001.

Denton, Nancy A. "Racial Identity and Census Categories: Can Incorrect Categories Yield Correct Information?" *Law and Inequality* 15, no. 1 (1997): 83–97.

Derthick, Martha, and Paul J. Quirk. *The Politics of Deregulation.* Washington, DC: Brookings Institution, 1985.

Douglas, Nathan. Leadership Roundtable. Washington, DC, March 31, 2000.

———. "Semantic Equality." *Interracial Voice,* July 20, 1996, http://www.web com.com/intvoice/nat_doug.html.

Douglass, Ramona. "AMEA Response to Mfume." *Interracial Voice,* November 1997, http://www.webcom.com/intvoice/ramona2.html.

———. "Beyond the 2000 Census: Community as Team." Speech delivered at the University of Michigan, Ann Arbor, April 5, 1997.

———. "Letters to the Editor." *Interracial Voice,* February 1997, http://www.webcom.com/intvoice/letter18.html.

———. "Multiracial People Must No Longer Be Invisible." *New York Times,* July 12, 1996, A14.

———. "Solidarity March." On-line posting, Interracial Individuals Listserv, July 25, 1995, http://soyokaze.biosci.ohio-state.edu/~jei/ii (accessed August, 1995).

———. "Upcoming Hearings." Memorandum to Nancy Brown and Faye Mandell, March 16, 1997.

Dovi, Suzanne. "Preferable Descriptive Representatives: Will Just Any Woman, Black, or Latino Do?" *American Political Science Review* 96, no. 4 (2002): 729–43.

Eagles, Charles W. "Toward New Histories of the Civil Rights Era." *Journal of Southern History* 66, no. 4 (2000): 815–48.

Eckler, A. Ross. *The Bureau of the Census.* New York: Praeger, 1972.

Eddings, Jerelyn, and Kenneth T. Walsh. "Counting a 'New' Type of American." *U.S. News and World Report,* July 14, 1997, 22.

Edmonston, Barry, Joshua Goldstein, and Juanita Tamayo Lott, eds. *Spotlight on Heterogeneity: The Federal Standards for Racial and Ethnic Classification.* Washington, DC: National Academy Press, 1996.

Edmonston, Barry, Sharon M. Lee, and Jeffrey S. Passel. "Recent Trends in Intermarriage and Immigration and Their Effects on the Future Racial Composition of the U.S. Population." In *The New Race Question,* ed. Joel Perlmann and Mary Waters. New York: Russell Sage Foundation, 2002.

Edmonston, Barry, and Charles Schultze, eds. *Modernizing the U.S. Census.* Washington, DC: National Academy Press, 1995.

Eisinger, Peter K. "The Conditions of Protest Behavior in American Cities." *American Political Science Review* 67 (March 1973): 11–28.

Erickson, Michelle. "Application for Enrollment into Magnet Schools." Letter to Sidney Yates. November 2, 1992.

———. "SB-406." Letter to Dan Cronin, May 3, 1995.

Erikson, Robert S., Gerald C. Wright, and John P. McIver. *Statehouse Democracy: Public Opinion and Policy in the American States.* Cambridge: Cambridge University Press, 1993.

Espiritu, Yen Le. *Asian American Panethnicity: Bridging Institutions and Identities.* Philadelphia: Temple University Press, 1992.

Evinger, Suzann. "How Shall We Measure Our Nation's Diversity?" *Chance* 8, no. 1 (winter 1995): 7–14.

———. "How to Record Race." *American Demographics,* May 1996, 36–41.

Farley, Reynolds. *The New American Reality: Who We Are, How We Got There, Where We Are Going.* New York: Russell Sage Foundation, 1996.

———. "Racial Identities in 2000: The Response to the Multiple-Response Option." In *The New Race Question: How the Census Counts Multiracial Individuals,* ed. Joel Perlmann and Mary Waters. New York: Russell Sage Foundation, 2002.

Fernández, Carlos A. "Government Classification of Multiracial/Multiethnic People." In *The Multiracial Experience: Racial Borders as the New Frontier,* ed. Maria P. P. Root. Thousand Oaks, CA: Sage Publications, 1996.

———. "La Raza and the Melting Pot: A Comparative Look at Multiethnicity." In *Racially Mixed People in America,* ed. Maria P. P. Root. Newbury Park, CA: Sage Publications, 1992.

———. "Message from the President." *Melange,* no. 1 (September 1989).

———. "Multiracial Designation." Letter to Tom Petri, July 29, 1997.

———. "The Wedowee Case: What Happened and What It Means for Us." *AMEA Networking News* 5, no. 1 (March 15, 1994): 2.

Fiore, Faye. "Multiple Race Choices to be Allowed on 2000 Census." *Los Angeles Times,* October 30, 1997, A1.

Fireside, Harvey. *Separate and Unequal: Homer Plessy and the Supreme Court Decision That Legalized Racism.* New York: Carroll & Graf, 2004.

Fitzpatrick, Jody L., and Rodney E. Hero. "Political Culture and Political Characteristics of the American States: A Consideration of Some Old and New Questions." *Western Political Quarterly* 41 (1998): 145–53.

Flowers, Gary. "New Racial Classifications: A Setback for Civil Rights Enforcement?" *Committee Report* 6, no. 1 (winter 1994): 1–6.

Foreman, Christopher H. *The African American Predicament.* Washington, DC: Brookings Institution Press, 1999.

Frey, William. "Melting Pot Suburbs: A Census 2000 Study of Suburban Diversity." *Brookings Institution Census 2000 Series* (June 2001): 1–17.

Frey, William, and William O'Hare. "Becoming Suburban, and Black." *American Demographics,* September 1992, 30–38.

———. "Vivan Los Suburbios!" *American Demographics,* April 1993, 30–37.

Frisby, Michael K. "Black, White or Other." *Emerge,* December 1996, 48–54.

Frymer, Paul. *Uneasy Alliances: Race and Party Competition in America.* Princeton: Princeton University Press, 1999.

Fu, Vincent Kang. "Racial Intermarriage Pairings." *Demography* 38, no. 2 (2001): 147–59.

Funderburg, Lise. *Black, White, Other: Biracial Americans Talk about Race and Identity.* New York: William Morrow, 1994.

Gallup Organization. "Civil Rights and Race Relations." January 2004.

Gallup Organization, CNN, and *USA Today.* "Gallup/CNN/USA Today Poll," March 9–11, 2001.

Gamson, William. *The Strategy of Social Protest.* Belmont, CA: Wadsworth, 1990.

———. *Talking Politics.* New York: Cambridge University Press, 1992.

Gilanshah, Bijan. "Multiracial Minorities: Erasing the Color Line." *Law and Inequality* 12 (1993): 183–204.

Gingrich, Newt. "Open Letter to Franklin Raines." July 1, 1997. http://www.speakernews.house.gov (accessed July 12, 1997).

"Gingrich Hails 9 Bills, 94 Days; But He Says Contract Was Just a Start." *St. Louis Post Dispatch*, April 8, 1995, 1A.

Glazer, Nathan. "On the Census, Race, and Ethnic Categories." *Poverty and Race* 4, no. 2 (March 1995): 15–17.

———. "Reflections on Race, Hispanicity, and Ancestry in the U.S. Census." In *The New Race Question: How the Census Counts Multiracial Individuals*, ed. Joel Perlmann and Mary Waters. New York: Russell Sage Foundation, 2002.

Goldstein, Joshua R. "Kinship Networks that Cross Racial Lines: The Exception or the Rule?" *Demography* 36, no. 3 (August 1999): 399–407.

Goldstein, Joshua R., and Ann J. Morning. "Back in the Box: The Dilemma of Using Multiple-Race Data for Single-Race Laws." In *The New Race Question: How the Census Counts Multiracial Individuals*, ed. Joel Perlmann and Mary Waters. New York: Russell Sage Foundation, 2002.

———. "The Multiple Race Population of the United States: Issues and Estimates." *Proceedings of the National Academy of Sciences* 97, no. 11 (2000): 6230–35.

Graham, Hugh Davis. *The Civil Rights Era: Origins and Development of National Policy: 1960–1972*. New York: Oxford University Press, 1990.

———. *Collision Course: The Strange Convergence of Affirmative Action and Immigration Policy in America*. New York: Oxford University Press, 2002.

———. "The Origins of Official Minority Designation." In *The New Race Question: How the Census Counts Multiracial Individuals*, ed. Joel Perlmann and Mary Waters. New York: Russell Sage Foundation, 2002.

———. "Race, History, and Policy: African-Americans and Civil Rights Since 1964." *Journal of Policy History* 6, no. 1 (1994): 12–39.

Graham, Susan. "Grassroots Advocacy." In *American Mixed Race: The Culture of Microdiversity*, ed. Naomi Zack. Lantham, MD: Rowman & Littlefield, 1995.

———. "Multiracial Life after Newt." November 9, 1998. http://www.projectrace.home.mindspring.com/director.html (accessed November 22, 1998).

———. "A Real Protest." April 1998. Flyer.

———. "The Real World." In *The Multiracial Experience: Racial Borders as the New Frontier*, ed. Maria P. P. Root. Thousand Oaks, CA: Sage Publications, 1996.

———. Third Multiracial Leadership Summit. Oakland, CA, June 7, 1997.

Graham, Susan, and James A. Landrith Jr. "Blood Pressure." *Multiracial Activist*, February 12, 2001, http://www.multiracial.com/news/bloodpressure.html.

Grieco, Elizabeth M. "The Native Hawaiian and Other Pacific Islander Population: 2000." *Census 2000 Brief*, December 2001. http://www.census.gov/prod/2001pubs/c2kbr01–14.pdf (accessed December 2, 2005).

———. "The White Population: 2000." *Census 2000 Brief*, August 2001. http://www.census.gov/prod/2001pubs/c2kbr01–4.pdf (accessed January 5, 2003).

Grieco, Elizabeth M., and Rachel C. Cassidy. "Overview of Race and Hispanic Origin." *Census 2000 Brief*, March 2001. http://www.census.gov/prod/2001pubs/c2kbr01–1.pdf.

Grofman, Bernard, ed. *Legacies of the 1964 Civil Rights Act*. Charlottesville: University Press of Virginia, 2000.

Grofman, Bernard, Robert Griffin, and Amihai Glazer. "The Effect of Black Population on Electing Democrats and Liberals to the House of Representatives." *Legislative Studies Quarterly* 17 (1992): 365–79.

Gross, Jane. "UC Berkeley at Crux of New Multiracial Consciousness and Diversity." *Los Angeles Times*, January 9, 1996, A1.

Guajardo, Raphael, "Walt Disney Magnet School Notification." Letter to Michelle Erickson, April 13, 1992.

Guinier, Lani. "From Racial Liberalism to Racial Literacy: *Brown v. Board of Education* and the Interest-Divergence Dilemma." *Journal of American History* 91, no. 1 (June 2004): 92–118.

Guinier, Lani, and Gerald Torres. *The Miner's Canary: Enlisting Race, Resisting Power, Transforming Democracy.* Cambridge: Harvard University Press, 2003.

Hacegaba, Noel, and Dowell Myers. "Multiracial Patterns in the 50 States." *Race Contours Census 2000, A University of Southern California and University of Michigan Collaborative Project.* http://www.usc.edu/schools/sppd/research/census2000/race_census/racecontours/US.htm.

Hacking, Ian. *The Social Construction of What?* Cambridge: Harvard University Press, 1999.

Haizlip, Shirlee Taylor. *The Sweeter the Juice.* New York: Simon & Schuster, 1994.

Haney López, Ian F. "The Birth of a 'Latino Race.'" *Los Angeles Times*, December 2, 2004, B11.

———. "The Social Construction of Race." In *Critical Race Theory: The Cutting Edge*, ed. Richard Delgado. Philadelphia: Temple University Press, 1995.

———. *White by Law: The Legal Construction of Race.* New York: New York University Press, 1996.

Harlan, Louis R., ed. *The Booker T. Washington Papers.* Vol. 3. Urbana: University of Illinois Press, 1974.

Harris, David. "The 1990 Census Count of American Indians: What Do the Numbers Really Mean?" *Social Science Quarterly* 75, no. 3 (1994): 580–91.

———. "Does It Matter How We Measure? Racial Classification and the Characteristics of Multiracial Youth." In *The New Race Question: How the Census Counts Multiracial Individuals*, ed. Joel Perlmann and Mary Waters. New York: Russell Sage Foundation, 2002.

Harris, David R., and Jeremiah Joseph Sim. "An Empirical Look at the Social Construction of Race: The Case of Multiracial Adolescents." *Research Report* 00–452. Ann Arbor: Population Studies Center, University of Michigan, 2000.

Harris, Marvin. *Patterns of Race in the Americas.* Westport, CT: Greenwood, 1964.

Harrison, Roderick J. "Inadequacies of Multiple-Response Data in the Federal Statistical System." In *The New Race Question: How the Census Counts Multiracial Individuals*, ed. Joel Perlmann and Mary Waters. New York: Russell Sage Foundation, 2002.

Harrison, Roderick J., and Claudette Bennett. "Racial and Ethnic Diversity." In *State of the Union: America in the 1990s, Social Trends*. Vol. 2, ed. Reynolds Farley. New York: Russell Sage Foundation, 1995.

Hawk, Steve. "Activists Rally around Family of Beaten Girl." *Orange County Register*, September 2, 1990, Metro 3.

Haynie, Kerry L. *African American Legislators in the American States.* New York: Columbia University Press, 2001.

Hero, Rodney E. *Faces of Inequality: Social Diversity in American Politics.* Oxford: Oxford University Press, 1998.

Hickman, Christine B. "The Devil and the One Drop Rule: Racial Categories, African Americans, and the U.S. Census." *Michigan Law Review* 95, no. 5 (1997): 1161–265.

Hirschman, Charles, Richard Alba, and Reynolds Farley. "The Meaning and Measurement of Race in the U.S. Census: Glimpses into the Future." *Demography* 37, no. 3 (2000): 381–93.

Hochschild, Jennifer L. "Multiple Racial Identifiers in the 2000 Census, And Then What?" In *The New Race Question: How the Census Counts Multiracial Individuals,* ed. Joel Perlmann and Mary Waters. New York: Russell Sage Foundation, 2002.

Hollinger, David. *Postethnic America: Beyond Multiculturalism.* New York: Basic Books, 1995.

Hollis, Yvette. Leadership Roundtable. Washington, DC, March 31, 2000.

Holmes, Steven A. "From One Problem to Bigger One for NAACP." *New York Times,* August 23, 1994, A18.

———. "Gingrich Outlines Plan on Race Relations." *New York Times,* June 19, 1997, B12.

———. "New Policy on Census Says Those Listed as White and Minority Will Be Counted as Minority." *New York Times,* March 11, 2000, A9.

Jacobson, Matthew Frye. "History, Historicity, and the Census Count By Race." In *The New Race Question: How the Census Counts Multiracial Individuals,* ed. Joel Perlmann and Mary Waters. New York: Russell Sage Foundation, 2002.

Japanese American Citizens League (JACL). "JACL Policy Position on the Multiracial Category." http://www.jacl.org (accessed July 22, 1997).

Johnson, Kevin R., ed. *Mixed Race America and the Law: A Reader.* New York: New York University Press, 2003.

Jones, Nicholas A. "We the People of More Than One Race in the United States." *Census 2000 Special Reports,* April 2005. http://www.census.gov/prod/2005pubs/censr-22.pdf.

Jones, Nicholas A., and Amy Symens Smith. "The Two or More Races Population: 2000." *Census 2000 Brief,* C2KBR/01–6, November 2001. http://www.census.gov/prod/2001pubs/c2kbr01–6.pdf (accessed May 25, 2005).

Jones-Correa, Michael, ed. *Governing American Cities: Inter-Ethnic Coalitions, Competition, and Conflict.* New York: Russell Sage Foundation, 2001.

Kadane, Joseph B., and Caroline Mitchell. "Statistics in Proof of Employment Discrimination Cases." In *Legacies of the 1964 Civil Rights Act,* ed. Bernard Grofman. Charlottesville: University Press of Virginia, 2000.

Kalmijn, Matthijs. "Intermarriage and Homogamy: Causes, Patterns, and Trends." *Annual Review of Sociology* 24 (1998): 395–421.

———. "Trends in Black-White Intermarriage." *Social Forces* 72, no. 1 (1993): 119–46.

Katzen, Sally. "Recommendations from the Interagency Committee for the Review of the Racial and Ethnic Standards to the Office of Management and

Budget Concerning Changes to the Standards for the Classification of Federal Data on Race and Ethnicity." *Federal Register* 62, no. 131 (July 9, 1997): 36874–946.

———. "Revisions to the Standards for the Classification of Federal Data on Race and Ethnicity." *Federal Register* 62, no. 210 (October 30, 1997): 58782–90.

———. "Standards for the Classification of Federal Data on Race and Ethnicity." *Federal Register* 60, no. 166 (August 28, 1995): 44674.

Kennedy, Randall. *Interracial Intimacies: Sex, Marriage, Identity, and Adoption.* New York: Pantheon, 2003.

———. "How Are We Doing With Loving?" In *Mixed Race America and the Law: A Reader,* ed. Kevin R. Johnson. New York: New York University Press, 2003.

Kertzer, David I., and Dominique Arel, eds. *Census and Identity: The Politics of Race, Ethnicity, and Language in National Censuses.* New York: Cambridge University Press, 2002.

Kimbrough, Ted. "Racial/Ethnic Section of the Options for Knowledge Form." Letter to Bernard Stone, June 1, 1992.

Laccetti, Susan. "Bill Would Add 'Multiracial' Category to Forms Seeking Race." *Atlanta Journal-Constitution,* March 24, 1994, B2.

Leadership Conference on Civil Rights. *Voting Records.* http://www.civilrights.org/research_center/voting_scorecards/voting_scorecards.html (accessed January 2, 1999).

Lee, Jennifer, and Frank Bean. "America's Changing Color Lines: Immigration, Race/Ethnicity and Multiracial Identification." *Annual Review of Sociology* 30 (2004): 221–42.

Lee, Sharon M. "Racial Classifications in the U.S. Census: 1890–1990." *Ethnic and Racial Studies* 16, no. 1 (1993): 75–88.

Leighley, Jan E. *Strength in Numbers? The Political Mobilization of Racial and Ethnic Minorities.* Princeton: Princeton University Press, 2001.

Lewis Mumford Center for Comparative Urban and Regional Research. *The New Ethnic Enclaves in America's Suburbs.* http://mumford1.dyndns.org/cen2000/suburban/SuburbanReport/page1.html (accessed July 9, 2001).

Libertarian Party. Press Release. July 10, 1997.

Lien, Pei-te. *The Making of Asian America through Political Participation.* Philadelphia: Temple University Press, 2001.

Lindsey, Daryl. "The Stakes Are a Bit Higher for Us: Interview with Hilary Shelton, NAACP Washington Bureau Chief." *Salon,* February 16, 2000. http://www.salon.com/news/feature/2000/02/16/naacp.

Lipsky, Michael. *Protest in City Politics.* Chicago: Rand McNally, 1970.

Liptak, Adam. "Bans on Interracial Unions Offer Perspectives on Gay Ones." *New York Times,* March 17, 2004, A22.

Locke, Michelle. "UC Regent Ward Connerly Pushes for Multiracial Category." *San Jose Mercury News,* March 17, 2004.

Logan, John R. *How Race Counts for Hispanic Americans.* Albany, NY: Lewis Mumford Center for Comparative Urban and Regional Research, 2003. http://browns4.dyndns.org/cen2000_s4/BlackLatinoReport/BlackLatino01.htm (accessed July 14, 2003).

Lopez, David, and Yen Espiritu. "Panethnicity in the United States: A Theoretical Framework." *Ethnic and Racial Studies* 13 (1990): 198–224.

Los Angeles Times. "Exit Poll." http://www.latimes.com/timespoll (accessed November 18, 2003).

Lott, Juanita T. "The Limitations of Directive 15." *Poverty and Race* 4, no. 1 (January 1995): 9–11.

Lublin, David. *The Paradox of Representation: Racial Gerrymandering and Minority Interests in Congress.* Princeton: Princeton University Press, 1997.

MacManus, Susan, and Lawrence Morehouse. "Redistricting in the Multiracial Twenty-First Century: Changing Demographic and Socioeconomic Conditions Pose Important New Challenges." In *Race and Representation*, ed. Georgia Persons. New Brunswick, NJ: Transaction, 1997.

Malcomson, Scott L. *One Drop of Blood: The American Misadventure of Race.* New York: Farrar, Straus, and Giroux, 2000.

Marriot, Michel. "Multiracial Americans Ready to Claim Their Own Identity." *New York Times*, July 20, 1996, A1.

Marx, Anthony. "Contested Citizenship: The Dynamics of Racial Identity and Social Movements." *International Review of Social History* 40 (1995): 159–83.

———. "Race Making and the Nation-State." *World Politics* 48 (1996): 180–208.

Maryland Task Force on Multiracial Designations. *Executive Summary.* http://www.mdarchives.state.md.us/msa/mdmanual/26excom/defunct/html /25mult.html (accessed June 26, 2004).

Matthews, Linda. "More than Identity Rides on a New Racial Category." *New York Times*, July 6, 1996, A1, A7.

Maushard, Mary. "School Labels Difficult for Multiracial Children." *Baltimore Sun*, August 5, 1997, B1.

McAdam, Doug. *Political Process and the Development of Black Insurgency, 1930–1970.* Chicago: University of Chicago Press, 1982.

McAdam, Doug, John D. McCarthy, and Mayer N. Zald, eds. *Comparative Perspectives on Social Movements: Political Opportunities, Mobilizing Structures, and Cultural Framings.* New York: Cambridge University Press, 1996.

McAdam, Doug, Sidney Tarrow, and Charles Tilly. *Dynamics of Contention.* New York: Cambridge University Press, 2001.

McBride, James. *The Color of Water: A Black Man's Tribute to His White Mother.* New York: Riverhead Books, 1996.

McCarthy, John, and Mayer N. Zald. "Resource Mobilization and Social Movements: A Partial Theory." *American Journal of Sociology* 82 (1977): 1212–41.

———. *The Trend of Social Movements in America: Professionalism and Resource Mobilization.* Morristown, NJ: General Learning Corporation, 1973.

McClain, Paula D., and Steven C. Tauber. "Racial Minority Group Relations in a Multiracial Society." In *Governing American Cities: Inter-Ethnic Coalitions, Competition, and Conflict*, ed. Michael Jones-Correa. New York: Russell Sage Foundation, 2001.

McKenney, Nampeo R., and Claudette E. Bennette. "Issues Regarding Data on Race and Ethnicity: The Census Bureau Experience." *Public Health Reports* 109, no. 1 (January 1994): 16–25.

Mfume, Kweisi. "NAACP's Views on New Multiracial Category." http://www.naacp.org (accessed November 15, 1996).

Moncrief, Gary, Joel Thompson, and William Cassie. "Revisiting the State of U.S. State Legislative Research." *Legislative Studies Quarterly* 21 (1996): 301–35.

Moran, Rachel F. *Interracial Intimacy: The Regulation of Race and Romance.* Chicago: University of Chicago Press, 2001.

Morris, Aldon D. *The Origins of the Civil Rights Movement: Black Communities Organizing for Change.* New York: Free Press, 1984.

Morris, Aldon D., and Carol McClurg Mueller, eds. *Frontiers in Social Movement Theory.* New Haven: Yale University Press, 1992.

Moseley-Braun, Carol. "Racial Classifications in the Chicago Public School System." Letter to Michelle Erickson, March 3, 1993.

Myrdal, Gunnar. *An American Dilemma: The Negro Problem and Modern Democracy.* New York: Harper and Brothers, 1944.

NAACP. *NAACP Rates Half of U.S. Senate, Congress with "F" Grade during Legislative Reform Press Conference Annual Convention.* http://www.naacp.org/news/2002/2002–07–10–2.html (accessed July 10, 2002).

National Research Council. Committee on National Statistics. Workshop on Race and Ethnicity Classification: An Assessment of the Federal Standard for Race and Ethnicity Classification. Washington, DC, 1994.

Navarro, Mireya. "When You Contain Multitudes." *New York Times,* April 2, 2005, 9–1.

Nobles, Melissa. "Lessons from Brazil: The Ideational and Political Dimensions of Multiraciality." In *The New Race Question: How the Census Counts Multiracial Individuals,* ed. Joel Perlmann and Mary Waters. New York: Russell Sage Foundation, 2002.

———. *Shades of Citizenship: Race and the Census in Modern Politics.* Palo Alto: Stanford University Press, 2000.

Norment, Lynn. "Am I Black, White, or In Between?" *Ebony,* August 1995, 108–12.

Oboler, Suzanne. *Ethnic Labels, Latino Lives: Identity and the Politics of (Re)Presentation in the United States.* Minneapolis: University of Minnesota Press, 1995.

Omi, Michael. "Racial Identity and the State: The Dilemmas of Classification." *Law and Inequality* 15, no. 7 (1997): 7–23.

Omi, Michael, and Howard Winant. *Racial Formation in the United States: From the 1960s to the 1990s.* 2d ed. New York: Routledge, 1994.

Ong, Paul, and David Lee. "Changing of the Guard? The Emerging Immigrant Majority in Asian American Politics." In *Asian Americans and Politics: Perspectives, Experiences, Prospects,* ed. Gordon Chang. Palo Alto: Stanford University Press, 2001.

Padilla, Felix M. *Latino Ethnic Consciousness: The Case of Mexican Americans and Puerto Ricans in Chicago.* Notre Dame, IN: University of Notre Dame Press, 1985.

Page, Clarence. "Biracial People Feel 'Boxed In' by Census Form." *Chicago Tribune,* July 28, 1996, B3.

Pascoe, Peggy. "Miscegenation Law, Court Cases, and the Ideologies of 'Race' in Twentieth-Century America." *Journal of American History* (June 1996): 44–69.

Passel, Jeffrey S. "The Growing American Indian Population, 1960–1990: Beyond Demography." *Population Research and Policy Review* 16, no. 1–2 (1997): 11–31.

Patterson, Orlando. "The Race Trap." *New York Times,* July 11, 1997, A25.

Patureau, Alan. "Principal Called Mixed-Race Pupil a 'Mistake.'" *Atlanta Journal Constitution,* March 10, 1994, A3.

Payson, Kenneth E. "Check One Box: Reconsidering Directive No. 15 and the Classification of Mixed-Race People." *California Law Review* 84 (1996): 1233–91.

Perlmann, Joel. "Multiracials, Intermarriage, Ethnicity." *Society* 34, no. 6 (1997): 20–23.

Perlmann, Joel, and Mary Waters. "Introduction." In *The New Race Question: How the Census Counts Multiracial Individuals,* ed. Joel Perlmann and Mary Waters. New York: Russell Sage Foundation, 2002.

Persily, Nathaniel. "Color by Numbers: Race, Redistricting, and the 2000 Census." *Minnesota Law Review* 85 (2001): 899–947.

———. "The Legal Implications of a Multiracial Census." In *The New Race Question: How the Census Counts Multiracial Individuals,* ed. Joel Perlmann and Mary Waters. New York: Russell Sage Foundation, 2002.

Persons, Georgia A., ed. *Race and Representation.* New Brunswick, NJ: Transaction, 1997.

Petersen, William. *Ethnicity Counts.* New Brunswick, NJ: Transaction, 1997.

———. "Politics and the Measurement of Ethnicity." In *The Politics of Numbers,* ed. William Alonso and Paul Starr. New York: Russell Sage Foundation, 1987.

Peterson, Paul, ed. *Classifying by Race.* Princeton: Princeton University Press, 1995.

Pew Research Center for the People and the Press. "The 2004 Political Landscape: Evenly Divided and Increasingly Polarized." November 5, 2003. http://people-press.org/reports/display.php3?ReportID=196.

Pinal, Jorge del. "Exploring Alternative Race-Ethnic Comparison Groups in Current Population Surveys." *Current Population Reports,* Series P-23-182. Washington, DC: U.S. Government Printing Office, 1992.

Pressley, Sue Anne. "The Color of Love: In a Country Transfixed by Race, Black-White Couples Turn to Each Other for Support." *Washington Post,* August 22, 1994, B1.

Prewitt, Kenneth. "Public Statistics and Democratic Politics." In *The Politics of Numbers,* ed. William Alonso and Paul Starr. New York: Russell Sage Foundation, 1987.

———. "Race in the 2000 Census: A Turning Point." In *The New Race Question: How the Census Counts Multiracial Individuals,* ed. Joel Perlmann and Mary Waters. New York: Russell Sage Foundation, 2002.

Project on Race and Ethnic Measurement in Federal Statistics. Working group meeting. New York, March 24, 2004.

———. Working group meeting. New School for Social Research, New York, November 11, 2002.

Project RACE. Mission Statement. http://www.projectrace.com (accessed August 27, 2002).

Raspberry, William. "What Ails the NAACP?" *Washington Post,* November 7, 1994, A23.

Reed, Adolph, Jr., ed. *Without Justice for All: The New Liberalism and Our Retreat from Racial Equality*. Boulder, CO: Westview Press, 1999.

Rhode, David W. *Parties and Leaders in the Post-Reform House*. Chicago: University of Chicago Press, 1991.

Rodriguez, Clara. *Changing Race: Latinos, the Census, and the History of Ethnicity in the United States*. New York: New York University Press, 2000.

Roediger, David R. *Colored White: Transcending the Racial Past*. Berkeley: University of California Press, 2002.

Root, Maria P. P. *Love's Revolution: Interracial Marriage*. Philadelphia: Temple University Press, 2001.

———, ed. *The Multiracial Experience: Racial Borders at the New Frontier*. Thousand Oaks, CA: Sage Publications, 1996.

———. *Racially Mixed People in America*. Newbury Park, CA: Sage Publications, 1992.

Rosin, Hanna. "Boxed In." *New Republic*, January 3, 1994, 12.

Samhan, Helen. Project on Race and Ethnic Measurement in Federal Statistics. Working group meeting, New York, November 11, 2002.

Saunders, Melissa. "Of Minority Representation, Multiple-Race Responses, and Melting Pots: Redistricting in the New America." *North Carolina Law Review* 79 (June 2001): 1367–81.

Schemo, Diane Jean. "Despite Options on Census, Many to Check 'Black' Only." *New York Times*, February 12, 2000, A1.

Schmitt, Eric. "Multiracial Identification Might Affect Programs." *New York Times*, March 14, 2001, A20.

Singh, Robert. *The Congressional Black Caucus: Racial Politics in the U.S. Congress*. Thousand Oaks, CA: Sage Publications, 1998.

Skerry, Peter. *Counting on the Census? Race, Group Identity, and the Evasion of Politics*. Washington, DC: Brookings Institution Press, 2000.

———. "Multiracialism and the Administrative State." In *The New Race Question: How the Census Counts Multiracial Individuals*, ed. Joel Perlmann and Mary Waters. New York: Russell Sage Foundation, 2002.

Skocpol, Theda. *Diminished Democracy: From Membership to Management in American Civic Life*. Norman: University of Oklahoma Press, 2003.

Skrentny, John David. *The Ironies of Affirmative Action: Politics, Culture and Justice in America*. Chicago: University of Chicago Press, 1996.

———. *The Minority Rights Revolution*. Cambridge: Belknap Press of Harvard University Press, 2002.

———, ed. *Color Lines: Affirmative Action, Immigration, and Civil Rights Options for America*. Chicago: University of Chicago Press, 2001.

Smith, Robert C. *We Have No Leaders: African-Americans in the Post-Civil Rights Era*. Albany: State University of New York Press, 1996.

Snipp, C. Matthew. "American Indians, Clues to the Future of Other Racial Groups." In *The New Race Question: How the Census Counts Multiracial Individuals*, ed. Joel Perlmann and Mary Waters. New York: Russell Sage Foundation, 2002.

———. "Some Observations about Racial Boundaries and the Experiences of American Indians." *Ethnic and Racial Studies* 20, no. 4 (1997): 667–89.

Sollors, Werner. "What Race Are You?" In *The New Race Question: How the Census Counts Multiracial Individuals*, ed. Joel Perlmann and Mary Waters. New York: Russell Sage Foundation, 2002.

————, ed. *Interracialism: Black-White Intermarriage in American History, Literature, and Law*. New York: Oxford University Press, 2000.

Spencer, Jon Michael. *The New Colored People: The Mixed-Race Movement in America*. New York: New York University Press, 1997.

Spencer, Rainer. "Census 2000: Assessments in Significance." In *New Faces in a Changing America: Multiracial Identity in the 21st Century*, ed. Loretta Winters and Herman DeBose. Thousand Oaks, CA: Sage Publications, 2003.

————. *Spurious Issues: Race and Multiracial Identity Politics in the United States*. Boulder, CO: Westview Press, 1999.

Spickard, Paul. *Mixed Blood: Intermarriage and Ethnic Identity in Twentieth-Century America*. Madison: University of Wisconsin Press, 1989.

Starr, Paul. "Social Categories and Claims in the Liberal State." *Social Research* 59, no. 2 (1992): 263–95.

Stone, Bernard. "Questionnaire Redesign." Letter to Ted Kimbrough, May 11, 1992.

Swain, Carol M. *Black Faces, Black Interests: The Representation of African-Americans in Congress*. Cambridge: Harvard University Press, 1993.

Swarns, Rachel L. "Other Race Stays on the Books." *New York Times*, November 23, 2004, A19.

Tafoya, Sonya M. "Check One or More: Mixed Race and Ethnicity in California." *California Counts* 1, no. 2 (2000): 1–11.

————. "Mixed Race and Ethnicity in California." In *The New Race Question: How the Census Counts Multiracial Individuals*, ed. Joel Perlmann and Mary Waters. New York: Russell Sage Foundation, 2002.

Tarrow, Sidney G. *Power in Movement: Social Movements, Collective Action, and Politics*. New York: Cambridge University Press, 1994.

Tate, Katherine. *Black Faces in the Mirror: African Americans and Their Representatives in the U.S. Congress*. Princeton: Princeton University Press, 2003.

————. *From Protest to Politics: The New Black Voters in American Elections*. New York and Cambridge: Russell Sage Foundation and Harvard University Press, 1993.

Taylor, Charles. "The Politics of Recognition." In *Multiculturalism and the Politics of Recognition*, ed. Charles Taylor and Amy Gutmann. Princeton: Princeton University Press, 1992.

Thomas, Deborah A. "Black, White, or Other?" *Essence*, July 1993, 118.

Tilles, Marc C. "Lawmaker Fights Creation of 'Colored' Race Category." *Michigan Chronicle*, March 22, 1995, A1.

Tilly, Charles. *Durable Inequality*. Berkeley: University of California Press, 1998.

Torres-Saillant, Silvio. "Inventing the Race: Latinos and the Ethnoracial Pentagon." *Latino Studies* 1, no. 1 (March 2003): 121–51.

Townsel, Lisa Jones. "Neither Black Nor White: Would a New Census Category Be a Dangerous Diversion or a Step Forward?" *Ebony*, November 1996, 45–50.

Traugott, Mark, ed. *Repertoires and Cycles of Collective Action*. Durham, NC: Duke University Press, 1995.

Tucker, Clyde, Ruth McKay, Brian Kojetin, Roderick Harrison, Manuel de la Puente, Linda Stinson, and Ed Robinson. *Testing Methods of Collecting Racial and Ethnic Information: Results of the Current Population Survey Supplement on Race and Ethnicity.* Statistical Note No. 40. U.S. Department of Labor, Washington, DC, 1996.

Uncommon Knowledge. "Strength in Numbers." Stanford University Television, February 22, 2002.

U.S. Commission on Civil Rights. *Briefing on the Consequences of Government Race Data Collection Bans on Civil Rights,* May 17, 2002. http://permanent .access.gpo.gov/lps26180/www.usccr.gov/pubs/racedata/trans.htm.

U.S. Congress. House. Subcommittee on Census, Statistics, and Postal Personnel. Committee on Post Office and Civil Service. *A Bill to Amend the Paperwork Reduction Act.* 104th Cong., 2d sess., H.R. 3920, *Congressional Record* 142, no. 114, daily ed., July 30, 1996: H8982.

———. *Hearings on the Review of Federal Measurements of Race and Ethnicity.* 103d Cong., 1st sess., 1993.

———. *Hearings on the Review of Federal Measurements of Race and Ethnicity.* Opening statement by Thomas Sawyer on April 14, 1993. 103d Cong., 1st sess., April 14, June 30, July 29, and November 3, 1993, 128, 197.

———. *Hearings on the Review of Federal Measurements of Race and Ethnicity.* Question from Tom Petri on June 30, 1993. 103d Cong., 1st sess., April 14, June 30, July 29, and November 3, 1993, 192.

———. *Hearings on the Review of Federal Measurements of Race and Ethnicity.* Response and testimony from Stephen Carbo on June 30, 1993. 103d Cong., 1st sess., April 14, June 30, July 29, and November 3, 1993, 179, 189, 193–94.

———. *Hearings on the Review of Federal Measurements of Race and Ethnicity.* Testimony by Daniel Akaka on July 29, 1993. 103d Cong., 1st sess., April 14, June 30, July 29, and November 3, 1993, 199.

———. *Hearings on the Review of Federal Measurements of Race and Ethnicity.* Testimony by Carlos Fernández on June 30, 1993. 103d Cong., 1st sess., April 14, June 30, July 29, and November 3, 1993, 127–28.

———. *Hearings on the Review of Federal Measurements of Race and Ethnicity.* Testimony by Arthur Fletcher on November 3, 1993. 103d Cong., 1st sess., April 14, June 30, July 29, and November 3, 1993, 273.

———. *Hearings on the Review of Federal Measurements of Race and Ethnicity.* Testimony by Barney Frank on July 29, 1993. 103d Cong., 1st sess., April 14, June 30, July 29, and November 3, 1993, 211.

———. *Hearings on the Review of Federal Measurements of Race and Ethnicity.* Testimony by Susan Graham on June 30, 1993. 103d Cong., 1st sess., April 14, June 30, July 29, and November 3, 1993, 108.

———. *Hearings on the Review of Federal Measurements of Race and Ethnicity.* Testimony by Rachel Joseph on July 29, 1993. 103d Cong., 1st sess., April 14, June 30, July 29, and November 3, 1993, 236.

———. *Hearings on the Review of Federal Measurements of Race and Ethnicity.* Testimony by Sally Katzen on July 29, 1993. 103d Cong., 1st sess., April 14, June 30, July 29, and November 3, 1993, 214–15, 226, 228.

———. *Hearings on the Review of Federal Measurements of Race and Ethnicity.* Testimony by Norman Mineta on July 29, 1993. 103d Cong., 1st sess., April 14, June 30, July 29, and November 3, 1993, 208.

———. *Hearings on the Review of Federal Measurements of Race and Ethnicity.* Testimony by Sonia Pérez on June 30, 1993. 103d Cong., 1st sess., April 14, June 30, July 29, and November 3, 1993, 172.

———. *Hearings on the Review of Federal Measurements of Race and Ethnicity.* Testimony by Henry Scarr on April 14, 1993. 103d Cong., 1st sess., April 14, June 30, July 29, and November 3, 1993, 3.

———. *Hearings on the Review of Federal Measurements of Race and Ethnicity.* Testimony by Billy Tidwell on July 29, 1993. 103d Cong., 1st sess., April 14, June 30, July 29, and November 3, 1993, 234.

U.S. Congress. House. Subcommittee on Government Management, Information, and Technology. Committee on Government Reform and Oversight. *Hearings on Federal Measures of Race and Ethnicity and the Implications for the 2000 Census.* 105th Cong., 1st sess., April 23, May 22, and July 25, 1997.

———. *Hearings on Federal Measures of Race and Ethnicity and the Implications for the 2000 Census.* Testimony by John Conyers on July 25, 1997. 105th Cong., 1st sess., April 23, May 22, and July 25, 1997, 535.

———. *Hearings on Federal Measures of Race and Ethnicity and the Implications for the 2000 Census.* Testimony by Newt Gingrich on July 25, 1997. 105th Cong., 1st sess., April 23, May 22, and July 25, 1997, 660.

———. *Hearings on Federal Measures of Race and Ethnicity and the Implications for the 2000 Census.* Testimony by Harold McDougall on May 22 and July 25, 1997. 105th Cong., 1st sess., April 23, May 22, and July 25, 1997, 309, 585.

———. *Hearings on Federal Measures of Race and Ethnicity and the Implications for the 2000 Census.* Testimony by Carrie Meek on April 23, 1997. 105th Cong., 1st sess., April 23, May 22, and July 25, 1997, 231–32.

———. *Hearings on Federal Measures of Race and Ethnicity and the Implications for the 2000 Census.* Testimony by Tom Petri on April 23, 1997. 105th Cong., 1st sess., April 23, May 22, and July 25, 1997, 225.

———. *Hearings on Federal Measures of Race and Ethnicity and the Implications for the 2000 Census.* Testimony by Tom Sawyer on April 23, 1997. 105th Cong., 1st sess., April 23, May 22, and July 25, 1997, 220–21.

U.S. Department of Commerce. U.S. Bureau of the Census. *Census of Population and Housing of the United States.* Summary File 1 (SF-1). Washington, DC: U.S. Government Printing Office, 2000.

———. *Census of Population and Housing of the United States.* Summary Tape File 1 (STF-1), Tables P-006 and P-008. Washington, DC: U.S. Government Printing Office, 1990.

———. *City and County Data Books.* Washington, DC: U.S. Government Printing Office, 1994.

———. "Composition of State Legislatures by Political Party Affiliation: 1994 to 2000." *Statistical Abstract of the United States,* 121st ed. Washington, DC: U.S. Government Printing Office, 2001.

———. "Composition of State Legislatures by Political Party Affiliation: 1990 to 1996." *Statistical Abstract of the United States,* 118th ed. Washington, DC: U.S. Government Printing Office, 1998.

———. "Findings on Questions on Race and Hispanic Origin Tested in the 1996 National Content Survey." Population Division Working Paper No. 16. Washington, DC: U.S. Government Printing Office, 1996.

———. "The Foreign-Born Population: 1994." *Current Population Reports*, Series P-20–486. Washington, DC: U.S. Government Printing Office, 1995.

———. "Interracial Married Couples: 1960 to Present." 1999. http://www.census.gov/population/socdemo/ms-la-tabms-3.txt (accessed April 2002).

———. "Marital Status and Living Arrangements." *Current Population Reports*, Series P-20–514. Washington, DC: U.S. Government Printing Office, 1998.

———. "Political Party Control of State Legislatures by Party: 1975 to 2000." *Statistical Abstract of the United States*, 121st ed. Washington, DC: U.S. Government Printing Office, 2001.

———. "Profile of the Foreign-Born Population in the United States: 2000." *Current Population Reports*, Series P-23–206. Washington, DC: U.S. Government Printing Office, 2001.

———. "Results of the 1996 Race and Ethnic Targeted Test." Population Division Working Paper No. 18 (May). Washington, DC: U.S. Government Printing Office, 1997.

———. *Statistical Policy Handbook*. Washington, DC: U.S. Government Printing Office, 1978.

U.S. Department of Labor. Bureau of Labor Statistics. *A Test of Methods for Collecting Racial and Ethnic Information: May 1995*, USDL 95–428. Washington, DC, 1995.

U.S. Executive Office of the President. Office of Management and Budget. "Exhibit F (Revised May 12, 1977): Race and Ethnic Standards for Federal Statistics and Administrative Reporting." *Circular No. A-46: Standards and Guidelines for Federal Statistics*, May 3, 1974, 3–4.

———. *Guidance on Aggregation and Allocation of Data on Race for Use in Civil Rights Monitoring and Enforcement*. OMB Bulletin 00–02, March 9, 2000, Washington, DC. http://whitehouse.gov/OMB/bulletins/b00–02.html (accessed December 5, 2005).

———. "Standards for the Classification of Federal Data on Race and Ethnicity; Notice." *Federal Register* 60, no. 166 (1995): 44673–93.

———. Tabulation Working Group of the Interagency Committee for the Review of Standards for Data on Race and Ethnicity. "Draft Provisional Guidance on the Implementation of the 1997 Standards for the Collection of Federal Data on Race and Ethnicity." *Federal Register*, February 17, 1999.

———. Tabulation Working Group of the Interagency Committee for the Review of Standards for Data on Race and Ethnicity. "Provisional Guidance on the Implementation of the 1997 Standards for Federal Data on Race and Ethnicity." Appendix C. *Federal Register*, December 15, 2000.

———. "To the Heads of Executive Departments and Establishments, Subject: Guidance on Aggregation and Allocation of Data on Race for Use in Civil Rights Monitoring and Enforcement." Bulletin 00–02, March 9, 2000, Washington, DC.

Wallman, Katherine K., Suzann Evinger, and Susan Schechter. "Measuring Our Nation's Diversity: Developing a Common Language for Data on Race/Ethnicity." *American Journal of Public Health* 90, no. 11 (2000): 1704–8.

Wallman, Katherine K., and John Hodgdon. "Race and Ethnic Standards for Federal Statistics and Administrative Reporting." *Statistical Reporter* 77, no. 10 (July 1977): 450–54.

Walton, Haynes, Jr. *When the Marching Stopped: The Politics of Civil Rights Regulatory Agencies.* Albany: State University of New York, 1988.

Waters, Mary C. *Ethnic Options: Choosing Identities in America.* Berkeley: University of California Press, 1990.

Webster, Yehudi. *The Racialization of America.* New York: St. Martin's Press, 1992.

Wheeler, David L. "A Growing Number of Scientists Reject the Concept of Race." *Chronicle of Higher Education,* February 17, 1995, 8–9, 15.

Whitby, Kenny J. *The Color of Representation: Congressional Behavior and Black Interests.* Ann Arbor: University of Michigan Press, 1997.

Whitby, Kenny J., and Franklin D. Gilliam Jr. "A Longitudinal Analysis of Competing Explanations for the Transformation of Southern Congressional Politics." *Journal of Politics* 53 (1991): 504–18.

White, Ruth. Leadership Roundtable. Washington, DC, March 31, 2000.

———. "Racial Classifications on Census Forms." C-SPAN News Conference, March 31, 2000.

White, Steve. Leadership Roundtable. Washington, DC, March 31, 2000.

White, Ruth and Steve. "APFU Response to Mfume." *Interracial Voice.* http://www.webcom.com/intvoice/a_place2.html (accessed October 3, 1997).

Williams, Gregory Howard. *Life on the Color Line: The True Story of a White Boy Who Discovered He Was Black.* New York: Plume Books, 1996.

Williams, Kim M. "Boxed In: The U.S. Multiracial Movement." PhD diss., Cornell University, 2001.

Williamson, Joel. *New People: Miscegenation and Mulattoes in the United States.* Baton Rouge: Louisiana State University Press, 1995.

Wing, Butch. "The Coalition that Kicked Proposition 54 out of the California Door." Lecture presented at the John F. Kennedy School of Government, Harvard University, Cambridge, MA, March 9, 2004.

Wright, Lawrence. "One Drop of Blood." *New Yorker,* July 25, 1994, 46–55.

Xie, Yu, and Kimberly Goyette. "The Racial Identification of Biracial Children with One Asian Parent: Evidence from the 1990 Census." *Social Forces* 76, no. 2 (December 1997): 547–70.

Yancey, George. *Who Is White? Latinos, Asians, and the New Black/Nonblack Divide.* Boulder, CO: Lynne Rienner, 2003.

Yanow, Dvora. *Constructing "Race" and "Ethnicity" in America: Category-Making in Public Policy and Administration.* Armonk, NY: M. E. Sharpe, 2003.

Yates, Sidney. Letter to Michelle Erickson, November 2, 1992.

———. "Michelle Erickson, My Constituent." Letter to Ronald Brown, June 4, 1993.

Younge, Gary. "Multiracial Citizens Divided on Idea of Separate Census Classification." *Washington Post,* July 19, 1996, A3.

Yzaguirre, Raúl, and Sonia M. Pérez. "Accurate Racial/Ethnic Data Should Drive Category Review." *Poverty and Race* 4, no. 1 (January 1995): 7–9.

Zack, Naomi, ed. *American Mixed Race: The Culture of Microdiversity.* Lanham, MD: Rowman & Littlefield, 1995.

———. *Race/Sex: Their Sameness, Difference, and Interplay.* New York: Routledge, 1997.

Zald, Mayer. "Ideologically Structured Action: An Enlarged Agenda for Social Movement Research." *Mobilization: An International Journal* 5 (2000): 1–16.

Zald, Mayer, and John McCarthy, eds. *The Dynamics of Social Movements: Resource Mobilization, Social Control, and Tactics.* Cambridge: Winthrop, 1979.

Zuberi, Tukufu. *Thicker than Blood: How Racial Statistics Lie.* Minneapolis: University of Minnesota Press, 2001.

Index

Note: Page numbers in italics indicate figures or tables.

1990, 19, 22; controversies of 2000, 20–21, 105–6; ethnicity and race questions, 2000, 137; minorities undercount in, 17–19, 153n45; top combinations of two or more races reporting, 2000, 113–14, *113. See also* hearings of 1993; hearings of 1997; mark one or more option

Census Bureau, U.S.: AMEA affiliates' goals for policy changes at, 13; AMEA plans to commemorate *Loving v. Virginia* and, 21; Graham's request for instruction from, 12; lack of autonomy and leadership difficulties for, 19–20; multiracial movement and stresses on, 16–17; Research Working Group and, 46; small populations tests using MOOM option and, 154n71; tabulation of multiple-race responses by, 58–63

Chase, JoAnn, 59

Civil Rights Act (1964), 4, 25

Civil Rights Acts (1866, 1870, 1871, and 1875), 23

Civil Rights Division, Department of Justice, 39–40

civil rights groups: on AMEA proposal to add mixed race category, 11, 25–26; Coalition Statement to Research Working Group, 47–48; disappointment in, 101–12; multiracial group leaders and, 96–98; resistance to multiracialism by, 126–30; tabulation decision and, 112, 160–61n1. *See also* blacks; *specific groups*

civil rights laws: enforcement of, racial census data and, 25, 26–27, 126–27; MOOM option and, 60, 116; Other Race reporting and, 117–19; U.S. Census and, 3–4

Civil War, population counts and, 23

Clinton, Bill, 121

college campuses, multiracial groups on, 34–35, 125–26, 147n21, 162–63n32

color-blindness theory: multiracial-

ism and, 124–25, 129–30. *See also* Campaign for a Color-Blind America

Commission on Civil Rights, U.S. "Briefing on the Consequences of Government Race Data Bans on Civil Rights," 128

Committee on Special Populations, 2000 Census and, 53–54

Connerly, Ward: Douglass debate with, 162n30; Proposition 54 on racial privacy and, 122; Racial Harmony Hall of Fame and, 105, 106–7, 122. *See also* Campaign for a Color-Blind America

Conyers, John, 57–58, 126, 128

C-SPAN, 106–7, 160n65

Current Population Survey: on interracial marriage statistics, 31–32; MOOM bridging analysis using, 62; and results of multiracial category tests, 52; Supplement on Race and Ethnicity to, 47, 58–59

Daniel, Reginald, 9

Darden, Edwin, 97–98

Davis, Gray, 123

Democrats: bill sponsorship in state legislatures by, 68–69, *68*; control in state legislatures, 66–68, *67*; hearings of 1993 and symbolic changes to racial classifications, 41; hearings of 1997 and, 56, *57*, 57–58; multiracial activists on support by, 107–8, *108*; multiracial category and, 5, 21–22; multiracial recognition, civil rights consequences and, 122; "New South" *versus* Deep South Democrats, 81

discrimination: against multiracial organization leaders, 87–88; against multiracial persons, 129

Douglass, Ramona: on AMEA organizational capacity, 15–16; on AMEA political agenda, 162n30; Census Advisory Committee and, 49, 53; civil rights movement and, 36–37; as first AMEA vice presi-